# fine
# Cooking
### A N N U A L

**VOLUME 2**

## a year of great recipes, tips & techniques

# fine Cooking

**VOLUME 2**

## A N N U A L

### a year of great recipes, tips & techniques

From the Editors and
Contributors of *Fine Cooking*

The Taunton Press

## The Taunton Press
Inspiration for hands-on living®

The Taunton Press, Inc., 63 South Main Street, PO Box 5506, Newtown, CT 06470-5506
email: tp@taunton.com

EDITORS: Pamela Hoenig, Martha Holmberg
COPYEDITOR: Li Agen
JACKET/COVER DESIGN: Sandra Mahlstedt
INTERIOR DESIGN: Alison Wilkes
LAYOUT: David Giammattei
PRINCIPAL PHOTOGRAPHER: Scott Phillips
ADDITIONAL PHOTO CREDITS: Photo p. 290 by Jamie Francis; photo p. 335 by Alan Richardson

LIBRARY OF CONGRESS CATALOGING-IN-PUBLICATION DATA

Fine Cooking Annual: a year of great recipes, tips & techniques from the
editors of Fine cooking /
  photography by Scott Phillips.
      p. cm.
  Includes bibliographical references and index.
  ISBN-13: 978-1-56158-916-6 (alk. paper) (vol. 1)
  ISBN-10: 1-56158-916-0 (alk. paper) (vol. 1)
  ISBN-13: 978-1-60085-005-9 (vol. 2)
  1.  Cookery.  I. Fine cooking.
  TX651.B4835 2006
  641.5--dc22
                        2006018123

Printed in China
10 9 8 7 6 5 4 3 2 1

The following manufacturer's/names appearing in *Fine Cooking Annual* are trademarks: Budweiser®, Bundt®, Crystal® hot sauce, Famous Chocolate Wafers®, Grand Marnier®, Jameson® whiskey, Jif® peanut butter, Kahlua®, KitchenAid®, Kraft® caramels, Lindt Excellence® chocolate, Pepperidge Farm® Classic white bread, Pom® pomegranate juice, Pyrex®, Real Torino® ladyfingers, Tabasco® pepper sauce, Thai Kitchen® fish sauce, Worcestershire® sauce.

The Taunton Press publishes *Fine Cooking*, the magazine for people who love to cook.

121

52

# Contents

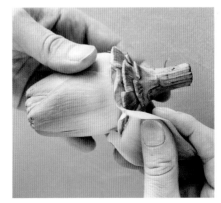

# Trends, yes, but not trendy

For the editors of *Fine Cooking,* this beautiful cookbook, a collection of the magazine's best recipes of the year, is not only a treat visually (the gorgeous photos from our pages look even better enlarged) but also a great way to reflect on the recipes themselves. Seeing the dishes here in all their glory, we get excited all over again and can't wait to make them in our own home kitchens. We also can't help but notice some trends from the past year. Pimentón, for example, the wonderfully smoky Spanish paprika, was a favorite spice among our many chef contributors, who included it in the expected (a shrimp tapas, for example) as well as the unexpected (the Thanksgiving turkey). As we flip through the chicken recipes, it becomes obvious that we favored dark meat this year, using thighs and legs to create deeply flavored roasts and braises. And there are crusts of all kinds (crispy, crunchy, nutty, and spicy) coating everything from bright and light fish fillets to a whole rack of lamb perfect for company. On the sweet side, fruit beat out chocolate this year's favorite dessert ingredient.

Despite such patterns, *Fine Cooking* does not aspire, as some cooking magazines do, to be trendy. Instead the focus is on giving readers recipes that are not only delicious but also reliable. As in the magazine, the recipes here are full of the details that make the difference. Scattered throughout the book are lots of quick tips as well as close-ups on techniques and ingredients that make it easy for you to cook with confidence (whether that includes pimentón or not).

If you're not already a *Fine Cooking* reader, we hope this book inspires you to become one. Look for the magazine on the newsstand or go to the website at FineCooking.com.

Enjoy!

—the editors

# 1

# Starters
# & Snacks

p21

p14

Seared Shrimp with Pimentón & Sherry
(recipe on page 34)

# Butter-Roasted Almonds

*Yields 2¼ cups.*

2 tablespoons unsalted butter

2 teaspoons kosher salt

2 teaspoons granulated sugar

12 ounces whole raw skin-on almonds (about 2¼ cups)

1 to 2 teaspoons extra-virgin olive oil

**These nuts are a deliciously simple snack, nibble, appetizer, or salad addition.**

Heat the oven to 400°F.

In a small saucepan over low heat, melt the butter with 1 teaspoon of the salt and the sugar, stirring. Put the almonds in a medium bowl, scrape the butter mixture into the bowl, and toss thoroughly to coat.

Scrape the almonds and anything remaining in the bowl onto a large rimmed baking sheet. Spread evenly. Roast until fragrant and darkened to a rich brown, 11 to 13 minutes (any exposed almond meat should be a deep golden brown). Be sure not to undercook; roasting thoroughly will dry them out all the way through and ensure that they're crunchy, not chewy.

Remove from the oven, drizzle with a little of the oil, and toss with the remaining 1 teaspoon salt. Let cool completely (they will get crunchier as they cool). Scrape the almonds and all the contents of the pan (there will be some yummy brown stuff) into an airtight container and store in the refrigerator for a week to 10 days. —*Susie Middleton*

# Goat Cheese Crackers with Hot Pepper Jelly

**Anyone from the South will recognize this simple hors d'oeuvre. This is so easy to make that we hesitate to call it a recipe because it comes together so quickly.**

Bring the goat cheese to room temperature. (If your goat cheese is especially crumbly, mash it in a bowl with a touch of heavy cream.) Spread about 1 teaspoon of the goat cheese on each cracker. Top each cracker with ¼ teaspoon hot pepper jelly. Sprinkle with chives and pass around.

*—Karen & Ben Barker*

*Yields 24 canapés; serves eight.*

One 5-ounce log fresh, mild goat cheese

Heavy cream, as needed

24 crackers (Bremner Wafers work well, but any good cracker will do)

3 tablespoons good-quality hot pepper jelly

Snipped fresh chives, for garnish

# Goat Cheese Spread with Herbs & Olive Oil

*Yields about 1¼ cups; serves six.*

8 ounces fresh goat cheese (about 1 cup), at room temperature

2 tablespoons heavy cream; more if needed

2 tablespoons extra-virgin olive oil; more for drizzling

2 tablespoons dry white wine

Kosher salt and freshly ground black pepper

2 tablespoons chopped fresh herbs (choose at least two from the following: parsley, chives, tarragon, dill)

1 tablespoon finely grated lemon zest

Good crackers or slices of walnut bread

About 1 pint cherry tomatoes

1 celery heart, cut into sticks

Garlanded with bright veggies, this creamy, cleverly molded spread feels special, but is so easy to throw together; it just needs to chill for 30 minutes before serving. (You can also refrigerate it overnight, if you're planning ahead.) You'll want to use the soft, spreadable logs of chalk-white goat cheese, which are sometimes labeled "chèvre." Imported and artisanally made goat cheeses tend to be milder; less expensive domestic varieties often have a more sharply "goaty" flavor. Since the olive oil is a star seasoning here, use a young extra-virgin oil for the best results.

Put the goat cheese, heavy cream, oil, and wine in a food processor (or mix in a bowl with a wooden spoon). Pulse just to blend. The mixture should be spreadable; if it's too thick, add 1 or 2 tablespoons more cream and pulse again. Season with salt and pepper, pulse again, and taste, adjusting the seasoning as necessary. Reserve 1 teaspoon of the herbs for sprinkling and add the rest to the processor. Add 2 teaspoons of the lemon zest. Pulse once more to blend.

Line a small (about 1½ cups) round bowl or cup with a sheet of plastic wrap and fill with the cheese mixture. Cover and chill for at least 30 minutes and up to 24 hours.

To serve, invert the bowl onto a serving platter and peel off the plastic. With the back of a spoon, level off the top of the cheese and make a small depression. Drizzle oil over the top. Sprinkle with the reserved herbs and lemon zest. Arrange the crackers or bread slices, tomatoes, and celery around the cheese and let guests serve themselves. *—Martha Holmberg*

# Cherry Tomatoes Stuffed with Mozzarella & Basil

*Yields about 3 dozen.*

½ pound fresh mozzarella, cut into tiny dice (to yield about 1¼ cups)

3 tablespoons extra-virgin olive oil

⅓ cup coarsely chopped fresh basil

½ teaspoon grated lemon zest (from about a quarter of a lemon)

Kosher salt and freshly ground black pepper

1 pint (about 18) cherry tomatoes, rinsed and stems removed

These are little bite-sized tastes of Italy's famous Caprese salad. Look for Sweet 100 cherry tomatoes—they're especially sweet and juicy—or mix in some yellow Sungolds to add more color to the platter. For authentic flavor, buy fresh water-packed mozzarella and use it within a few days of purchasing.

In a medium bowl, stir together the cheese, oil, basil, lemon zest, ½ teaspoon salt, and ¼ teaspoon pepper. Refrigerate for at least 2 hours and up to 4 hours before assembling.

When ready to assemble, slice each tomato in half (either direction is all right) and scoop out the insides with the small end of a melon baller or a teaspoon. Sprinkle lightly with salt. Invert onto a paper towel and let the tomatoes drain for 15 minutes.

Fill each tomato half with a scant teaspoon of the cheese mixture and arrange on a serving tray. Serve immediately, or wrap and refrigerate for up to 2 hours. —*Jessica Bard*

# Grilled Zucchini & Goat Cheese Roll-Ups

*Yields 8 to 10 roll-ups.*

3 ounces goat cheese, at room temperature

1 tablespoon finely chopped oil-packed sun-dried tomatoes, drained well

Heaping ½ teaspoon fresh thyme leaves, chopped

1 to 1½ tablespoons olive oil

Kosher salt

3 small zucchini

2 tablespoons freshly grated Parmigiano-Reggiano

Like eggplant, zucchini often benefits from salting before cooking: Salt draws out excess moisture, giving the zucchini more flavor and prompting better browning. To try it with this recipe, slice the zucchini, then generously sprinkle the slices with salt and layer in a colander set over a medium bowl for about 30 minutes. Pat the zucchini dry with paper towels and proceed with the recipe. If outdoor grilling is not an option, you can cook the zucchini in a heavy-duty grill pan.

In a small bowl, combine the goat cheese, tomatoes, thyme, 1 teaspoon of the oil, and ⅛ teaspoon salt.

Trim the ends of the zucchini and cut it lengthwise into ¼-inch-thick slices. Brush both sides of each slice with plenty of olive oil and season with salt. Heat a gas grill to high. Lay the slices of zucchini on the hot grate at a 45-degree angle to the grates and grill, covered, until well browned and limp, 3 to 4 minutes per side. When done, drape them over a cooling rack to keep them from steaming as they cool.

Line a baking sheet with parchment or foil. Spread 1 heaping teaspoon of the filling thinly over one side of each grilled zucchini strip (use a mini spatula or your fingers to spread). Roll up the zucchini (not too tightly; this is more like folding) and put them on the baking sheet. Refrigerate if not using within an hour; (you can assemble them several hours ahead, but bring back to room temperature before broiling).

Heat the broiler. Position a rack 4 inches from the broiler element. Sprinkle the rolls with a little grated Parmigiano and brown under the broiler, about 1 minute.

*—Susie Middleton*

# Garlic-Parmesan Bread

A delicious flavored butter with a fresh twist—finely grated lemon zest—makes this garlic bread special enough to stand on its own with other hors d'oeuvres and savory snacks. You can keep the butter in the fridge for a week, or up to several months in the freezer.

Heat the oven to 425°F.

In a food processor or a large bowl, combine the butter, Parmigiano, oil, garlic, lemon zest, ¼ teaspoon salt, and ⅛ teaspoon pepper. Pulse a few times to blend but don't overprocess or the butter might separate. If mixing by hand, mash together with a fork or a wooden spoon.

Slice the bread 1-inch thick, cutting almost but not all the way through the bottom crust, so it's easy to pull apart. Spread a light, even coating of the butter mixture on both sides of each slice of bread. (You may not need all the butter; refrigerate any leftover for up to a week or freeze for up to three months.) Wrap the bread in foil and put the loaf on a baking sheet to catch any butter that runs out. Heat in the oven for about 15 minutes, then open the top of the foil to slightly crisp the top of the loaf, about 5 more minutes. Serve while hot. *—Martha Holmberg*

*Serves six.*

½ cup (1 stick) salted butter, softened

¼ cup lightly packed finely grated Parmigiano-Reggiano

1 tablespoon extra-virgin olive oil

2 large cloves garlic, very finely minced or grated on a rasp-style grater

1 teaspoon finely grated lemon zest

Kosher salt and freshly ground black pepper

1 medium loaf artisan-style bread with a tight crumb (wide bâtard shapes work better than baguettes)

# Bruschetta with Herbed Tomatoes

*Serves six to eight.*

2 large ripe tomatoes, cut in ¼-inch-thick slices (you should have 12 slices)

4 tablespoons Rosemary-Garlic Oil (see recipe, below)

1 teaspoon chopped fresh thyme

A scant ¼ teaspoon crushed red pepper flakes

Kosher salt

Twelve ¾-inch-thick slices from a crusty artisan-style loaf (from about ½ pound bread)

1 teaspoon good balsamic vinegar, preferably aged

For these bruschetta, the quality of the tomatoes makes all the difference. In the summer, use good ripe ones from your garden or pick some up at the local farmers' market. Salting the tomatoes extracts some of the juices, which prevents the toasts from getting soggy and concentrates the tomato flavor. Long-aged balsamic vinegars achieve a syrupy texture and complexity of flavor that make them more of a condiment than a simple salad dressing ingredient. The longer they age, the more expensive they are—but that doesn't mean you have to spend a mint. For this recipe, try to use a balsamic that's just a step above the everyday bottle you use to dress salads; look for one that's been aged for several years or more at a specialty foods store or well-stocked supermarket.

Heat a gas grill to medium or prepare a medium-hot charcoal fire. (Or heat the broiler to high.)

Set the tomato slices on a small rack set over a rimmed baking sheet and sprinkle with 1 tablespoon of the oil, the thyme, red pepper, and 1 teaspoon salt. Let sit at room temperature for at least 10 minutes or up to a couple of hours.

Brush both sides of the bread with the remaining 3 tablespoons oil.

Sprinkle lightly with salt. Grill (or broil) until crisp with prominent grill marks (or nicely browned), about 2 minutes. Flip and cook the other side in the same manner. Transfer to a platter and let cool to room temperature (they can sit for up to 2 hours, loosely covered).

Pour the tomato juices from the baking sheet into a small bowl. Before serving, brush these juices on the bread. Top with the tomatoes and a drop or two of vinegar and serve. *—Tony Rosenfeld*

## Rosemary-Garlic Oil

*Yields 1½ cups.*

Using the flat side of a chef's knife to smash each garlic clove makes it a snap to peel and opens it up just enough to infuse the oil. To smash the garlic, place the blade, flat side down, on top of the clove and give the blade a good whack with the heel of your hand. You can make this flavored oil up to five days ahead; keep it chilled.

1½ cups extra-virgin olive oil

6 cloves garlic, smashed and peeled

3 sprigs fresh rosemary

Heat the oil and garlic in a small saucepan over medium heat, stirring occasionally, until the garlic starts to bubble steadily, 3 to 4 minutes. Add the rosemary, remove from the heat, and let cool to room temperature. Transfer to a clean glass jar or other storage container, cover, and refrigerate. Use within five days.

# Bruschetta with Grilled Eggplant & Vidalia Onion

*Serves six to eight.*

1 medium eggplant (1 to 1¼ pounds)

1 medium-large (about 12-ounce) Vidalia onion (or other sweet variety, like Texas Sweet or Walla Walla)

½ cup heavy cream

4 cloves garlic, thinly sliced

2 teaspoons fresh thyme leaves, chopped

¼ cup extra-virgin olive oil; more for the bread

Kosher salt and freshly ground black pepper

¼ cup freshly grated Parmigiano-Reggiano

About ½ baguette, sliced diagonally into ½-inch-thick slices

**Cream and Parmesan add richness to these savory and substantial bruschetta; they're especially delicious served warm. You can substitute almost any fresh herb you have on hand for the thyme: fresh oregano, mint, summer savory, or chervil would be nice. Or use a mix of any that you like.**

Prepare a medium-hot grill fire.

Trim off ½ inch from the top and bottom of the eggplant. Cut the eggplant lengthwise into ½-inch-thick slices. Cut the onion crosswise into ½-inch-thick slices. To keep the rings together, insert toothpicks or small skewers horizontally through the rings of each slice.

In a small saucepan over medium-high heat, bring the cream, garlic, and thyme to a boil. Reduce the heat to medium and simmer gently until the cream has reduced by half, 3 to 5 minutes. Remove from the heat.

When the grill is ready, brush both sides of the eggplant and onion slices with the ¼ cup oil. Arrange the vegetables on the grill and cook with the lid closed until the first sides have started to soften and get grill marks, 2 to 3 minutes for the eggplant and 5 to 6 minutes for the onion. Flip and cook with the lid closed until the eggplant is tender and the onion is nicely charred but not necessarily fully tender, 2 to 3 minutes more for the eggplant and 5 to 6 minutes more for the onion. Transfer the eggplant to a cutting board and sprinkle with ¼ teaspoon salt and ¼ teaspoon pepper. Transfer the onion to a large sheet of foil, stack the slices, wrap tightly, and let rest until residual heat has softened the onion, about 5 minutes. Remove the skewers from the onion slices. Coarsely chop the eggplant and onion and combine in a medium bowl. Add the cream mixture and Parmigiano; stir to combine. Taste and add salt and pepper as needed.

Brush the bread slices on both sides with oil and grill until lightly golden brown, 30 seconds to 1 minute per side. Top each slice with a generous dollop of the eggplant mixture and serve. —*Jessica Bard*

# Three-Cheese Quesadillas with Garlic Butter

*Serves eight to twelve.*

2 small cloves garlic, unpeeled

2 tablespoons salted butter, at room temperature

8 ounces Monterey Jack, coarsely grated (2 cups)

1¼ ounces Parmigiano-Reggiano, finely grated (½ cup)

4 ounces fresh goat cheese, crumbled (¾ cup)

Four 9- or 10-inch flour tortillas (burrito size)

A simple cheese quesadilla is a perennial hit at parties as well as a satisfying anytime snack. This recipe is a great example of how to kick things up a notch with just a few tweaks: Crumbling over a fresh cheese, such as the tangy goat cheese here, and adding a sprinkling of a rich aged cheese like Parmesan to a mild melter like Monterey Jack is an easy way to add a tasty variation. A swipe of a quick garlic butter on each tortilla really makes it party-worthy. Boiling the garlic cloves mellows their pungency a bit and softens them enough to blend with the butter.

Position a rack in the center of the oven; heat the oven to 200°F.

Bring a small saucepan of water to a boil. Add the garlic cloves and cook until soft, about 5 minutes. Drain the garlic, let it cool slightly, peel, and place in a small bowl. With a fork, mash the garlic to a coarse paste, then add the butter and mix well.

In a medium bowl, combine the three cheeses. Spread the garlic butter on one side of each tortilla and set them on a work surface, buttered side down. Distribute the cheese mixture among the tortillas, covering only half of each and leaving a 1-inch margin at the edge. Fold in half to enclose the filling, creating a half-moon.

In a 10- or 12-inch nonstick skillet over medium heat, cook two of the quesadillas, covered, until golden brown, about 4 minutes. Uncover and flip the quesadillas. Cook until the second side is golden brown and the cheese has melted completely, about 2 minutes. Transfer them to the oven to keep warm and repeat with the remaining two quesadillas. (You can hold them in the warm oven for up to 30 minutes.) Cut the quesadillas into wedges and serve. *—Laura Werlin*

# Mozzarella, Tomato & Basil Quesadillas with Parmesan Crust

*Serves eight to twelve.*

3 tablespoons unsalted butter, at room temperature

1 ounce Parmigiano-Reggiano, finely grated (½ cup)

Four 9- or 10-inch flour tortillas (burrito size)

8 ounces mozzarella (see note above), coarsely grated (about 2 cups)

2 medium-size ripe tomatoes (about ¾ pound total), seeded and coarsely chopped (about 1 cup)

⅓ cup coarsely chopped fresh basil

Kosher salt and freshly ground black pepper

**If you want a really melty, cheesy quesadilla, use deli-style mozzarella (the kind used on pizza); it has a lower moisture content than fresh water-packed mozzarella, which makes it grate and melt easily. If you prefer the fresh-style mozzarella, just cut it into small pieces before using.**

Position a rack in the center of the oven; heat the oven to 200°F.

In a small bowl, combine the butter and Parmigiano. Spread this on one side of each tortilla and set them on a work surface, buttered side down. Distribute the mozzarella among the tortillas, covering only half of each and leaving a 1-inch margin at the edge. Follow with the tomatoes and basil, and sprinkle with ¼ teaspoon each salt and pepper. Fold the tortillas in half to enclose the filling, creating a half-moon.

In a 10- or 12-inch nonstick skillet over medium heat, cook two of the quesadillas, covered, until golden brown on the first side, about 3 minutes. Uncover, flip, and cook until the second side is golden brown and the cheese has melted completely, about 2 minutes. (Watch carefully as the Parmigiano crust can burn easily; lower the heat if it's getting too dark.) Transfer them to the oven to keep warm and repeat with the remaining two quesadillas. (You can hold them in the warm oven for up to 30 minutes.) Cut the quesadillas into wedges and serve. *—Laura Werlin*

## Four tips for perfect quesadillas

**1** Use 9- or 10-inch flour tortillas, often labeled "burrito size."

**2** Spread butter on the outside of the tortillas to add flavor.

**3** Grate the cheese to help it melt quickly.

**4** Fold to encase the filling and keep the ingredients from overflowing.

# Mushroom & Fontina Quesadillas

**Because it melts so easily and smoothly, Fontina makes a fabulous quesadilla cheese. It also has a creamy nuttiness that pairs deliciously with the earthy mushrooms in this variation. These also make a satisfying main course for four; just add a bowl of soup or green salad.**

Position a rack in the center of the oven; heat the oven to 200°F.

In a 10- or 12-inch nonstick skillet, heat the oil over medium high until hot. Add the mushrooms and cook, stirring occasionally, until they release most of their juices and are slightly browned, 5 to 7 minutes. Add the garlic, thyme, 1/2 teaspoon salt, and 1/4 teaspoon pepper. Taste and adjust the seasoning as needed. Transfer the mushrooms to a medium bowl.

Spread the butter on one side of each tortilla and set the tortillas on a work surface, buttered side down. Distribute the Fontina among the tortillas, covering only half of each and leaving a 1-inch margin at the edge. Distribute the mushrooms on top of the cheese. Fold the tortillas in half to enclose the filling, creating a half-moon.

Wipe out the skillet with a paper towel. Over medium heat, cook two of the quesadillas, covered, until golden brown, about 4 minutes. Uncover and flip the quesadillas. Cook until the second side is golden brown and the cheese has melted completely, about 2 minutes. Transfer them to the oven to keep warm and repeat with the remaining two quesadillas. (You can hold them in the warm oven for up to 30 minutes.) Cut the quesadillas into wedges and serve. —*Laura Werlin*

*Serves eight to twelve.*

1 tablespoon extra-virgin olive oil

8 ounces white button or cremini mushrooms, trimmed coarsely chopped (about 2½ cups)

2 small cloves garlic, minced

1½ tablespoons fresh thyme leaves, finely chopped

Kosher salt and freshly cracked black pepper

2 tablespoons salted butter, at room temperature

Four 9- or 10-inch flour tortillas (burrito size)

8 ounces Fontina, coarsely grated (about 2 cups)

# Warm Black Bean & Chipotle Dip

*Serves ten to twelve.*

2 tablespoons extra-virgin olive oil; more for the baking dish

2 medium-size ripe tomatoes, cored and cut into medium dice

2 teaspoons kosher salt; more as needed

1 large yellow onion, finely diced

3 large cloves garlic, minced

1 tablespoon chili powder

Two 15.5-ounce cans black beans, rinsed and drained well

2 canned chipotles (from a can of chipotles in adobo sauce), minced (about 1 tablespoon), plus 3 tablespoons adobo sauce

3 tablespoons cider vinegar

1½ cups fresh or frozen corn kernels (if frozen, thaw first)

6 ounces sharp Cheddar cheese, grated (1½ cups)

6 ounces Monterey Jack cheese, grated (1½ cups)

¾ cup chopped fresh cilantro

Freshly ground black pepper

Tortilla chips, for serving

**This is a great party dip that can be fully assembled up to 2 days ahead. Keep covered in the refrigerator until ready to bake.**

Heat the oven to 425°F. Grease a 1½-quart baking dish with oil and line a baking sheet with foil.

Set the tomatoes in a colander over the sink and sprinkle with 1 teaspoon of the salt.

Heat the oil in a 12-inch skillet over medium-high heat until shimmering hot. Reduce the heat to medium, add the onion, sprinkle with 1 teaspoon salt, and cook, stirring, until softened and translucent, 4 to 6 minutes. Add the garlic and chili powder and cook, stirring, for 1 minute. Add half of the beans, the chipotles and adobo sauce, and ¾ cup water and bring to a boil. Cook until the liquid reduces by about half, 2 to 3 minutes.

Transfer the bean mixture to a food processor, add the vinegar, and process until smooth. Let cool for a couple of minutes, then transfer to a large bowl. Add the rest of the beans, the tomatoes, corn, half of each of the cheeses, and ½ cup of the cilantro. Mix well and season to taste with salt and pepper.

Transfer to the baking dish and sprinkle with the remaining cheese. Bake on the foil-lined baking sheet (to catch dips) until the cheese melts and browns around the edges, about 15 minutes (longer if refrigerated). Sprinkle with the remaining cilantro and serve with the tortilla chips for dipping.

*—Tony Rosenfeld*

# Pork Shiu Mai

*Yields about 5 dozen shiu mai.*

1 pound ground pork

1 cup thinly sliced Napa cabbage, plus extra leaves for lining the steamer

½ cup chopped scallions (both white and green parts)

¼ cup chopped fresh cilantro

1½ tablespoons soy sauce

1 tablespoon finely chopped garlic

1 tablespoon rice vinegar

1 tablespoon cornstarch; more for dusting

2 teaspoons peeled and finely chopped fresh ginger

1½ teaspoons Asian sesame oil

1 teaspoon granulated sugar

½ teaspoon freshly ground black pepper

1 large egg white

55 to 60 shiu mai wrappers or wonton wrappers

Soy Dipping Sauce (see recipe, below)

## Soy Dipping Sauce

*Yields about 1 cup.*

**If you're not making all of the shiu mai, you won't need the full recipe; you can either make a half-batch or use the leftover sauce in a stir-fry. Mirin, a sweet Japanese rice wine, is available in Asian grocery stores and some supermarkets.**

⅓ cup soy sauce

⅓ cup rice vinegar

⅓ cup thinly sliced scallions (about 3, both white and green parts)

2 tablespoons mirin

1 tablespoon Asian sesame oil

1 teaspoon peeled and finely chopped fresh ginger

Combine all the ingredients in a small bowl. Use within a day of making.

**Packaged shiu mai wrappers and wonton wrappers are made from the same kind of dumpling dough, though shiu mai wrappers are generally thinner and round, while wonton wrappers are square. Round wrappers are preferred in this recipe, but either will work just fine. The dumplings can be conveniently frozen ahead of time and popped directly into the steamer when you're ready to serve them.**

In a large bowl, stir together the pork, sliced cabbage, scallions, cilantro, soy sauce, garlic, vinegar, 1 tablespoon cornstarch, ginger, sesame oil, sugar, pepper, and egg white.

Sprinkle a rimmed baking sheet liberally with cornstarch. Set a small bowl of water on the work surface. If the wrappers are larger than 3 inches across in any direction, trim them with a cookie cutter to 3-inch rounds. Working with one wrapper at a time, and keeping the remaining wrappers covered with plastic wrap so they don't dry out, place a heaping teaspoon of the pork filling in the center of each one. Using a pastry brush or your fingers, dab a bit of water around the edge of the wrapper to moisten. Crimp the wrapper up and around the filling, squeezing slightly with your fingers to bring it together like a beggar's pouch. Place on the cornstarch-coated baking sheet, cover with plastic wrap, and repeat with the remaining wrappers and filling until you run out of one or the other. You can steam the shiu mai immediately or freeze and steam them later.

**To freeze:** Freeze the uncooked shiu mai on the baking sheet. When frozen, transfer them to an airtight container, setting parchment or plastic wrap between layers, or seal them in a plastic bag. Store in the freezer, where they'll keep for about a month.

**To steam:** If frozen, do not thaw the shiu mai before cooking. If using a bamboo steamer, follow the manufacturer's directions for set-up. For a metal steamer, put 2 inches of water in the bottom of the pot. Line the steamer insert with cabbage leaves to keep the shiu mai from sticking. (Do this with a bamboo insert, too.) Set the steamer (or wok if using a bamboo steamer) over medium-high heat and cover. When steam begins to escape from the steamer, remove from the heat and carefully take off the lid. Arrange the shiu mai in the steamer so they don't touch, otherwise they will stick together (you'll have to cook them in batches). Cover the steamer and return to medium-high heat. Steam until the pork is cooked through (cut into one to check), 5 to 7 minutes if fresh, 10 to 12 minutes if frozen. Serve with the dipping sauce. *—Kate Hays*

**tip:** Shiu mai wrappers are available in Asian markets, or else use wonton wrappers, which can be found in most supermarkets.

# Bacon, Leek & Cheddar Mini Quiches

*Yields about 4 dozen mini quiches.*

¾ pound bacon, cut into medium dice

3 cups medium-diced leeks, washed well and drained (about 3 leeks, white and light green parts only)

1¼ cups half-and-half

4 ounces extra-sharp Cheddar cheese, grated (1 cup)

2 large eggs

2 large egg yolks

2 tablespoons chopped fresh thyme

1 teaspoon kosher salt

½ teaspoon freshly ground black pepper

¼ teaspoon ground nutmeg

Cooking spray

Two 1.1-pound packages frozen puff pastry sheets (preferably Pepperidge Farm® brand), thawed according to package directions

Flour as needed for rolling out the dough

**Once you get the hang of making these tasty bites, you can improvise with other fillings. Substitute smoked salmon for the bacon and Fontina cheese for the Cheddar, or make the quiches vegetarian by using chopped sun-dried tomatoes instead of the bacon.**

In a medium skillet over medium-high heat, cook the bacon until browned and crispy, 6 to 8 minutes. Using a slotted spoon, transfer it to a plate lined with a paper towel. Pour off all but 1 to 2 tablespoons of the fat in the skillet. Set the skillet over medium heat and cook the leeks, stirring occasionally, until softened, about 5 minutes. Let cool slightly.

Meanwhile, combine the half-and-half, Cheddar, whole eggs, egg yolks, thyme, salt, pepper, and nutmeg in a medium bowl. Add the cooled leeks and bacon and stir to combine.

Lightly spray four mini muffin tins (or two if your tins have two dozen cups) with cooking spray. (If you don't have enough muffin tins, you can assemble the quiches in batches, storing the remaining egg mixture and dough in the refrigerator until you're ready to use it.)

Working with one sheet of puff pastry dough at a time, use a floured rolling pin to roll the dough on a lightly floured work surface into a 10x18-inch rectangle. Stamp out 3-inch circles of dough with a cookie cutter and gently press the rounds into the mini muffin tins, making sure that each round is centered and that the dough extends up to the top of the tin. Fill each with about 1 tablespoon of filling—you can fill right to the top of the dough. Repeat with the remaining dough and filling until all the filling is used. You may not

need all the dough; save leftovers for another use. You can bake the quiches immediately or freeze and bake them later.

**To freeze:** Freeze the unbaked quiches in the muffin tins for about 2 hours, until set. Remove them from the tins and transfer to an airtight container, setting parchment or plastic wrap between layers, or seal them in a plastic bag. Store in the freezer, where they'll keep for about a month.

**To bake:** If frozen, do not thaw the quiches before baking. Put the quiches back into the muffin tins. Heat the oven to 400°F and position racks in the top and bottom thirds of the oven. Bake the quiches, switching the position of the tins halfway through baking, until the filling is puffed and the crust is golden brown, about 20 minutes if fresh or 30 to 35 minutes if frozen. *—Kate Hays*

# Goat Cheese, Lemon & Chive Turnovers

Be sure to thaw the frozen puff pastry overnight in the fridge before you plan to make these. You can fill and shape the turnovers up to 2 hours ahead of cooking. Cover tightly with plastic wrap or brush with melted butter before refrigerating.

Position a rack in the center of the oven and heat the oven to 400°F.

In a medium bowl, mash the goat cheese with a fork. Add the chives, onion, lemon zest, ½ teaspoon salt, and ¼ teaspoon pepper. Stir until well combined.

On a lightly floured work surface, unfold the pastry sheet and lightly dust with flour. Use a rolling pin to roll the sheet into a 12-inch square. Cut the dough into 9 squares. Put equal amounts of the filling (about 1 tablespoon) in the center of each square. Moisten the edges of a square with a fingertip dipped in water. Fold the dough over to form a triangle, gently pressing to remove air pockets around the filling and pressing the edges of the dough together. Use the tines of a fork to crimp and seal the edges of the turnover. Repeat this process with the other dough squares.

Arrange the turnovers on a cookie sheet and bake until puffed and golden all over, 15 to 18 minutes. Let cool on a rack for a few minutes and serve warm. *—Jessica Bard*

*Yields 9 turnovers.*

4 ounces fresh goat cheese (about ½ cup), at room temperature

¼ cup thinly snipped fresh chives

¼ cup minced yellow onion

1 teaspoon finely grated lemon zest

Kosher salt and freshly ground black pepper

Flour for dusting

1 sheet frozen puff pastry (preferably Pepperidge Farm brand), thawed overnight in the refrigerator

# Spinach, Feta & Sun-Dried Tomato Phyllo Triangles

*Yields about 6 dozen phyllo triangles.*

Two 10-ounce packages frozen chopped spinach, thawed and squeezed dry

2 cups crumbled feta cheese (about 12 ounces)

¾ cup roughly chopped fresh mint

½ cup roughly chopped oil-packed sun-dried tomatoes

½ cup pitted and roughly chopped Kalamata olives

4 large eggs, lightly beaten

3 tablespoons chopped garlic

2 tablespoons fresh lemon juice

1 tablespoon finely grated lemon zest

¾ teaspoon freshly ground black pepper

½ teaspoon kosher salt

One 1-pound package frozen phyllo dough (preferably a twin-pack), thawed according to package directions

1 cup (2 sticks) unsalted butter, melted; more as needed for baking

**Think of these savory little jewels as spanikopita (the Greek spinach-and-cheese pies) with an added punch of flavor and color. You can bake them all for a large party or freeze half for another time.**

In a large bowl, combine the spinach, feta, mint, sun-dried tomatoes, olives, eggs, garlic, lemon juice and zest, pepper, and salt. Mix well.

Unroll the phyllo and lay it flat on a clean, dry work surface. Cover completely with plastic wrap. Working with one sheet of phyllo at a time, and keeping the rest covered with the plastic wrap to keep it from drying out, place a sheet vertically in front of you. Brush the phyllo with butter and cover with another sheet. Butter the top sheet and cut the phyllo lengthwise into equal 3-inch-wide strips. Spoon 2 teaspoons of filling on the lower end of each strip as shown at right. Fold up the phyllo strips as you would a flag to create a neat triangle, being careful not to roll too tightly or the triangles will crack when baked. Transfer to a baking sheet and cover with plastic wrap. Repeat with the rest of the phyllo and filling until you run out of filling. You can bake the triangles immediately or freeze and bake them later.

**To freeze:** Freeze the uncooked triangles on the baking sheet. When frozen, transfer them to an airtight container, setting parchment or plastic wrap between layers if needed. Store in the freezer, where they'll keep for about a month.

**To bake:** If frozen, do not thaw the triangles before baking. Position racks in the top and bottom thirds of the oven and heat the oven to 375°F. Butter two baking sheets. Arrange the phyllo triangles on the prepared baking sheets in a single layer. Brush the tops with melted butter and bake until golden brown, 15 to 20 minutes for fresh triangles, 20 to 25 minutes for frozen, switching the positions of the pans halfway through baking. *—Kate Hays*

## Making neat phyllo triangles

**1** Starting with 2 teaspoons of filling at the end of a strip of phyllo, lift a corner up and over the filling to form a triangle.

**2** Lift a corner of the triangle and roll it over, wrapping the filling in another layer of phyllo.

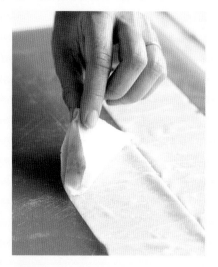

**3** Continue lifting a corner of the triangle and rolling it over until you get to the end of the strip.

# Pan-Fried Halloumi with Fennel, Olive & Mint Compote

*Serves four to six.*

3 tablespoons extra-virgin olive oil

½ medium fennel bulb, cored and cut into ¼-inch dice (about 1¼ cups)

½ medium yellow onion, cut into ¼-inch dice (about ¾ cup)

Kosher salt and freshly ground black pepper

12 pitted Kalamata olives, slivered (about ⅓ cup)

1 teaspoon finely grated lemon zest

⅓ cup minced fresh mint

One 8-ounce package halloumi cheese, cut into ¼- to ⅜-inch-thick slices

A sheep's milk cheese from Cyprus, halloumi resembles fresh mozzarella, but it has a springier texture that just softens—but doesn't melt—when grilled or fried, while the surface turns a light, crisp golden. Its mild flavor makes it a great foil for assertive Mediterranean ingredients like the ones in the compote. The interplay of textures and flavors in this recipe is absolutely delicious, but a simpler preparation—a drizzle of olive oil and squeeze of lemon over the warm cheese—is also satisfying. Try this as a prelude to (or even alongside) grilled fish or lamb chops.

Heat 2 tablespoons of the oil in a heavy, 10-inch sauté pan over medium heat until hot. Add the fennel and onion and cook gently, stirring occasionally, until the vegetables begin to soften (but don't let them brown), 4 to 5 minutes. Reduce the heat to medium low, add ¼ teaspoon salt and ¼ teaspoon pepper and continue to cook until the vegetables soften completely, another 3 to 5 minutes. Turn the heat to low and stir in the olives, lemon zest, mint, and the remaining 1 tablespoon oil. Remove from the heat and cover to keep warm.

Set a large (preferably 12-inch) nonstick skillet over medium-high heat (no oil is necessary) until hot, about 1 minute. Working in batches if necessary to avoid crowding the pan, cook the halloumi until golden in spots, about 2 minutes. Flip and cook until the other side is golden, about 2 minutes more. Reduce the heat as needed if the halloumi is browning too fast.

Place the halloumi slices on a serving platter, overlapping them. Stir the compote and spoon half of it over the halloumi. Serve immediately with the remaining compote on the side. *—Jessica Bard*

## Discover halloumi, a cheese you can grill

Halloumi, from Cyprus, has a lot going for it. Traditionally made from goat's and sheep's milk, this cheese has a great chewy texture and a mellow yet briny flavor that hints of mint. Though halloumi is perfectly tasty when eaten fresh with bread and fruits and vegetables like watermelon, figs, cucumbers, tomatoes, or olives, the coolest thing about halloumi is that, when heated, it softens but doesn't melt, so you can grill it, pan-fry it, or pop it under the broiler. Cooked halloumi gets a tasty brown crust and a soft gooey center.

A marinade makes halloumi even better. Soak sliced halloumi in olive oil, lemon juice, red pepper flakes, chopped garlic, and fresh oregano for several hours, then eat it right out of the marinade or throw it on the grill—it's delicious in a BLT or tucked into a pita with a slab of ripe tomato and a drizzle of the marinade. For grilling, slices that are about ⅓ inch thick work best.

If halloumi is too salty for your taste, simmer it in water for about 5 minutes. This also softens the cheese, so if you intend to grill it, chill it until firm.

Look for halloumi in the cheese section of your local market; it keeps well in the refrigerator and can also be frozen.

# Smoked Salmon & Pea Fritters with Scallion Sour Cream

*Yields about 18 fritters.*

1 cup sour cream

1 bunch scallions, thinly sliced (white and green parts kept separate)

2 tablespoons capers, drained, rinsed, and roughly chopped

2 large eggs

¾ cup whole milk

¼ pound smoked salmon, cut into ¼-inch dice (about ¾ cup)

1 cup frozen peas

1¼ cups all-purpose flour

2 teaspoons baking powder

Kosher salt

¼ teaspoon ground white pepper

1½ cups vegetable oil

**Smoked salmon stars in this elegant dish that's a snap to whip up. Try substituting sweet corn kernels for the peas or crème frâiche for the sour cream.**

Position a rack in the center of the oven and heat the oven to 200°F.

In a medium bowl, mix together the sour cream, scallion greens, and capers. Set aside.

In a large bowl, whisk the eggs until frothy. Whisk in the milk. Stir in the salmon, peas, and scallion whites. Add the flour, baking powder, ½ teaspoon salt, and the white pepper and whisk until well combined.

Pour the oil into a 10-inch skillet that's 2 inches deep (the oil should be about ½ inch deep) and heat over medium-high heat until shimmering hot. (A good way to tell if it's hot enough is to drop a 1-inch cube of bread in the oil; it should turn golden brown in about 30 seconds.) Add the batter to the oil one heaping tablespoon at a time. Cook the fritters in batches of six (don't crowd the pan) until golden brown on the first side, 2 to 3 minutes. Using a slotted spatula or spoon, turn and cook until the second side is golden brown, about 2 minutes. Transfer the fritters to a rimmed baking dish lined with paper towels and keep warm in the oven. Continue to cook the remaining fritters.

Serve the fritters hot with the scallion sour cream. *—Jessica Bard*

# Seared Shrimp with Pimentón & Sherry

*Serves eight.*

1½ pounds large (31 to 40 per pound) shrimp, peeled, deveined, and patted dry with paper towels

Kosher salt

3 tablespoons extra-virgin olive oil

6 medium cloves garlic, very thinly sliced

Heaping ¼ teaspoon sweet pimentón (or paprika)

Heaping ⅛ teaspoon crushed red pepper flakes

3 tablespoons fino sherry

¼ teaspoon finely grated lemon zest

1½ tablespoons thinly snipped fresh chives

Fresh lemon juice to taste

**Pimentón, or Spanish smoked paprika, is the sweetly smoky flavor in everything from chorizo sausage to paella. Look for *dulce* (sweet) and *de la Vera* on the label: Peppers from the La Vera region are always smoke-dried; in some other regions they are sun-dried. Pimentón can be found at some specialty food stores and from online sources.**

Sprinkle the shrimp with ¾ teaspoon salt, toss, and let sit for 10 minutes (or refrigerate for up to 1 hour).

In a 12-inch skillet, heat the oil on high heat. Add the shrimp to the skillet, sprinkle with ¾ teaspoon salt, and sear until they're pink and a little golden on one side, about 1 minute. Sprinkle the garlic, pimentón, and red pepper over the shrimp, and cook, stirring, until the shrimp are almost completely pink, another minute. Add the sherry and cook, stirring to deglaze the bottom of the pan, until the shrimp are pink all over (the sherry will evaporate quickly but you should still have some juices in the pan).

Remove the pan from the heat. Add the lemon zest and chives and toss with the shrimp. Pour the shrimp and juices into a serving dish, squeeze on lemon juice to taste, and serve. *—Sarah Jay*

## A bite-size buffet: tapas at home

Tapas, the small bites and plates of food offered in the bodegas of Spain, are so simple and sociable, they make great cocktail party fare. It's easy to create your own "tapas bar" at home when you invite friends over for drinks—just start with our recipes and the suggestions that follow.

**Make one or more of these recipes:**
- Seared Shrimp with Pimentón & Sherry (at left)
- Sautéed Chorizo with Red Wine (p. 30)
- Manchego Marinated in Olive Oil & Herbs (p. 40)

**Set out in little bowls:**
- Buttery Marcona almonds from Spain (they're fried in olive oil and sprinkled with sea salt)
- Simple salted almonds
- Marinated olives and olives stuffed with piquillo peppers
- Boquerones, which are Spanish white anchovies

**Top toasted breads with:**
- A mixture of tuna, onion, capers, and olive oil
- A dollop of aioli and serrano ham, Manchego cheese, or roasted piquillo pepper
- A rub of garlic and tomato and a drizzle of olive oil; add a slice of Manchego cheese or Serrano ham if you like

To drink, try fino sherry (serve it well-chilled), Spanish rosé, white Rueda, cava (Spain's sparkling wine), red Rioja crianza, or your favorite beer

# Sautéed Chorizo with Red Wine

*Serves eight.*

3 tablespoons extra-virgin olive oil

1½ pounds cured but soft chorizo, cut into ½-inch-thick slices

⅓ cup dry red wine

Good country bread, cut into large cubes

**Hard, fully cured Spanish chorizo is a classic tapa. For this recipe, you'll need a softer cured chorizo, such as Bilbao chorizo, or one labeled "soft for cooking." You can find domestic cured chorizos in Hispanic markets and gourmet markets or from online sources.**

Heat the olive oil in a 12-inch skillet over medium heat. Add the chorizo slices and cook until they begin to turn deep brown on one side, 3 to 5 minutes. Stir and continue to cook, stirring a few times, until the chorizo is deeply browned all over, about 5 minutes more. Carefully add the wine (be ready in case it flames) and let it simmer, scraping the bottom of the pan to deglaze it, until it has reduced somewhat but is still saucy, 1 to 3 minutes.

Pour the chorizo and juices into a serving dish. Serve with the bread, for dipping into the sauce. *—Sarah Jay*

# Sautéed Mushrooms with Garlic & Parsley

*Serves eight.*

**5 tablespoons extra-virgin olive oil**

**1 pound white or cremini mushrooms, trimmed and cut into quarters (or sixths, if large)**

**Kosher salt**

**5 to 6 medium cloves garlic, minced (1½ tablespoons)**

**1 tablespoon sherry vinegar**

**2 tablespoons chopped fresh flat-leaf parsley**

**For the best flavor, brown the mushrooms well.**

Heat the oil in a 12-inch skillet over high heat until it's hot and shimmering. Add the mushrooms, season with ¾ teaspoon salt, stir to coat in the oil, then let the mushrooms cook undisturbed until the liquid they release evaporates and they're deep golden brown, 5 to 7 minutes. Stir and continue to cook, stirring a few times, until most sides are nicely browned, 3 to 5 minutes more. Reduce the heat to medium, add the garlic, and cook just to soften it, 15 to 30 seconds. Add the vinegar and stir, scraping up any browned bits in the pan, until the vinegar evaporates, about 15 seconds. Remove the pan from the heat and toss in the parsley. Season to taste with more salt, if you like.

Transfer to a dish and serve with toothpicks for spearing the mushrooms or a serving spoon for putting on individual plates. —*Sarah Jay*

# Olives & Peppers on a Pick with Scallion Vinaigrette

**These little skewers are good with just olives and peppers, or you can add a third element, such as pickled onions or feta.**

Finely grate enough of the lemon zest to get ¼ teaspoon packed zest. Cut the lemon in half and squeeze to get 2 tablespoons juice. Put the zest and juice in a small bowl. Whisk in the oil, scallion, thyme, chile, and salt and pepper to taste. Let the vinaigrette sit for at least 20 minutes (or up to 12 hours in the fridge; bring to room temperature before using) to meld the flavors and soften the scallion.

Cut the peppers lengthwise into ½-inch-wide strands, then cut the strands in half crosswise—you'll need 40 pieces of pepper. Fold a piece of pepper in half and thread it onto a toothpick. Spear an olive onto the pick. Then spear either an onion or a cube of feta on the end, if using. Set the pick in a shallow serving dish. Repeat with the remaining ingredients. If not serving right away, refrigerate.

About 30 minutes before serving, give the vinaigrette a good whisk to emulsify as best you can, then drizzle it over the olive picks. —*Sarah Jay*

*Serves eight; yields about 40 skewers.*

**1 lemon**

**¼ cup extra-virgin olive oil**

**1 small scallion (white and light green parts), very thinly sliced (1 tablespoon)**

**½ teaspoon chopped fresh thyme**

**½ teaspoon seeded and minced red serrano chile or jalapeño**

**Kosher salt and freshly ground black pepper**

**7 jarred piquillo peppers or 2 jarred roasted red peppers**

**40 small pitted green olives (from about a 2.5-ounce jar)**

**40 pickled sour cocktail onions (from about two 3.5-ounce jars; optional)**

**12 ounces feta (creamy feta holds together better than dry, crumbly feta), cut into ½- to ¾-inch cubes (optional)**

# Manchego Marinated in Olive Oil & Herbs

*Serves eight.*

1 cup extra-virgin olive oil; more if needed

3 large sprigs fresh thyme

Two 4-inch sprigs fresh rosemary

1 small dried red chile, cut in half or thirds

8 ounces Manchego (more aged is better), rind cut off and cut into ½- to ¾-inch cubes

**This is an easy way to make supermarket-quality Manchego cheese taste extra special. You should eat the cheese within three days, but you can keep the infused olive oil refrigerated and use it for sautéing for up to ten days.**

In a small saucepan, heat the oil, thyme, rosemary, and chile over medium heat until the oil is hot (160°F) and looks shimmery, about 2 minutes. Set aside to cool completely at room temperature.

Put the Manchego in a glass or ceramic bowl. Pour the cooled oil mixture on top. Add more oil to cover, if needed. Cover and refrigerate for at least 4 hours.

Remove the bowl from the refrigerator a few hours before serving to return the oil to room temperature.

To serve, transfer everything to a pretty bowl, with toothpicks alongside for spearing the cheese. —*Sarah Jay*

# Chorizo

Consisting primarily of pork, pimentón, and garlic, this dry-cured sausage adds a meaty note to stews, pastas, and eggs. Some dry-cured chorizos are hard and ready to eat. Others are softer (though not raw) and benefit from a little cooking.

# Jamón Serrano

Sliced paper thin and set on a plate alone or with Manchego cheese, jamón (pronounced ha-MOHN) serrano is the simplest tapa of all. This cured ham looks just like Italian prosciutto, but its unique curing and aging process translates into more complex and intense flavors. Salty, sweet, rich, and mellow, jamón serrano surely makes the best ham sandwich you'll ever have. It's just starting to appear in regular supermarkets in the United States and is usually available in specialty food shops.

# Sherry vinegar

Sharply acidic with sweet sherry undertones, this vinegar may become your everyday vinegar at home. Use it instead of red-wine vinegar and you'll never go back.

# Manchego

Spain's most well-known cheese is made from sheep's milk and always features a basket-weave pattern on its rind. Look for aged Manchego (1 year or older), which has a firmer texture and nutty flavor.

# Piquillo peppers

These pointy-tipped little peppers (piquillo means "little beak") are slow-roasted over a wood fire, peeled by hand, and canned or jarred in nothing but their juices. They have a wonderfully sweet flavor with a kick. Traditionally they're stuffed with salt cod, but they're also delightful in pastas, sandwiches, omelets, sauces, or anywhere else you might use a roasted bell pepper.

# Pimentón

This is Spanish smoked paprika, and it can be sweet (*dulce*), spicy (*picante*), or sweet-spicy (*agridulce*). Use it as you would paprika, and you'll find its smoky flavor adds an intriguing background note to whatever you're cooking.

# Crispy Potatoes with Tangy Tomato Sauce (Patatas Bravas)

*Serves eight.*

**For the sauce:**

1½ tablespoons extra-virgin olive oil

⅓ cup chopped onion (½ small)

⅓ cup chopped carrot (1 small)

2 medium cloves garlic, smashed and peeled

1 tablespoon dry white wine

¼ teaspoon sweet pimentón (or paprika)

¼ teaspoon ground cumin

1½ cups canned tomatoes with juice, chopped coarsely

3 large sprigs fresh thyme

1 teaspoon granulated sugar

¼ teaspoon Tabasco®; more to taste

Kosher salt and freshly ground black pepper

¼ teaspoon sherry vinegar

**For the potatoes:**

2½ pounds (about 8 medium) Yukon Gold, white, or red potatoes, scrubbed and cut into 1-inch pieces (no need to peel)

½ cup extra-virgin olive oil

Kosher salt

1 teaspoon chopped fresh rosemary (optional)

**Roasting the potatoes in a good amount of olive oil gives them a crispy fried flavor without the hassle of deep frying. The sauce can be made up to three days ahead.**

**Make the sauce:** In a 1- or 2-quart saucepan, heat the oil over medium heat. Add the onion, carrot, and garlic and cook, stirring frequently, until softened but not browned, about 5 minutes. Add the wine and let it reduce until almost evaporated, about 1 minute. Add the pimentón and cumin and stir for about 15 seconds. Add the tomatoes and juice, thyme, sugar, Tabasco, ¼ teaspoon salt, and a few grinds of pepper. Reduce the heat to a gentle simmer and cook, uncovered, stirring occasionally, to reduce the sauce somewhat and intensify its flavor. This should take about 1 hour; depending on how much juice you started with, you may need to add up to ½ cup water during simmering to keep the consistency saucy rather than dry.

Fish out the spent thyme sprigs. Purée the sauce with a hand-held blender or in a regular blender until it's smooth and creamy; you can thin with a little water if needed. Stir in the vinegar. Taste and add salt and pepper, if needed. The sauce should be slightly spicy, and you should have about 1½ cups.

**Roast the potatoes:** Heat the oven to 425°F. Toss the potatoes with the ½ cup oil, 1 teaspoon salt, and the rosemary (if using) on a large rimmed baking sheet. Roast, turning the potatoes with a metal spatula every 15 minutes, until they're browned and crisp outside and tender inside, about 45 minutes.

Put the potatoes in a serving dish and put the sauce in a small dish next to the potatoes, along with a spoon. *—Sarah Jay*

# 2 Soups

p56

p62

**Russett Potato Soup with Pancetta Croutons (recipe on page 54)**

# Silky Asparagus Soup

*Yields 7 to 8 cups; serves six to eight.*

2 pounds asparagus

3½ tablespoons unsalted butter

2 small ribs celery, coarsely chopped (about 1 cup)

1 large yellow onion, coarsely chopped (about 2 cups)

1 large leek (white and green parts), halved lengthwise, rinsed well, and thinly sliced crosswise (keep dark green parts separate from light green and white parts)

6 cups cold water

8 black peppercorns

5 sprigs fresh flat-leaf parsley

2 sprigs fresh thyme

Kosher salt

2 medium cloves garlic, chopped

1 large or 3 small red potatoes (about ½ pound total), peeled and cut into ½-inch dice (1 heaping cup)

¼ cup heavy cream

Freshly ground white pepper

**Both thick and thin asparagus spears will work in this soup, which is as delicious served cold as it is hot. To speed things up, make the vegetable stock a day ahead.**

Snap off the tough ends of the asparagus, but don't discard them. Cut about 1½ inches of the tips off the asparagus spears and cut the spears crosswise in thirds; set the spears and tips aside separately.

Melt 1½ tablespoons of the butter in a 3-quart saucepan over medium-low heat. Add the asparagus ends, about half of the celery, the onion, and the dark green parts of the leek. Cook, uncovered, stirring occasionally, until the vegetables look very soft, about 30 minutes (if the vegetables show any sign of browning, reduce the heat to low).

Add the cold water, peppercorns, parsley, thyme, and ½ teaspoon salt. Bring to a boil, reduce the heat to medium low, cover, and simmer for 30 minutes to make a flavorful vegetable stock.

Meanwhile, bring a 2-quart pot of salted water to a boil over high heat. Add the asparagus tips and cook until just tender, 2 to 3 minutes. Drain in a colander, shower with cold running water to stop the cooking, and drain again. Set aside.

In another 3-quart (or larger) saucepan, melt the remaining 2 tablespoons butter over medium-low heat. Add the white and light green sliced leek and the remaining celery and season with a generous pinch of salt. Cook, stirring occasionally, until the leeks look soft but not browned, 3 to 4 minutes. Add the garlic and cook for 1 minute more. Add the asparagus spears and potato. Set a wire mesh strainer over the pot and pour in the stock from the other pot; discarding the solids. Stir well and bring to a boil. Reduce the heat to medium low, cover, and cook at a lively simmer until the potato and asparagus are very tender, about 20 minutes. Turn off the heat and let cool slightly.

Purée the soup in a blender in two or three batches. Return the puréed soup to the soup pot, add the cream, and stir well. Reheat gently over medium-low heat. Season to taste with more salt and a large pinch of white pepper. Ladle the soup into bowls or soup plates, scatter in the asparagus tips, distributing them evenly among the servings, and serve. *—Ruth Lively*

# Tortellini Soup with Carrots, Peas & Leeks

**You can make most of this speedy soup ahead of time, but don't add the tortellini until you're ready to eat or they'll become mushy.**

Trim the roots and dark green leaves from the leeks. Slice the white and light green part in half lengthwise, then slice the halves thinly crosswise. Rinse well and drain.

Melt the butter in a 4-quart saucepan over medium heat. Add the garlic, leeks, and carrot. Season with a couple pinches of salt and cook, stirring occasionally, until tender, 5 to 7 minutes. (It's fine if the vegetables brown lightly.) Stir in ¼ teaspoon pepper and cook for about 20 seconds, then add the broth and bring to a boil. Add the tortellini and cook for 3 minutes. Reduce the heat to a simmer and add the peas. Continue to simmer until the tortellini are cooked, 3 to 5 minutes.

Season to taste with salt and pepper. Portion the soup into warm bowls, top each with some of the cheese, and serve. *—Joanne McAllister Smart*

*Serves four.*

2 medium leeks (12 ounces)

1 tablespoon unsalted butter

3 cloves garlic, finely chopped (about 1 tablespoon)

½ medium carrot, peeled and finely diced (2 tablespoons)

Kosher salt

Freshly ground black pepper

5 cups homemade or canned low-salt chicken broth

8 ounces frozen cheese tortellini

1 cup frozen peas

¼ cup freshly grated Parmigiano-Reggiano or Grana Padano

# Summer Squash Soup with Pesto

*Yields about 8 cups soup and ³⁄₄ cup pesto; serves four.*

3 large cloves garlic, peeled

¹⁄₃ cup plus 2 tablespoons extra-virgin olive oil

1 medium-size sweet onion (such as Vidalia), cut into small dice (about 2 cups)

Kosher salt and freshly ground black pepper

4 small zucchini or yellow squash (or a mix), quartered lengthwise, seeded, and cut into medium dice (about 3 cups)

2 cups small-diced tomatoes (from about 2 medium-large tomatoes)

1 quart homemade or canned low-salt chicken broth

1¹⁄₃ cups fresh basil leaves (reserve the stems)

¹⁄₂ cup freshly grated Parmigiano-Reggiano (plus 1 large piece of the rind, optional)

1 cup water

¹⁄₄ cup pine nuts

2 teaspoons chopped fresh marjoram

**A generous dollop of pesto gives this soup great color and a bright hit of summery herbal perfume. To streamline your prep, dice the squash and tomatoes while the onion and garlic are cooking.**

Finely chop 2 cloves of the garlic. Heat 2 tablespoons of the oil in a 4-quart saucepan over medium-low heat. Add the onion, chopped garlic, ³⁄₄ teaspoon salt, and ¹⁄₄ teaspoon pepper; cook, stirring occasionally, until the onion is very soft and just beginning to brown, about 15 minutes.

Add the squash, increase the heat to medium, and cook, stirring occasionally, until the squash just begins to soften, 4 to 5 minutes. Add the tomatoes, broth, basil stems, Parmigiano rind (if using), and water and bring to a simmer. Simmer until the squash is tender, about 5 minutes.

While the soup is simmering, put the remaining clove of garlic in a food processor and pulse until coarsely chopped. Scrape down the bowl. Add the basil leaves, grated Parmigiano, pine nuts, ¹⁄₄ teaspoon salt, and ¹⁄₈ teaspoon pepper and process until roughly chopped. With the motor on, slowly add the remaining ¹⁄₃ cup oil. Season to taste with salt and pepper.

Using tongs, remove the basil stems and Parmigiano rind (if using) from the soup. Add the marjoram and season to taste with salt and pepper. Serve the soup topped with a generous dollop of pesto and pass the remaining pesto at the table. —*Allison Ehri*

This is a task that a cook might perform several times during the course of preparing a big meal, so it's worth knowing how to do it quickly, safely, and easily. The first step, of course, is making sure your knife is sharp.

1 Trim the ends but leave much of the root intact. Cut the onion in half from end to end and peel each half. Lay one half on its cut side. Make parallel vertical cuts from root to stem end, but not completely through the root end. Space the cuts as wide as you want your dice.

2 Make one or two horizontal cuts, again being careful not to cut through the root end. Whether you make one or two horizontal cuts depends on the size of the onion.

3 Make a series of cuts perpendicular to the cuts from step 1, again spacing them as wide as you want the dice to be. Keep the fingers of your guiding hand curled so you don't cut your fingertips.

4 When you get close to the root end and the cutting becomes awkward, flip the onion root side up as shown and slice across it one or two times.

5 Flip the onion back to how it was in step 3. The top is now flat and easier to dice. Finish dicing down to the root. Discard the root and repeat with the other onion half.

# Creamy Tomato Soup with Zucchini

*Serves four as a light main course.*

6 tablespoons (¾ stick) unsalted butter

3 medium zucchini (about 1½ pounds total), cut into medium dice

Kosher salt

2 cloves garlic, minced

1 cup chopped yellow onion

Three 15-ounce cans peeled whole tomatoes, drained

1½ cups homemade or canned low-salt chicken broth

½ cup dry white wine

1 cup heavy cream

½ cup fresh basil leaves, chopped, for garnish

**Sautéed zucchini makes this light and bright soup a little more substantial. To make it even more of a meal, serve it with slices of toasted, garlic-rubbed baguette or a pesto and mozzarella panini.**

Melt 4 tablespoons (½ stick) of the butter in a large stockpot over medium-high heat. Add the zucchini and 1 teaspoon salt and cook, stirring occasionally, until the zucchini is crisp-tender but not browned, about 5 minutes. Add the garlic and cook for 1 minute. Using a slotted spoon, transfer the zucchini mixture to a medium bowl.

Melt the remaining 2 tablespoons butter in the pot over medium-high heat. Add the onion and cook, stirring, until it becomes translucent, about 3 minutes. Increase the heat to high, add the tomatoes and 1 teaspoon salt, and cook, stirring constantly for 1 minute. Add the broth and wine and bring to a boil. Reduce the heat to a simmer and cook, stirring occasionally, until the liquid has reduced by half, about 20 minutes.

Remove the pot from the heat and let the tomato mixture cool slightly. Purée the soup in the pot with a hand blender or in batches in a regular blender. If you use a regular blender, return the soup to the pot. Add the cream. Bring to a boil and cook until heated through, about 2 minutes. Stir the zucchini into the soup. Garnish each serving with some of the chopped fresh basil and serve. *–Julianna Grimes Bottcher*

# Roasted Tomato & Fennel Soup

*Yields 5½ to 6 cups; serves four to six.*

¼ cup extra-virgin olive oil

2½ pounds plum tomatoes, cored, halved lengthwise, and seeded

1 medium-large fennel bulb (about 1 pound), cored and cut into medium dice (plus some chopped fennel fronds for garnish; optional)

1 medium yellow onion, cut into medium dice

2 cloves garlic, chopped

Kosher salt and freshly ground black pepper

2 cups homemade or canned low-salt chicken broth

½ cup whole or low-fat milk

2 teaspoons chopped fresh thyme

¼ cup crumbled fresh goat cheese

**Broiling makes quick work of peeling fresh tomatoes and, as a bonus, it gives the tomatoes a deep, roasted flavor. Don't be afraid to broil the tomatoes until they're good and charred, even on parts of the flesh under the skin. If you're in a hurry, you can purée this soup right in the pot with a hand blender; if you prefer a smoother, more refined texture, use a regular blender.**

Position a rack directly under the broiler element and heat the broiler on high. Grease a rimmed baking sheet with 1 tablespoon of the oil and arrange the tomatoes on the sheet, cut side down. Drizzle 1 tablespoon of the oil over the tomatoes and rub it all over the tomato skins. Broil until the skins are very charred and shrunken, turning as necessary, 8 to 10 minutes total. Let cool for a few minutes, then slip the skins off the tomatoes. Discard the skins.

Meanwhile, heat the remaining 2 tablespoons oil in a 4- to 6-quart saucepan or pot over medium heat. Add the fennel, onion, garlic, and ½ teaspoon salt. Cook, stirring frequently, until softened and golden, 10 to 15 minutes. Add the broth and scrape the bottom of the pot to release the browned bits. Add the tomatoes and any juices from the baking sheet, bring to a simmer over medium-high heat, and cook until the fennel is very tender, about 5 minutes.

Purée the soup with a hand blender, or in two batches in a regular blender (if using a regular blender, return the soup to the pot). Add the milk and thyme and heat gently over medium-low heat for 5 minutes. Season to taste with salt and pepper. Top each serving with a scattering of the goat cheese and chopped fennel fronds (if using) and serve. *–Jennifer Armentrout*

# Creamy Onion Soup with Bacon & Thyme

**When the chopped bacon gets puréed, it leaves behind little nubbins that add a welcome texture to the creamy soup.**

Heat the oil in a heavy, 4-quart saucepan over medium-low heat. Add the bacon and cook until most of its fat has rendered but the bacon has not begun to crisp, about 5 minutes. Add the onions, garlic, and thyme. Season lightly with salt and pepper, cover the pot, and cook for 5 minutes. Uncover the pot and continue to cook, stirring occasionally, until the onions are very soft and golden brown, another 15 to 20 minutes.

Add the potato and broth, raise the heat to high, and bring to a boil. Reduce the heat to medium low and simmer until the potato is very tender, 15 to 20 minutes.

Stir in the cream. Using a hand blender, purée the soup right in the pot. Season to taste with salt and pepper. Serve hot with a sprinkling of thyme leaves. *—Joanne McAllister Smart*

*Yields about 4¹/₂ cups; serves four.*

1 tablespoon olive oil

2 strips bacon, cut into a medium dice

2 medium onions (7 to 8 ounces each), thinly sliced (about 3 cups)

2 cloves garlic, smashed and peeled

1 tablespoon fresh thyme leaves; more for garnish

Kosher salt and freshly ground black pepper

1 medium-small Yukon Gold potato (about 6 ounces), peeled and cut into medium dice (about 1 cup)

2¹/₂ cups homemade or canned low-salt chicken broth

¹/₂ cup heavy cream

# Russet Potato Soup with Pancetta Croutons

See photo on page 45.

*Yields about 8 cups; serves six as a main course or eight as a first course.*

2 tablespoons unsalted butter

2 medium onions (8 ounces total), chopped (about 2 cups)

Kosher salt and freshly ground black or white pepper

3 large cloves garlic, thinly sliced

2 pounds russet potatoes (3 to 4 medium), peeled and cut into ¾- to 1-inch chunks

4 cups homemade or canned low-salt chicken broth

2 bay leaves, preferably fresh

1 cup whole milk

½ cup light or heavy cream, plus more as needed for garnish

Pancetta Croutons (see recipe below)

**Potato soup is like a bowl of pure comfort, but it can be a little drab without a bit of embellishment. Here crusty bread and savory pancetta add a hearty, flavorful touch.**

Melt the butter in a 4-quart saucepan over medium heat. Add the onions, season with salt and pepper, and cook gently, stirring occasionally, until translucent but not at all browned, 8 to 10 minutes. Add the garlic and cook another 2 minutes. Add the potatoes, stir, pour in the broth, and add the bay leaves. Bring to a simmer over medium-high heat, partially cover, reduce the heat to medium low or low, and simmer gently until the potatoes are very tender, 25 to 30 minutes. Discard the bay leaves.

Working in batches, purée the soup in a blender. If the soup is too thick to blend, add a little of the milk. Pulse the blender in short bursts and avoid overworking the soup.

Rinse the soup pot and return the soup to it. Stir in the milk and cream and heat through. Season with salt and pepper to taste. Ladle the soup into bowls and top each with a generous handful of the pancetta croutons. Garnish with a thread of cream, if you like. *—Molly Stevens*

## Pancetta Croutons

*Yields 2 cups.*

**Toasted bread and crisp pancetta turn a good potato soup into a great one. (They also make an addictive kitchen snack or a delicious addition to a salad.) In fact, you might want to plan on having leftovers. These can be made up to 2 hours ahead and kept at room temperature. If you have leftovers, refrigerate them.**

4 ounces country-style bread, cut into ½-inch cubes (about 3 cups)

4 ounces pancetta, cut into ¼- to ½-inch dice (about ¾ cup)

1 tablespoon extra-virgin olive oil

Freshly ground black pepper

Position a rack in the center of the oven and heat the oven to 350°F. Spread the bread cubes and pancetta on a rimmed baking sheet. Sprinkle with the oil and a few grinds of pepper and toss to combine. Bake, stirring a few times, until the pancetta is crisp and the bread cubes are golden, about 20 minutes. Let cool.

# Lemony Chicken Noodle Soup with Ginger, Chile & Cilantro

**Because fish sauce varies in saltiness from brand to brand, it's a good idea to prepare the soup with the modest amount specified in this recipe; then, at serving time, pass around the fish sauce so people can season their portions with a touch more if they wish.**

Finely grate 1 teaspoon of zest from the lemon and put it in a small dish. Add the cilantro and ginger, and mix together. Cut the zested lemon in half and squeeze it to obtain 3 tablespoons of juice. Thinly slice two of the chile halves crosswise.

In a large saucepan, bring the broth to a boil over medium-high heat. Add the lemon juice, noodles, fish sauce, and the 2 remaining chile halves to the boiling broth. Reduce the heat, cover, and simmer the soup until the noodles are almost cooked, about 3 minutes.

Remove the chile halves. Stir in the chicken and chile slices and return to a boil. Remove the pan from the heat, making sure the chicken slices are just cooked through. Taste and add a touch more fish sauce, if you like. Portion the soup evenly among four serving bowls. Divide the cilantro mixture among the bowls, stir, and serve. *—Jennifer McLagan*

*Yields 7 cups; serves four.*

1 lemon

¼ cup chopped fresh cilantro

1 teaspoon peeled and finely grated fresh ginger

2 serrano chiles, stemmed, halved, and seeded

6 cups homemade or canned low-salt chicken broth

4 ounces fresh Chinese egg noodles (look in the produce section of your supermarket)

2 tablespoons fish sauce (preferably Thai Kitchen® brand); more to taste

1 boneless, skinless chicken breast half, cut into ¼-inch-thick slices (this is easier if the chicken is partially frozen)

# Barley Minestrone

*Yields about 3 quarts;*
*serves six to eight.*

2 tablespoons extra-virgin
    olive oil

¼ cup finely diced pancetta
    (about 1 ounce)

2 cups large-diced Savoy
    cabbage

1 cup medium-diced yellow
    onion

1 cup sliced carrot (¼ inch thick)

¼ cup medium-diced celery

2 cloves garlic, minced

2 quarts homemade or canned
    low-salt chicken broth

One 14.5-ounce can diced
    tomatoes, with their juices

½ cup pearl barley, rinsed

2 large sprigs fresh rosemary

One 2-inch-square Parmigiano-
    Reggiano rind (optional)

Kosher salt

1 cup water

1 cup rinsed and drained canned
    kidney beans

Freshly ground black pepper

Freshly grated Parmigiano-
    Reggiano, for serving

**This rendition of the classic Italian vegetable and bean soup uses barley instead of pasta. Simmering a piece of the rind from Parmigiano-Reggiano in the soup is a traditional way of adding flavor. When you finish off a wedge of Parmigiano, just stash the rind in the freezer so you always have it on hand when you need it.**

Heat the oil in a heavy 6-quart or larger pot over medium heat. Add the pancetta and cook, stirring frequently, until it becomes slightly golden, 2 to 3 minutes. Add the cabbage, onion, carrot, celery, and garlic. Cook, stirring frequently, until the vegetables begin to soften, about 6 minutes. Add the broth, the tomatoes with their juices, the barley, rosemary, Parmigiano rind (if using), ½ teaspoon salt, and water. Bring to a boil, then reduce the heat to a simmer and cook until the barley and vegetables are tender, about 20 minutes.

Discard the rosemary sprigs and Parmigiano rind. Stir in the beans and season to taste with salt and pepper. Serve sprinkled with the grated Parmigiano. *−Jennifer Armentrout*

## The real thing is worth the price

Worth the cost at almost any price, true Parmigiano-Reggiano is full of intensely savory flavor that's crucial to so many dishes, from pastas to hearty soups. Keep a chunk in the fridge for grating fresh right before you need it (once grated, it starts losing its flavor, so don't bother buying it already grated). When the cheese is used up, stash the rind in the freezer for simmering in the next pot of soup or beans. A well-wrapped chunk of Parmigiano will maintain its best flavor in the fridge for about a month.

# White Bean Soup with Wild Mushrooms & Chive Mascarpone

*Yields 8 cups; serves six to eight.*

1 tablespoon fennel seeds

½ cup plus 2 tablespoons extra-virgin olive oil

Leaves from 1 small sprig fresh rosemary

1 chile d'árbol (or other small, hot dried chile), stemmed and crumbled

1 cup chopped yellow onion

½ cup chopped fennel bulb

1 tablespoon plus 1 teaspoon fresh thyme leaves

2 cups dried cannellini beans, picked through and rinsed

3 quarts water

Kosher salt

½ cup mascarpone

1 tablespoon minced shallot

1 tablespoon minced fresh chives

Freshly ground black pepper

1 tablespoon unsalted butter

½ pound wild mushrooms (such as shiitake, oyster mushrooms, or chanterelles), stems trimmed and caps thinly sliced

1 tablespoon chopped fresh flat-leaf parsley

**This soup thickens as it sits. If you make it in advance, save any extra cooking liquid to thin it with before serving. The herbed mascarpone can also be made ahead—and the leftovers swirled into mashed potatoes.**

**Make the soup:** Toast the fennel seeds in a small skillet over medium heat until they release their aroma and are golden brown, 2 to 3 minutes. Pound them coarsely in a mortar or grind coarsely in a spice grinder.

Heat a heavy, 6- to 8-quart pot over high heat for 2 minutes. Pour in ½ cup of the oil and add the rosemary leaves and chile. Let them sizzle in the oil for about 1 minute. Add the onion, fennel, fennel seeds, and 1 tablespoon of the thyme and cook until the onion is softened, 3 to 4 minutes.

Add the beans to the pot and cook a few more minutes, stirring to coat well. Add the water and bring to a boil. Turn the heat to low and place a circle of parchment over the beans to keep them underwater. Simmer, stirring occasionally. After 30 minutes, add 1½ tablespoons salt and continue cooking at a low simmer until the beans are tender, another 1 to 1½ hours.

While the soup is cooking, stir together the mascarpone, shallot, and chives in a small bowl. Season to taste with salt and pepper, cover with plastic wrap, and refrigerate.

Separate the bean mixture from the liquid by straining the soup over a bowl. Put half the bean mixture into a blender with ½ cup of the liquid (you will need to purée the soup in batches). Process on the lowest speed until the mixture is puréed. With the blender running at medium speed, slowly pour in more of the liquid, until the soup is the consistency of heavy cream. Turn the speed up to high and blend until completely smooth, about 1 minute. Set aside and repeat with the second batch. (Save any extra liquid for thinning the soup later, if necessary.) Taste and adjust the seasoning with salt and pepper. Keep the soup warm in a pot on the stove. If making ahead, cool completely before refrigerating.

**Sauté the mushrooms:** Turn on the exhaust fan. Heat a 12-inch skillet over high heat for 1 minute. Swirl in the remaining 2 tablespoons oil and the butter. When the butter melts, scatter the mushrooms into the pan. Season with ¼ teaspoon salt and a pinch of pepper. Cook the mushrooms, stirring a few times, until they are tender, browned, and a little crispy, about 5 minutes. Stir in the parsley and the remaining 1 teaspoon thyme and remove from the heat.

Ladle a cup of hot soup into each warm bowl. Scatter warm mushrooms over the top, add a dollop of the mascarpone, and serve. *—Suzanne Goin*

## Toast spices to draw out their flavor

Whether they're whole or ground, spices generally taste better when they're toasted. The heat opens up their complex flavors, making them full and smooth instead of harsh and raw. Toasting is quick and easy, so it's worth taking this extra step. To toast whole or ground spices, put them in a dry skillet over medium-low to medium heat and stir frequently just until they become very fragrant and darken slightly (or pop, in the case of mustard seeds). It shouldn't take more than a few minutes; watch carefully so they don't burn. Immediately transfer to a dish to cool (if left in the hot pan, they could burn).

To grind the spices to a coarse or fine powder, use a mortar and pestle or an electric coffee grinder dedicated to spices.

# Creamy Chickpea Soup with Crisp Chorizo

*Yields about 6 cups; serves four.*

1 cup dried chickpeas, cooked until tender following the Basic Beans method below

3 tablespoons extra-virgin olive oil

1 yellow onion, diced

1 medium carrot, peeled and diced

1 inner rib celery, diced

Kosher salt and freshly ground black pepper

1 clove garlic, minced

2 teaspoons chopped fresh thyme

¼ cup heavy cream

1 tablespoon sherry vinegar

10 ounces chorizo, cut into ½-inch dice

3 tablespoons thinly snipped fresh chives

Spicy chorizo sausage cuts through the starchiness of the chickpeas in this creamy, full-flavored soup. For the chickpeas, or any dried bean, you can avoid overcooked beans and washed-out flavors by gently cooking the peas or beans separately. Use the method below left whenever you want flavorful chickpeas for soup, salad, and pasta.

Separate the cooked chickpeas from their liquid. There should be 4 cups liquid, if not, add more water to equal this amount.

Heat 1½ tablespoons of the oil in a large saucepan over medium-high heat for 30 seconds. Add the onion, carrot, and celery, season with salt, and cook, stirring occasionally, until the vegetables soften and start to brown, about 7 minutes. Add the garlic and cook for 30 seconds, stirring. Add the chickpeas and their cooking liquid and half of the thyme. Season well with salt and pepper. Bring to a boil, reduce the heat to a bare simmer, and cook for 30 minutes so that the chickpeas soften a little more but don't break up. Working in batches, purée the chickpeas and broth in a blender. Return the puréed soup to the saucepan, stir in the cream, vinegar, and remaining thyme, and keep warm over low heat, stirring occasionally to prevent scorching. Taste for salt, pepper, and vinegar.

Set a large skillet over medium-high heat for 1 minute. Cook the chorizo in the remaining 1½ tablespoons oil until it's brown and crisp, about 8 minutes. With a slotted spoon, transfer half the chorizo to a plate lined with paper towels and stir the rest into the soup. Reserve the cooking oil from the chorizo if you like.

Ladle the soup into shallow bowls. Sprinkle with the chorizo, scatter with the chives, and drizzle with a bit of the reserved chorizo oil, if you like. Serve immediately.

*—Tony Rosenfeld*

## Basic Beans

*One cup dried beans yields about 3 cups cooked.*

Canned chickpeas or beans work fine for many recipes, but for the best flavor, cook up a pot from scratch, adding aromatics such as herbs and garlic.

2 bay leaves

2 cloves garlic, smashed and peeled

2 to 3 sprigs fresh herbs (such as rosemary, thyme, or flat-leaf parsley)

1 to 1½ cups dried beans or chickpeas, picked through and rinsed

2 quarts water, more if needed

1 teaspoon kosher salt

Wrap the bay leaves, garlic, and herbs in cheesecloth and tie with twine. Put the beans or chickpeas in a large pot and cover with water by 2 inches. Add the herb bundle and salt. Bring to a boil, then lower the heat to maintain a very gentle simmer, cover, and cook until tender (try biting into one) but not splitting and falling apart, 2 hours for chickpeas and less for other beans (check occasionally to be sure the beans aren't boiling and are covered with liquid; add water if needed).

Discard the herb bundle. Use the beans and their cooking liquid right away, or let the beans cool in the liquid and refrigerate for up to 3 days.

# Shrimp, Chickpeas & Spinach with Ginger & Cumin

*Serves three to four.*

¾ pound large (31 to 40 per pound) shrimp, peeled and deveined

Kosher salt

2 tablespoons extra-virgin olive oil

½ large lemon, cut into 5 wedges

1 small onion, chopped

1½ tablespoons peeled and finely chopped fresh ginger

2 small cloves garlic, minced

1 teaspoon ground cumin

Pinch cayenne

1½ cups water

One 14- to 16-ounce can chickpeas, rinsed and drained

10 ounces mature spinach, washed well, stemmed, and coarsely chopped

¼ cup chopped fresh cilantro

**More a stew than a soup, the Indian flavors of this dish would go well with toasted pita wedges or crisped pappadams.**

In a small bowl, toss the shrimp with ½ teaspoon salt. Heat 1 tablespoon of the oil in a 12-inch nonstick skillet over medium-high heat until hot. Add the shrimp and cook until one side is pink, about 2 minutes. Turn the shrimp over and continue to cook until pink all over, still a bit translucent in the center, and not quite cooked through, 1 to 2 minutes. Take the skillet off the heat and transfer the shrimp to a plate. Squeeze one of the lemon wedges over the shrimp.

Put the skillet over medium heat, add the remaining 1 tablespoon oil, then the onion. Sprinkle with a big pinch of salt and cook until the edges of the onion begin to brown, about 5 minutes. Add the ginger and garlic and cook, stirring, until fragrant, 1 minute. Add the cumin and cayenne and cook, stirring, until fragrant, about 20 seconds. Add the water, chickpeas, and ½ teaspoon salt. Simmer over medium-high heat for 5 minutes to develop the flavors.

Using a potato masher, mash about half of the chickpeas right in the pan. Add the spinach and cilantro. Using tongs, carefully toss the greens to help them cook evenly and wilt, about 2 minutes. Add the shrimp and any juices that have accumulated on the plate. Cook for another 1 or 2 minutes to reheat the shrimp and cook them fully (be careful not to overcook them). Season with salt to taste. Portion into warm bowls and serve with the remaining lemon wedges on the side. —*Joanne McAllister Smart*

# Seafood Chowder with Bacon, Thyme & Jalapeño

**The cream in this soup tempers most of the jalapeño's heat, but you can still taste its bright, fresh flavor, which plays beautifully off the salty bacon and sweet seafood.**

In a heavy, 4-quart saucepan or Dutch oven, cook the bacon over medium heat, stirring occasionally, until browned and crisp, about 8 minutes. Transfer the bacon to a small dish lined with paper towels, leaving the fat behind in the pan.

Add the shallot and 1 tablespoon of the jalapeño to the bacon fat and cook over medium heat, stirring a few times, until the shallot is softened, about 2 minutes. Add the flour and cook, stirring, for 1 minute. Gradually stir in all the clam juice (from the cans and the bottles). Add the cream, potatoes, and thyme and bring to a simmer over medium-high heat, stirring occasionally. Reduce the heat as necessary and continue to simmer, stirring occasionally, until the potatoes are tender, about 10 minutes.

Add the fish fillets and cook for 3 minutes. Stir in the clams and continue stirring until the fish has broken into chunks. Cook until the fish is cooked through and the clams are heated, about another 2 minutes.

Season the soup to taste with salt and pepper. Portion into warm soup bowls and sprinkle each serving with the reserved bacon and the remaining jalapeño. *–Joanne McAllister Smart*

*Serves four.*

- 4 strips bacon, cut crosswise into ¼-inch-wide strips
- 1 medium shallot, minced
- 1 large jalapeño, seeded and very finely chopped (about 2 tablespoons)
- 2 tablespoons all-purpose flour
- Two 6.5-ounce cans chopped clams, clams and juice separated (about 1 cup juice)
- Two 8-ounce bottles clam juice
- 1 cup heavy cream
- 8 to 10 ounces red-skinned potatoes (about 2 medium), scrubbed, left unpeeled, and cut into ½-inch dice
- ½ teaspoon dried thyme
- ¾ pound skinless haddock or cod fillets
- Kosher salt and freshly ground black pepper

# Vietnamese Beef Noodle Soup with Fresh Herbs (Faux Phở)

*Serves four as a main course.*

3 whole star anise

2 whole cloves

One 2-inch cinnamon stick

½ teaspoon fennel seeds

2½ cups canned low-salt chicken broth

2½ cups canned low-salt beef broth

3 tablespoons fish sauce

One 3-inch-long piece fresh ginger (1 to 1½ inches thick), unpeeled and thinly sliced

8 ounces ⅛- to ¼-inch wide rice noodles

8 ounces cooked steak (see page 184), very thinly sliced and cut into bite-size pieces (about 1⅓ cups)

⅓ cup thinly sliced scallion greens

⅓ cup coarsely chopped fresh cilantro

⅓ cup coarsely chopped fresh basil

1 medium shallot, sliced into thin rings

1 cup bean sprouts, rinsed

1 lime, cut into eight wedges

Chile paste, such as sambal oelek, or thinly sliced fresh hot red chiles (optional)

Phở is a classic Vietnamese beef noodle soup garnished with bright, fresh ingredients. Authentic phở (pronounced fuh) involves making a long-simmering spiced beef broth from scratch to pour over cooked rice noodles and thinly sliced raw beef, so the heat of the broth cooks the beef. This superfast version calls for doctoring store-bought broth with the same spices you'd find in real phở and, in place of the raw meat, it uses thinly sliced leftover steak. (If you don't have leftover steak, use some uncooked rib eye or tenderloin, slice it thinly, and just be sure the broth is extremely hot when you add it to the bowls, so it will cook the beef.) It's not the real thing, but it comes close to being just as tasty, especially on a busy weeknight.

In a dry 3-quart or larger saucepan over medium heat, combine the star anise, cloves, cinnamon stick, and fennel seeds. Toast them, shaking the pan occasionally, until quite fragrant, 1 to 2 minutes. Add the chicken and beef broths, fish sauce, and ginger and bring to a boil. Reduce the heat to medium low or low, cover, and simmer gently for 30 minutes.

Meanwhile, soak the rice noodles in cold water for 20 minutes. Bring 2 quarts water to a boil in another 3-quart or larger saucepan. Drain the rice noodles and add them to the boiling water. Give the noodles a quick stir and cook until just tender, 1 to 2 minutes—don't overcook or the noodles will get gummy. Drain the noodles and portion them into four large soup bowls.

Portion the steak, scallions, cilantro, basil, and shallot into the four bowls, scattering them over the noodles. Strain the broth into a heatproof container, preferably one with a pouring spout, such as an 8-cup Pyrex® measuring cup. You should have about 5 cups broth; if not, add water to equal 5 cups and quickly reheat the broth if necessary. Divide the broth among the four bowls, pouring it over the noodles and other ingredients. Top with the bean sprouts. Serve with the lime wedges and chile paste or chiles (if using) on the side for diners to add individually to taste. *—Jennifer Armentrout*

## With bean sprouts, freshness is key

Mung bean sprouts, which are used in many Asian dishes, are extremely perishable, so you need to pay extra attention when you're buying or storing them. Here are some tips:

**How to buy:** Look for sprouts that have crispy, white roots with yellow and light green leaves. Darkening roots, sliminess, and a musty odor are all signs that sprouts may be over the hill. The USDA recommends that sprouts be stored at 32°F, which is colder than most grocery store produce department shelves. If the sprouts on display don't look very fresh, ask if there are more in the back cooler. Don't buy sprouts too far in advance because they'll fade after a couple of days.

**How to store:** If not using the sprouts the day you buy them, rinse them in a colander under cold water, transfer to a zip-top plastic bag lined with paper towels, and refrigerate in the vegetable bin. If you need to keep them longer than a couple of days, try storing them submerged in a covered container of ice water in the refrigerator, changing the water

and adding more ice daily. This can prolong their life for up to 5 days.

**Easy ways to use up sprouts:** Pile them on a sandwich or in a wrap—they add a great juicy crunch and are especially tasty with avocado. Toss them into an Asian-style slaw made with Napa cabbage, carrot, scallion, chopped peanuts, sliced jalapeño, mint, cilantro, lime juice, and peanut oil. Sprouts also add a nice crunch to soups and go well in any stir-fry; just don't cook them for more than a few minutes or they'll get soggy.

# 3 Salads

p72

p80

**Vietnamese Noodle Salad with Pork Patties (Bún Cha) (recipe on page 92)**

# Simple Green Salad with Herbs

*Serves six.*

6 cups mixed salad greens (6 to 7 ounces), washed and dried

1 cup mixed fresh herb leaves, such as flat-leaf parsley, dill, cilantro, basil, and mint, washed and dried; tear large leaves into bite-size pieces

4 to 6 tablespoons vinaigrette of your choice (see recipes below)

Kosher salt and freshly ground black pepper

**Use a bagged mix of salad greens or combine some of your favorite lettuces.**

Combine the greens and herbs in a salad bowl. Toss with enough vinaigrette to coat lightly. Sprinkle with about 2 pinches salt and several grinds of pepper. Toss again just to distribute the seasoning. —*Jennifer Armentrout*

## Spicy Ginger-Lime-Garlic Vinaigrette

*Yields about ½ cup.*

**This vinaigrette tastes best after it sits for about half an hour.**

1 teaspoon peeled and finely minced fresh ginger

½ teaspoon finely grated lime zest

½ teaspoon minced garlic

¼ teaspoon Dijon mustard

¼ teaspoon table salt

⅛ teaspoon granulated sugar

2 tablespoons plus 2 teaspoons fresh lime juice

1 teaspoon white-wine vinegar

6 drops Tabasco; more to taste

¼ cup grapeseed oil or other neutral-flavored oil

In a small bowl, whisk the ginger, lime zest, garlic, mustard, salt, sugar, lime juice, vinegar, and Tabasco. Slowly whisk in the oil until the dressing is creamy and blended. Taste and adjust the seasonings. —*Martha Holmberg*

## Blue Cheese & Balsamic Vinaigrette

*Yields about ⅔ cup.*

**Be sure to use good-quality blue cheese for this vinaigrette; it will really enhance the flavor.**

¼ cup crumbled good-quality blue cheese

2 tablespoons balsamic vinegar

6 tablespoons extra-virgin olive oil

Kosher salt and freshly ground black pepper

Using a fork, mash 2 tablespoons of the blue cheese with the vinegar in a small bowl. Gradually whisk in the oil. Stir in the remaining 2 tablespoons blue cheese and season to taste with salt and pepper. —*Jennifer Armentrout*

## Mustard Vinaigrette

*Yields about ½ cup.*

**Two types of mustard add depth to this vibrant vinaigrette.**

2 teaspoons whole-grain Dijon mustard

½ teaspoon Dijon mustard

½ teaspoon honey

¼ teaspoon table salt

⅛ teaspoon freshly ground black pepper

3 drops Tabasco

2 tablespoons white-wine vinegar

6 tablespoons good-quality extra-virgin olive oil

In a small bowl, whisk the mustards, honey, salt, pepper, Tabasco, and vinegar. Slowly whisk in the oil until the dressing is creamy and blended. Taste and adjust the seasonings. —*Martha Holmberg*

Ready-to-go salad mixes are all the rage these days, judging by the amount of shelf space devoted to them in supermarket produce sections. One of these popular mixes is mesclun, also known as spring mix or mixed baby greens. This blend contains 10 or more varieties of tender, young lettuces and other greens, some of which may be familiar to you and others that probably aren't. So for all you curious types who have been wondering which leaf is the Lollo Rossa and which is the Tango, here's a little guide to some of the greens you're likely to encounter in a bag of spring mix.

## Arugula
peppery & assertive

## Lollo Rossa
delicate & mildly bitter

## Red oak leaf
mildly bitter

## Red romaine
earthy & savory

## Green romaine
sweet & juicy

## Spinach
dense & mineraly

## Mizuna
biting & mustardy

## Mâche
delicate & floral

## Green oak leaf
sweet & mild

## Red chard
salty & rich

## Frisée
bittersweet

## Tango
sweet & pungent

## Tatsoi
succulent & spicy sweet

# Frisée Salad with Blue Cheese, Dried Cherries & Walnut Vinaigrette

*Serves six.*

⅓ cup dried tart cherries

½ cup hot water

2 tablespoons minced shallot (about 1 medium shallot)

2 tablespoons sherry vinegar

1 teaspoon Dijon mustard

Kosher salt and freshly ground black pepper

6 tablespoons walnut oil

2 tablespoons extra-virgin olive oil

1 large head frisée (about 8 ounces), washed, spun dry, and torn into bite-size pieces

4 ounces good-quality blue cheese, crumbled (about 1 cup)

Walnut oil and dried cherries add an autumnal note to this salad, but it's so good you'll want to make it year-round. Sherry vinegar combines the lightness and acidity of wine vinegar with the complexity of aged balsamic; it may be the perfect vinaigrette vinegar. Look for it and walnut oil at gourmet markets and well-stocked supermarkets.

In a small bowl, soak the dried cherries in the hot water until plumped, 5 to 10 minutes.

Meanwhile, in another small bowl, combine the shallot, vinegar, and mustard. Season with salt and pepper, then whisk to combine. Drizzle in the walnut oil, whisking as you go, followed by the olive oil. Drag a piece of frisée through the vinaigrette and taste for seasoning.

Drain the cherries. Put the frisée in a large bowl. Pour on about two-thirds of the vinaigrette and toss to coat. Add more if needed to evenly but lightly coat the leaves (you may not need all of it). Arrange the frisée on six salad plates. Top each with some of the blue cheese and dried cherries and serve.
—Molly Stevens

# Grilled Corn & Tomato "Salad" with Basil Oil

*Serves six to eight.*

2 ears corn, husks removed

2 tablespoons extra-virgin olive oil

Kosher salt and freshly ground black pepper

3 to 4 large ripe beefsteak tomatoes

Basil Oil (see recipe below)

Small leaves of Dark Opal or Purple Ruffles basil, or gently torn larger ones, for garnish (optional)

**Purple basil leaves add fragrance and a beautiful contrast on the plate. Look for purple basil at your farmer's market; purple Thai basil is sold at some Asian markets. If you can't find purple basil, garnish the salad with sweet green basil instead. Serve the salad with grilled bread (which you could brush with some of the Basil Oil before grilling).**

Cut the corn cobs in half crosswise, put them in a large bowl, and toss with the olive oil, ½ teaspoon salt, and ¼ teaspoon pepper.

Heat a grill to medium high. Grill the corn until the tips of the kernels are nicely browned all around, about 2 minutes on each of three sides. Return the corn to the bowl with the oil and toss again. When the ears are cool enough to handle, place the flat end of a cob on a cutting board so the cob is upright and slice the kernels off with a sharp knife. You should have about 1 cup kernels. Set aside until ready to assemble.

Slice the tomatoes ½-inch thick and generously season each slice with salt and pepper. On serving plates, arrange one, two, or three slices of tomato per person, depending on how big the tomatoes are. Scatter the corn over the tomato slices. Drizzle basil oil generously over each serving. Garnish with fresh purple basil leaves, if using. *—Jessica Bard*

## Basil Oil

*Yields about ¾ cup.*

**Sweet basil is the familiar green-leafed variety sold in most supermarkets. A mild, non-virgin olive oil works best here; an assertively flavored oil would compete with the basil. Use any leftover in a vinaigrette or drizzle it over a Caprese salad.**

1 cup mild olive oil

2 cups tightly packed sweet basil leaves

½ teaspoon kosher salt

Put the measured oil in the refrigerator while you prepare the basil. Bring a pot of water to a boil. Have a bowl of ice water ready. Blanch the basil leaves in the boiling water for about 10 seconds. Remove them quickly with a strainer and dunk in the ice water, swishing them around to be sure they're all cold. Remove from the water and squeeze gently to remove the excess water.

Roughly chop the basil and put it in a blender. Add the oil and salt; blend until the basil is puréed. The mixture will be very frothy. Let the purée settle for about 30 minutes. Strain through a cheesecloth-lined fine strainer, very gently pushing on the solids to extract the oil. Use immediately or refrigerate for up to a week. For the best flavor, let the oil come to room temperature before using.

# Spinach & Grilled Radicchio Salad

When grilled, radicchio's sturdy leaves soften a bit, and its natural sugars caramelize, adding a mellow sweetness and taming the chicory's distinctive bite. Radicchio is delicious with Italian antipasto meats such as prosciutto and salami. This salad would also be right at home alongside charcoal-grilled steaks.

Heat a gas grill to medium or prepare a medium-hot charcoal fire.

Brush the radicchio with 2 tablespoons of the oil and sprinkle with ¾ teaspoon salt. Grill the radicchio (covered if using a gas grill) until it browns and chars lightly in spots on one side, 3 to 4 minutes. Flip and grill until the other side is browned and the radicchio is softened and wilting, 3 to 4 minutes. (If using a large radicchio, you may need to grill it on a third side for a few more minutes to fully soften it.)

Let the radicchio cool on a cutting board for a couple of minutes, then trim off the cores and coarsely chop. In a serving bowl, toss the radicchio with the spinach and cheese. Just before serving, toss the salad with the remaining 5 tablespoons oil and the vinegar and season with salt and pepper to taste.

—*Tony Rosenfeld*

*Serves six to eight.*

- ¾ to 1 pound radicchio (2 small or 1 large), trimmed and quartered through the core
- 7 tablespoons extra-virgin olive oil
- Kosher salt and freshly ground black pepper
- 6 ounces baby spinach (about 6 cups), rinsed well and spun dry
- 3½ to 4 ounces Pecorino Romano or Parmigiano-Reggiano, shaved (use a vegetable peeler to do this) (about 1 cup)
- 2 tablespoons balsamic vinegar

# Tomato, Feta & Preserved Lemon Salad

*Serves four to six.*

1 to 2 preserved lemons
   (page 75)

1 serrano chile

½ pound feta (preferably one
   more creamy than crumbly),
   cut into ½-inch cubes
   (1¾ cups)

1½ cups grape or small cherry
   tomatoes, halved

½ cup pitted Kalamata olives,
   drained and rinsed

¼ cup extra-virgin olive oil

1 teaspoon cumin seeds,
   toasted (see page 59)

2 tablespoons coarsely chopped
   fresh flat-leaf parsley

This salad is delicious—bright with bold, briny flavors. To keep the salt in check, soak brine-packed feta in fresh cold water for about 10 minutes before using. A milder feta also helps: try French or Bulgarian fetas, which are dependably creamy and mild. Serve the salad over undressed salad greens, if you like, with grilled bread on the side.

Rinse one of the preserved lemons well, cut it into quarters, and slice the quarters crosswise into thin slices (you need about ½ cup—cut up another lemon if needed). Remove any seeds. Discard the stem from the chile, then cut it in half lengthwise and remove the seeds. Slice the chile halves thinly crosswise. Put the sliced preserved lemon, chile, feta, tomatoes, and olives in a bowl. Pour in the oil and sprinkle with the cumin seeds and parsley. Toss gently to mix and then serve. —*Jennifer McLagan*

# Preserved Lemons

*Yields 1 quart.*

A staple of the Moroccan kitchen, preserved lemons have a soft, silky-smooth texture and a salty, pickled taste. The only hard thing about making them is waiting for them to cure, which takes about four weeks. You can buy preserved lemons at some specialty foods stores and at Middle Eastern markets, but they don't compare to the homemade version.

1 wide-mouthed quart-size canning jar, sterilized

6 small thin-skinned lemons

½ cup kosher salt

One 2-inch piece cinnamon stick

2 whole cloves

1 bay leaf

Make these in a wide-mouthed glass jar that has a hinged glass lid. This way, it's easy to pack the lemons into the jar without metal coming into contact with the lemon juice and salt. The lemons will keep in the fridge for up to 6 months.

Wash and scrub 4 of the lemons thoroughly. Cut them lengthwise into quarters from the tip to within ½ inch of the stem end, so the quarters stay together at one end. (If you don't have a wide-mouthed jar, go ahead and separate the quarters.) Juice the remaining 2 lemons. Put the cut-up lemons in a large bowl with the salt and toss to coat, packing the salt into the cut edges of the lemon.

Reform them into lemon shape and pack them tightly into the sterilized jar with any extra salt and the cinnamon, cloves, and bay leaf. Pour in the lemon juice and cover the jar. Store in a cool place for 1 week, tipping the jar once a day to mix in the salt.

After a week, put the jar in the refrigerator and keep for 3 more weeks before using. Rinse preserved lemons before using to remove excess salt.

## Ways to enjoy preserved lemons

- **Dice the lemons** and mix with a bit of their juices and olive oil for a dressing.

- **Add chopped preserved lemons** to braised meats or when making gravy or sauce.

- **Mix the finely diced rind** into mayonnaise with a little crushed garlic and chopped fresh mint; use as a dip for crudites or serve with fried fish in place of tartar sauce.

- **Stir chopped preserved lemons** into guacamole, salsa, relish, chutney, or even tuna salad.

- **Mince the rind** and toss with sautéed shrimp or scallops.

- **Mix the minced rind** into softened butter, and use in sandwiches or on grilled fish, steak, veggies, or lobster.

- **Use slices as a garnish** for grilled chicken or fish.

# Arugula, Mint & Apple Salad with Walnuts & Buttermilk Dressing

*Serves six.*

## For the dressing:

2 tablespoons finely diced shallot (about 1 medium shallot)

1 tablespoon fresh lemon juice

½ teaspoon kosher salt; more to taste

¼ cup crème fraîche

¼ cup buttermilk

½ cup mayonnaise

Freshly ground black pepper

## For the salad:

¾ cup walnuts (about 3 ounces)

1 teaspoon extra-virgin olive oil

Kosher salt

2 apples (preferably Gala, Fuji, or Pink Lady)

½ pound baby arugula, washed and spun dry

1 medium head radicchio (about 4 ounces), washed, spun dry, and torn into bite-size pieces

1 cup small fresh mint leaves (or large leaves torn into small pieces), washed and spun dry

Serve this bright, tangy salad as a refreshing counterpoint to all manner of robust, cool-weather foods. It would be delicious with everything from a hearty bean soup to a luxurious prime rib. The dressing may be made a day ahead.

**Make the dressing:** Combine the shallot, lemon juice, and ½ teaspoon salt in a small bowl and let sit for 5 minutes. Whisk in the crème fraîche and buttermilk, then the mayonnaise. Adjust the seasoning with salt and pepper to taste.

**Assemble the salad:** Position a rack in the center of the oven and heat the oven to 375°F. Spread the walnuts on a baking sheet and toast them, stirring once or twice, until they smell nutty and are lightly browned, 8 to 10 minutes. When the nuts have cooled slightly, toss them with the oil and a generous pinch of salt. Crumble half of them with your hands.

Core, then cut the apples into ⅛-inch-thick slices and put them in a large salad bowl. Dress the apples with half of the buttermilk dressing, then very gently toss in the arugula, radicchio, and mint. The salad should be lightly dressed—add more salad dressing only if needed (you will have leftover dressing, which will keep for a few days in the fridge).

Arrange the salad on six plates, scatter the toasted walnuts (both crumbled and whole) over the top, and serve. *—Suzanne Goin*

# Arugula & Radicchio Salad with Ruby Grapefruit & Toasted Almonds

*Serves six.*

2 medium ruby grapefruit

1 tablespoon fresh lime juice

2 teaspoon honey

¼ teaspoon kosher salt

6 tablespoon extra-virgin olive oil

2 tablespoon chopped fresh mint, plus leaves for garnish

6 to 8 large handfuls arugula (about 8 ounces), tough stems removed

1 head radicchio, cored and cut into strips

⅓ cup sliced almonds, lightly toasted on a baking sheet in a 350° F oven for 5 to 7 minutes

**Segments of juicy pink grapefruit sparkle like jewels in this pretty winter starter. Ruby grapefruit varieties such as Rio Red and Star Ruby are the sweetest of them all; they have a bright sweet-tartness but lack the puckery acidity of white grapefruit. If you have ripe blood oranges in season, they can stand in for the grapefruit.**

With a sharp knife, cut away both ends of one of the grapefruit. Stand the fruit on one of its cut ends and slice off the skin in strips (try to get all the white pith). Working over a bowl, cut the segments free from the membrane, letting each one fall into the bowl as you go. When you've removed all the segments, squeeze the membrane to extract all the juice. Repeat with the second fruit. Spoon out the grapefruit segments from the bowl and set them aside on a plate. Remove any seeds from the juice.

Measure out 3 tablespoons of the juice into a small bowl. Save the rest for another use (or drink it). Whisk the lime juice, honey, and salt into the grapefruit juice. Whisk in the oil, then the chopped mint. Drag an arugula leaf though the vinaigrette and taste for seasoning. Drizzle about 1 tablespoon of the vinaigrette over the grapefruit segments.

Combine the arugula and radicchio in a large bowl. Toss with enough of the vinaigrette to evenly but lightly coat the leaves (you may not need all of it). Arrange the greens on six salad plates, garnish with the grapefruit segments, almonds, and a few mint leaves, and serve. *—Molly Stevens*

## Treviso: A more delicate radicchio

If your market has an especially good produce section, then you may have encountered a vegetable that looks like a head of romaine lettuce crossed with a radicchio. This isn't a new hybrid; it's a variety of radicchio that's long been popular in Italy. Radicchio rosso di Treviso, commonly known as Treviso in the U.S., has elongated, variegated red leaves that taste more delicate and less bitter than the more familiar ball-shaped Radicchio rosso di Chioggia.

Raw Treviso adds vivid color and a juicy crunch to salads, but this vegetable also stands up well to cooking. It's particularly tasty when halved lengthwise and grilled or broiled until slightly softened and lightly charred, then garnished with olive oil, balsamic vinegar, and shavings of Parmigiano-Reggiano. For a real treat, wrap the halves in thinly sliced pancetta or bacon before grilling.

# Roasted Butternut Squash & Pear Salad with Spiced-Pecan Vinaigrette

*Serves six.*

½ cup pecans, very coarsely chopped

2 tablespoons unsalted butter, melted

½ teaspoon ancho chile powder

3 cups peeled butternut squash cut into ¾-inch dice (from about a 2-pound squash)

⅓ cup plus 2 tablespoons extra-virgin olive oil

Kosher salt

¼ cup very thinly sliced shallots

3 tablespoons balsamic vinegar

1 tablespoon Dijon mustard

2 teaspoons light brown sugar

6 cups loosely packed mixed salad greens

1 small ripe pear, halved, cored, and thinly sliced

If available at a farmers' market, red and bronze heirloom lettuces (such as Lolla Rossa, Red Salad Bowl, and oak leaf varieties) would be a gorgeous addition to the mix of salad greens. This would make a nice Thanksgiving starter—a delicious, unexpected way to serve squash at the big meal.

Give the pear at least a few days to ripen after you bring it home; it's ripe when it yields to gentle pressure at the stem end (it will still feel firm in the middle). To safely peel squash, trim both ends, then cut the squash in half crosswise. Stand each piece on one of its cut ends and slice off the peel in strips, working from top to bottom.

Position a rack in the center of the oven and heat the oven to 450°F.

Put the pecans and butter in an 8-inch-square Pyrex dish and toss to coat. Sprinkle with the chile powder and toss. Bake the nuts until toasted, about 5 minutes. Set aside to cool.

Put the squash on a heavy-duty rimmed baking sheet. Drizzle 2 tablespoons of the oil over the squash and sprinkle with ¾ teaspoon salt. Toss to coat. Roast the squash until browned on the bottom, about 20 minutes. Flip with a metal spatula and continue to roast until the squash is tender and nicely browned on the other side, 5 to 10 minutes more. Set aside to cool.

Put the shallots in a small bowl, cover with hot water, and let soak for 15 minutes; drain in a colander.

Combine the vinegar, mustard, brown sugar, and ¼ teaspoon salt in a small bowl. While whisking vigorously, slowly pour in the remaining ⅓ cup oil.

Combine the salad greens and shallots in a large bowl; sprinkle with ½ teaspoon salt. Drizzle just enough of the dressing over the salad to coat lightly, then toss gently. Divide the greens among six plates and scatter the pecans, squash, and pears over the greens. Drizzle with a little more dressing if desired and serve. *—Julianna Grimes Bottcher*

# Grilled Sourdough Panzanella

**Panzanella is just one of many ingenious dishes devised by thrifty Tuscan cooks (it's traditionally made with day-old bread and tomatoes). In a new twist, fresh bread is grilled, leaving it toasty on the outside, tender on the inside. If you don't feel like grilling the bread, you can toast it in a grill pan or under a low broiler.**

Heat a gas grill with all burners on medium. Brush the bread with ¼ cup of the oil and season it with ¼ teaspoon salt and a few grinds of pepper. Grill the bread on both sides, checking frequently, until nicely browned, 3 to 4 minutes per side. When the bread is cool enough to handle, cut it into ½-inch cubes.

In a small bowl, soak the shallot in the vinegar for 10 minutes. With a slotted spoon, transfer the shallot to a large bowl, reserving the vinegar. Sprinkle the garlic with ¼ teaspoon salt and mash it into a paste on a cutting board with the side of a chef's knife. Whisk the mashed garlic, the remaining ¼ cup oil, ¼ teaspoon salt, and ⅛ teaspoon pepper into the reserved vinegar.

Toss the bread cubes, tomatoes, cucumber, basil, mint, capers, and vinaigrette in the bowl with the shallot. Season the panzanella to taste with salt and pepper and serve. *—Allison Ehri*

*Serves four to six.*

Four ½-inch-thick slices (about 8 ounces) from the center of a round sourdough loaf (a boule)

½ cup extra-virgin olive oil

Kosher salt and freshly ground black pepper

1 small shallot, sliced into thin rings

3 tablespoons red-wine vinegar

1 small clove garlic, coarsely chopped

1½ pounds ripe, meaty tomatoes, cut into ½-inch dice (about 3½ cups)

1 small English cucumber, seeded and cut into ½-inch dice (about 1½ cups)

3 tablespoons chopped fresh basil

3 tablespoons chopped fresh mint

2 tablespoons capers, drained and rinsed

# Roasted Potato Salad with Green Beans, Feta & Mint

*Serves six.*

¾ pound green beans, trimmed and cut diagonally into 1½-inch pieces

⅓ cup chopped fresh mint

Simple Roasted Potatoes (see recipe below)

5 tablespoons extra-virgin olive oil

1½ tablespoons fresh lemon juice

Kosher salt and freshly ground black pepper

¼ pound feta, crumbled (1 scant cup)

Fresh mint sprigs, for garnish (optional)

Lemon wedges, for garnish (optional)

**Tangy Greek flavors make this satisfying salad a great match with grilled tuna, broiled lamb chops, or Turkish-style ground lamb or beef kebabs (kofta kebabs).**

Bring a pot of salted water to a boil. Add the green beans and cook until crisp-tender, 4 to 7 minutes. Drain.

Add the green beans and chopped mint to the potatoes and toss. In a small bowl, whisk together the oil and lemon juice. Add to the salad and toss. Season with salt and pepper to taste. Crumble the feta on top and serve garnished with mint sprigs and lemon wedges, if using. *—Joanne Weir*

## Simple Roasted Potatoes

*Serves six.*

**Roasting potatoes at a high temperature produces a crunchy outside and tender inside that boiled or steamed potatoes can only dream of. Plus, it's the easiest possible way to prepare them. Leaving the skins on adds rustic appeal—and more nutrients.**

2 pounds small red-skinned potatoes or small Yukon Gold potatoes, scrubbed and cut into ¾-inch chunks

3 tablespoons extra-virgin olive oil

Kosher salt and freshly ground black pepper

Position a rack in the center of the oven and heat the oven to 450°F. Spread the potatoes on a heavy-duty rimmed baking sheet. Drizzle with the oil, sprinkle with 1 teaspoon salt and several grinds of pepper, and roll them around to evenly coat them with the oil. Spread the potatoes in a single layer, preferably with a cut side down. Roast until they're tender when pierced with a fork, 20 to 30 minutes, depending on the potatoes. The potatoes should be browned on the sides touching the pan.

Loosen the potatoes from the pan with a thin metal spatula and transfer them to a large serving bowl to be tossed with the salad ingredients and dressing. They can be tossed while still warm or at room temperature.

# Roasted Potato Salad with Shaved Fennel & Salsa Verde

*Serves six.*

½ cup chopped fresh flat-leaf parsley

¼ cup extra-virgin olive oil

3 tablespoons thinly snipped fresh chives

3 tablespoons drained, rinsed, and chopped capers

1 teaspoon finely grated orange zest

2 tablespoons fresh orange juice

1 tablespoon white-wine vinegar or Champagne vinegar

1 teaspoon chopped fresh thyme

1 medium shallot, finely chopped

1 medium clove garlic, finely chopped

Kosher salt and freshly ground black pepper

1 medium fennel bulb

Simple Roasted Potatoes (see page 82)

**Salsa verde, the Italian olive-oil based sauce flavored with garlic, herbs, and other seasonings, adds wonderful zest not only to potatoes, but to beef, lamb, and fish. Try this salad with grilled or sear-roasted salmon, chicken breasts, or rib-eye.**

In a medium bowl, stir together the parsley, oil, chives, capers, orange zest and juice, vinegar, thyme, shallot, and garlic to make the salsa verde. Season with salt and pepper to taste.

Cut off the top and the bottom of the fennel bulb, then slice it in half from top to bottom. Lay each half flat on its cut surface, then slice each half crosswise as thinly as possible. Stop slicing when you hit the core (a little core is all right, but you don't want wide areas of core in your slices). Discard the remainder or save for another use.

Add the salsa verde and shaved fennel to the bowl of roasted potatoes. Toss well, season with salt and pepper to taste, and serve. *—Joanne Weir*

# Roasted Potato Salad with Crispy Prosciutto & Mustard Vinaigrette

*Serves six.*

4 thin slices prosciutto (about 2 ounces)

¼ cup extra-virgin olive oil

2 medium shallots, finely chopped

½ cup finely diced (¼ inch) cornichons or gherkins

3 tablespoons grainy or whole-grain Dijon mustard

2 tablespoons white-wine vinegar

Kosher salt and freshly ground black pepper

Simple Roasted Potatoes (see page 82)

3 tablespoons coarsely chopped fresh flat-leaf parsley

**To ensure that the potatoes absorb the maximum amount of flavor, toss them while still warm with the warm vinaigrette. This salad is good with grilled pork chops, roasted pork tenderloin, and grilled sausages.**

Heat the oven to 400°F. Cut the prosciutto crosswise into ½-inch-wide strips. Arrange the strips in a single layer on a baking sheet and bake, watching closely, until crisp and light golden, 6 to 8 minutes. With a metal spatula, loosen the prosciutto from the pan and set aside.

Heat 1 tablespoon of the oil in a small skillet over medium heat. Add the shallots and cook, stirring frequently until softened, 2 to 3 minutes. Add the remaining 3 tablespoons oil, the cornichons, mustard, and vinegar. Season with salt and pepper to taste and mix well.

Add the warm shallot-mustard vinaigrette to the potatoes along with the reserved prosciutto and the parsley. Toss, taste for seasoning, and add more salt and pepper if necessary. Serve immediately. *—Joanne Weir*

tip: Cornichons add a tangy edge to this potato salad. These French-style sour gherkins are unripe baby cucumbers that have been pickled. If you don't have these or gherkins on hand, you can substitute baby dill pickles.

# Chopped Shrimp "Waldorf" Salad

The original Waldorf salad was created at the Waldorf-Astoria Hotel in New York in the late 1890s by Chef Oscar Tschirky. It was considered the height of sophistication and originally was nothing more than apples, celery, and mayonnaise. Chopped nuts and grapes came later. This version features shrimp.

Put the shrimp in a steamer basket over simmering water and steam until just cooked through, about 3 minutes (the center should still be slightly translucent). Let cool.

In a medium bowl, whisk together the mayonnaise, buttermilk, lemon juice, tarragon, and mustard. Season with salt and pepper to taste.

Cut the shrimp into ½-inch pieces and mix in a large bowl with the apples, grapes, celery, and almonds. Toss with enough of the dressing to coat the ingredients well (you may not need it all). Taste and add more salt, pepper, or lemon juice as needed. Sprinkle with the chives, if using. Serve the salad on beds of lettuce leaves or put the leaves next to the salad and have guests spoon some of the salad into a leaf and roll it up to eat out of hand. *–John Ash*

*Serves six to eight.*

- 1 pound large (31 to 40 per pound) shrimp, peeled and deveined
- ½ cup mayonnaise
- ⅓ cup buttermilk
- 1 tablespoon fresh lemon juice; more to taste
- 1 tablespoon roughly chopped fresh tarragon
- 1 teaspoon Dijon mustard
- Kosher salt and freshly ground black pepper
- 2 cups cored and diced (¼ inch) sweet apples, preferably Fuji (about 1½ apples)
- 2 cups red seedless grapes, halved
- 1½ cups diced (¼ inch) celery (3 to 4 ribs)
- ⅓ cup slivered blanched almonds, toasted on a baking sheet in a 375° F oven until lightly colored, 4 to 8 minutes
- 1 tablespoon thinly snipped fresh chives (optional)
- 12 tender butter lettuce leaves

# Chopped Greek Salad with Garlic Croutons

*Serves six to eight.*

### For the garlic croutons:

3 cups ¾-inch bread cubes (cut from day-old sturdy bread with crusts removed)

⅓ cup extra-virgin olive oil

2 large cloves garlic, thinly sliced

2 tablespoons finely chopped fresh flat-leaf parsley

1 teaspoon finely grated lemon zest

Kosher salt and freshly ground black pepper

### For the dressing:

½ cup extra-virgin olive oil

¼ cup red- or white-wine vinegar (or fresh lemon juice)

2 tablespoons finely chopped shallot

1 teaspoon Dijon mustard

1 teaspoon chopped fresh oregano

1 teaspoon mashed oil-packed anchovies (2 to 4 fillets), or to taste

Kosher salt and freshly ground black pepper

### To assemble:

4 cups gently packed baby arugula, washed and spun dry

3 medium-size firm, ripe tomatoes, cored, seeded, and cut into ½-inch dice (about 2 cups)

1 medium English cucumber, seeded and cut into ½-inch dice (about 2 cups)

1 cup meaty black olives, preferably Cerignola or Kalamata, pitted and quartered

8 ounces firm feta, cut into ½-inch dice (about 1½ cups)

**Bread salads are famous in both Italy (where they're called *panzanella*) and the Middle East (*fattoush*). Sometimes the bread component is mixed in ahead to soak up the vegetable juices; other times, the bread is added at the last moment, so it keeps some of its texture, as in this recipe. Remember that a bread salad is only as good as the bread that goes into it: For best results, use an artisan-style country loaf.**

**Make the garlic croutons:** Position a rack in the center of the oven and heat the oven to 375°F. Put the bread cubes in a large bowl. In a small saucepan, heat the oil and garlic over medium heat until the garlic just begins to color, 3 to 5 minutes. Be careful it doesn't burn or it will become bitter. Pour the oil through a strainer onto the bread cubes. Toss until the cubes are evenly coated with oil (discard the garlic). Transfer to a rimmed baking sheet and toast the bread in the oven, flipping occasionally, until it's nicely golden on all sides, about 12 minutes. The croutons should be toasty on the surface but still somewhat soft in the middle. Return them to the large bowl and, while still warm, toss them with parsley, lemon zest, ¼ teaspoon salt, and a few grinds of pepper.

**Make the dressing:** In a medium bowl, whisk the oil with the vinegar, shallot, mustard, oregano, and anchovies. Add salt and pepper to taste. Let sit for at least 10 minutes to let the flavors blend.

**Assemble the salad:** Lay the arugula on a large platter and artfully arrange the tomatoes, cucumber, olives, feta, and croutons in stripes or piles on top of the arugula. Whisk the dressing to recombine and serve it in a pitcher. Encourage guests to spoon elements of the salad onto their plates and drizzle over some of the dressing. Or drizzle the dressing over the salad platter just before serving. You may not need all of the dressing. *—John Ash*

# Chopped Mexican Salad with Roasted Peppers, Corn, Tomatoes & Avocado

*Serves eight.*

**For the peppers and corn:**

2 large orange or red bell peppers

2 ears fresh corn

1 tablespoon extra-virgin olive oil

Kosher salt and freshly ground black pepper

**For the vinaigrette:**

1 small clove garlic

Kosher salt

3 tablespoons fresh lime juice

3 tablespoons fresh orange juice

2 teaspoons finely chopped shallot

1 tablespoon honey; more to taste

¾ teaspoon cumin seeds, toasted and finely ground

¼ cup extra-virgin olive oil

Freshly ground black pepper

**To assemble:**

2 large firm, ripe tomatoes, cored, seeded, and cut into ¼-inch dice (about 1¾ cups)

1 small jícama, peeled and cut into ¼-inch dice (2 cups)

2 large firm, ripe Hass avocados, pitted, peeled, and cut into ¼-inch dice (about 2½ cups)

One 15-ounce can black beans, drained and rinsed (or 1½ cups home-cooked black beans)

¼ cup coarsely chopped fresh cilantro

Serve the vegetables on a bed of greens, add grilled chicken, steak, or shrimp, and this easily makes a satisfying main course for four. You can chop all the salad ingredients up to four hours ahead and store them separately covered in the fridge. Toast whole cumin seeds in a dry sauté pan over medium heat until fragrant, shaking the pan for even browning. Grind the toasted seeds in a mortar and pestle or in an electric coffee grinder dedicated to spices.

**Roast the peppers and corn:** Position a rack in the center of the oven and heat the oven to 425°F. Line a heavy-duty rimmed baking sheet with foil. Cut the peppers in half lengthwise and remove the stem, seed core, and ribs. Put the pepper halves on the baking sheet cut side down. Husk the corn and put the ears on the baking sheet. Drizzle the oil over the peppers and corn and rub it around to coat the pepper skins and corn kernels evenly. Sprinkle the corn with salt and pepper. Roast until the peppers are soft and slightly shriveled and browned and the corn kernels are lightly browned in a few spots, about 20 minutes (rotate the corn occasionally as it roasts).

When the vegetables are done, let them rest until cool enough to handle. Scrape away the pepper skin and cut the flesh into ½-inch dice. Cut the corn kernels from the cob. You should have about 1½ cups kernels.

**Make the vinaigrette:** Mince and mash the garlic into a paste with ¼ teaspoon salt. In a medium bowl, whisk the garlic paste with the lime and orange juices, shallot, honey, and toasted ground cumin. Slowly add the oil in a thin stream, whisking until well blended. Season to taste with pepper and more salt and honey, if you like.

**Assemble the salad:** Artfully arrange the corn, tomatoes, peppers, jícama, avocados, and black beans in stripes or piles on a small platter or other wide, shallow serving dish. Sprinkle with the cilantro. Serve the vinaigrette in a pitcher. Encourage guests to spoon elements of the salad onto their plates and drizzle over some of the vinaigrette. Or drizzle the vinaigrette over the salad platter just before serving. *—John Ash*

# Vietnamese Noodle Salad with Pork Patties (Bún Cha)

*Serves two to three.*

8 or 9 ounces rice vermicelli noodles (thin rice sticks)

Kosher salt

½ cup very thin carrot strips (julienne)

½ cup very thin daikon radish or jícama strips (julienne)

3 teaspoons granulated sugar

1 teaspoon red-wine vinegar

Vietnamese Dipping Sauce (see page 93)

1 pound ground pork (ask the butcher for coarsely ground pork butt)

5 small or 4 large scallions (white and green parts), thinly sliced

1½ teaspoons fish sauce

Freshly ground black pepper

6 large leaves romaine lettuce, torn into bite-size pieces

1 cup roughly chopped fresh mint

1 cup roughly chopped fresh cilantro

**This popular dish is one of many versions of *bún*, salads composed of noodles served at room temperature with cool garnishes and warm toppings. Drizzled with a lively dressing, it becomes an intricately flavored dish of contrasting tastes, textures, and temperatures. A handheld julienne slicer or peeler is a great tool for making the very fine, wispy julienne slices of carrot and radish that are added to the sauce. Rice vermicelli noodles can be found in the Asian foods section of many supermarkets and at Asian groceries.**

Soak the rice vermicelli in a large bowl of warm water for 15 minutes. Meanwhile, bring about 2 quarts water and 1 teaspoon salt to a boil in a large saucepan. Drain the noodles and add them to the boiling water, stirring with chopsticks to gently separate the strands. When the water returns to a boil (after about 2 minutes), drain the noodles in a colander (push the strands against the sides of the colander with chopsticks to help them drain completely). Put the noodles on a platter and fluff them with chopsticks. Set aside until cool, at least 30 minutes and up to 2 hours.

Put the carrots and daikon or jícama in a colander. Sprinkle on 1 teaspoon of the sugar, the vinegar, and ¼ teaspoon salt and mix well. Let the colander sit in the sink for 10 minutes, then gently squeeze the vegetables to get rid of the liquid. Add the vegetables to the bowl of dipping sauce.

Put the pork in a medium bowl. Add the scallions, the remaining 2 teaspoons sugar, the fish sauce, ⅛ teaspoon salt, and ⅛ teaspoon pepper and mix gently with your hands. Shape the meat into small patties about 2 inches wide and ¾ inch thick; you should have ten patties.

Grill the patties over a medium-hot gas or charcoal grill (or in an oiled grill pan or skillet over medium-high heat on the stove) until they're well browned outside and cooked through but still moist inside, 8 to 10 minutes on a grill; 15 minutes in a grill pan (cut into one to check—it's fine if the pork is still a little pink inside). Add the patties, still warm, to the bowl of sauce and vegetables and let sit for 5 to 10 minutes before serving.

Serve the noodles on the platter, along with the lettuce, mint, and cilantro. Remove the pork patties from the sauce and put them on a different platter. Give everyone a large bowl and let people serve themselves noodles, lettuce, and herbs, then top that with pork patties and a generous drizzle of the dipping sauce and the vegetables in it. Toss gently. *—Thai Moreland*

# Vietnamese Dipping Sauce (Nuoc Cham)

*Yields 2¼ cups.*

**The sauce keeps for two weeks in the refrigerator.**

3 large cloves garlic, minced

1 hot red chile (such as serrano), thinly sliced

1 cup water

½ cup fish sauce

½ cup red-wine vinegar

½ cup granulated sugar

Stir all the ingredients together in a medium bowl. Set aside.

# Mexican-Style Slaw with Jícama, Cilantro & Lime

*Serves six to eight.*

1 small or ½ medium red or green cabbage (or use a mix of both, about 1½ pounds total), bruised outer leaves removed, cored, and cut into six wedges

Kosher salt

1 medium jícama (about 1 pound), peeled and quartered

4 scallions (white and green parts), thinly sliced on the diagonal (about ½ cup)

¼ cup chopped fresh cilantro

¼ cup plus 2 tablespoons mayonnaise

¼ cup fresh lime juice; more to taste

1 jalapeño, seeded (if you like) and minced

**This creamy slaw is reminiscent of the garnish on Baja-style fish tacos. Use it as a topping for fish or chicken soft tacos, or spoon it alongside lime-grilled chicken, fish, or shrimp. Use a mandoline, V-slicer, or the coleslaw setting on your food processor to slice the cabbage into thin strips.**

Thinly slice the cabbage in a food processor using the 4mm slicing disk (see the box below) or by hand; you should have about 6 packed cups. Put the cabbage in a colander and toss it with 1 tablespoon salt. Lay a plate that fits inside the colander on top of the cabbage and set a heavy can or jar on top. Drain the cabbage in the sink or over a bowl for 2 hours.

If using a food processor, switch to the grating disk and grate the jícama (position it as shown in the box below) or cut it into very thin (julienne) strips by hand; you should have about 2 cups. Put the jícama in a large bowl and toss in the scallions and cilantro.

In a small bowl, whisk together the mayonnaise, lime juice, and jalapeño.

Turn the cabbage out onto a clean dishtowel or paper towels and pat it thoroughly dry. Toss the cabbage with the jícama and lime mayonnaise. Season to taste with more salt and lime juice if needed. *—Allison Ehri*

## For quicker slaws use a food processor

You can slice the ingredients for slaws by hand, but a food processor does the job in seconds. To get the long, thin strands that make a great slaw, you need to use the appropriate blade attachment, then orient the vegetables in a certain way. Here's how to do it.

### Pick the right disk

Most food processors come with these attachments: a 4mm slicing disk, shown on top at left, and a medium grating disk (it may be called a 4mm or medium shredding disk).

### Position the vegetable correctly

For cabbage, use the slicing disk. Put the wedge of cabbage in the feed tube with a cut side on the disk so you get nice long ribbons.

For carrots, celery root, jícama, and mangos, use the grating disk. Cut them into lengths the same size as the feed tube opening, then stack the pieces in the tube with a long side on the disk to get long shreds.

# 4 Pasta

p118

p130

Pasta with Mushrooms, Peas, Prosciutto
& Sour Cream (recipe on page 124)

# Linguine with Hot Chile, Caramelized Onion & Gremolata

*Serves four to six.*

2 tablespoons extra-virgin
olive oil

1 large yellow onion, very
thinly sliced

½ teaspoon crushed red
pepper flakes

Kosher salt

1 serrano or other fresh small,
hot red or green chile, seeded
and finely diced

½ cup (1 stick) unsalted butter,
cut into about 5 pieces

3 tablespoons fresh lemon juice

1 pound dried linguine

⅓ cup roughly chopped fresh
flat-leaf parsley

1 large clove garlic, finely
chopped

1 teaspoon finely chopped
lemon zest

½ cup grated Pecorino Romano;
more for sprinkling

**Gremolata—a combination of lemon zest, garlic, and parsley—adds a nice, fresh touch to this and many other dishes. Try sprinkling it on a creamy pasta, risotto, grilled shrimp, sautéed spinach, or steamed green beans.**

Bring a large pot of well-salted water to a boil.

Meanwhile, heat the oil in a 10-inch straight-sided sauté pan over medium heat. Add the onion and red pepper, season with a big pinch of salt, and cook, stirring frequently, until tender and nicely browned, about 15 minutes (reduce the heat to medium low if the onion is browning too fast). Add the chile and continue to cook for 1 minute. Turn off the heat, add the butter, and swirl the pan to melt. Add the lemon juice and another pinch of salt. Keep warm.

Cook the linguine in the boiling water until al dente, about 10 minutes.

**Meanwhile, make the gremolata:** Combine the parsley, garlic, and lemon zest on a cutting board and chop them together with a chef's knife until the parsley is finely chopped and mixed well with the lemon and garlic.

Drain the pasta and return it to its cooking pot. Over medium heat, add the onion mixture and toss to combine. Add the Pecorino, quickly toss again, and add salt to taste. Transfer the pasta to a platter or shallow bowls. Sprinkle liberally with the gremolata and more Pecorino and serve. *—Tasha DeSerio*

tip : Instead of grating the lemon for the gremolata, use a zester, then finely chop the long strips of zest with a chef's knife. This zest is a little chunkier and easier to sprinkle.

# Fettuccine with Tuna, Lemon & Fried Capers

*Serves four.*

Kosher salt

1 lemon, scrubbed

¼ cup plus 2 tablespoons
   extra-virgin olive oil; more
   for drizzling

¼ cup small (nonpareil)
   capers, rinsed, drained,
   and patted dry

3 cloves garlic, thinly sliced

One 12-ounce or two 6-ounce
   cans solid white tuna packed
   in water, drained well

⅛ teaspoon crushed red
   pepper flakes

¾ pound dried fettuccine

Freshly ground black pepper

3 tablespoons chopped fresh
   flat-leaf parsley

**Tuna stands up well to the vibrant flavors of crisp capers, thin slivers of garlic, and bright strips of lemon zest. Be sure to enhance the flavor of the pasta by adding a couple tablespoons of kosher salt to the cooking water. The water should taste as salty as the ocean.**

Bring a large pot of well-salted water to a boil.

Meanwhile, using a zester tool (called a channel knife), zest the lemon into thin strips or, using a vegetable peeler, shave off the zest, then slice into very thin strips. Juice the lemon to get 2 tablespoons juice.

Heat ¼ cup of the oil in a 10-inch straight-sided sauté pan over medium heat. Add the capers and cook until they start to brown and get crisp, 3 to 5 minutes. Stir in the lemon zest and cook until it starts to crisp and curl up, about 1 minute. Using a slotted spoon, transfer the capers and zest to a plate lined with a paper towel—it's fine if a few capers remain in the pan.

Reduce the heat to medium low, add the garlic to the remaining oil in the pan and cook, stirring, until it browns lightly but doesn't burn, 2 to 3 minutes. Add the tuna and red pepper and cook until the tuna just heats through, about 2 minutes. Remove from the heat.

Meanwhile, cook the fettuccine in the boiling water, stirring often, just until al dente (see the package for cooking time). Reserve ½ cup of the pasta water and drain the pasta.

Return the sauté pan to medium heat. Add the drained pasta, ¼ cup of the reserved pasta water, the lemon juice, and the remaining 2 tablespoons oil. Cook, tossing and stirring, for 1 to 2 minutes to blend the flavors. If the pasta isn't tender, add the remaining cooking water and continue to cook and stir until done. Season to taste with salt, pepper, and more lemon juice.

Serve immediately, drizzled with a little olive oil and sprinkled with the capers, lemon strips, parsley, and a few grinds of black pepper.
—*Tony Rosenfeld*

# Spaghetti with Arugula, Tomato & Ricotta Salata

*Serves four to six.*

1 pound dried spaghetti

5 ounces baby arugula (about 6 cups, loosely packed), washed, spun dry, and long stems removed

½ cup extra-virgin olive oil

2 teaspoons dried oregano

3 beefsteak tomatoes, cut into ½-inch dice (about 3 cups)

Kosher salt and freshly ground black pepper

5 ounces ricotta salata, grated

This pasta is so easy but so good. The flavor of ricotta salata is unbeatable with arugula. But if you can't find this dry cheese at an Italian market or at a cheese shop, use a smaller amount of mozzarella or Parmesan instead (the soft ricotta that comes in a tub won't work). Whichever cheese you use, grate it slowly on a grater with large holes to get long strands of cheese.

Bring a large pot of well-salted water to a boil.

Meanwhile, place the arugula in a large bowl.

Cook the spaghetti in the boiling water until just al dente. Drain well, place in the bowl with the arugula, add the oil, oregano, and tomatoes, and season with salt and pepper. Gently toss and divide among bowls. Top with the ricotta salata and serve immediately. —*Tony Mantuano*

# Angel Hair Pasta with Lemon Cream Sauce

*Serves four as a first course.*

Kosher salt

2 lemons

1 cup heavy cream

½ cup gin

12 ounces fresh angel hair pasta

Freshly ground black pepper

¼ cup chopped fresh
   flat-leaf parsley

**If you happen to have some grappa on hand, the fiery Italian spirit is a delicious alternative for the gin in this recipe.**

Bring a large pot of well-salted water to a boil.

Meanwhile, finely grate the zest of one of the lemons; set aside. Cut a thick slice off both ends of the zested lemon to expose the flesh. Stand the fruit upright, then, cutting from the top down, remove the peel, including all the white pith. Holding the fruit over a bowl to catch the juice, use a paring knife to cut along either side of each segment to free it from the membranes; let each segment fall into the bowl as you go. Once you've removed all the segments, squeeze any juice from the membranes into the bowl, then discard the membrane. Remove the seeds and set the segments aside in another small dish. Cut the remaining lemon in half and squeeze to obtain 2 tablespoons juice total.

Put the cream, gin, and lemon segments in a 12-inch skillet over medium heat and bring just to a boil. Lower the heat and simmer until the cream thickens slightly, 5 to 8 minutes. Remove from the heat.

When the water boils, cook the pasta just until al dente. Drain.

Reheat the cream sauce over medium-low heat. Add the lemon juice, along with the drained pasta and half of the grated lemon zest. Toss the pasta in the warm sauce to coat thoroughly. Season to taste with salt and pepper. Serve in warmed pasta bowls. Sprinkle with the remaining lemon zest and the parsley.

*—Jennifer McLagan*

## Tips for zesting...

- Thick-skinned lemons, which tend to have pebbly-textured skin, are easiest to zest.
- Before zesting, scrub the lemon's skin well to remove any residues (a soak in warm water can help remove any wax coating).
- Remove just the thin yellow layer of rind, not the white pith below.
- Zest a lemon before you juice it.
- Use a vegetable peeler to get wide strips of zest for adding to slow-cooked dishes.
- A channel zester gives you long, skinny strips of zest, but this tool doesn't give you as much zest as a grater does.
- A rasp-style grater is the ideal tool for finely grated zest. It's so easy to use and it gives you the most zest.
- Save the flavor: You can freeze lemon zest in a sealed container for up to 3 months.

## ...and clever ways to use it

- Add grated zest to breadcrumbs and use for coating cutlets and topping gratins.
- Mix grated zest into ground meats when making meatballs and hamburgers.
- Stir grated zest with chopped capers and parsley to top cooked meat and fish.
- Add a long, wide strip of zest when braising vegetables or meat or when making stock.
- Make lemon sugar by putting strips of zest in granulated sugar. Use in cookies, cakes, or tea; or sprinkle on French toast.
- Make lemon vodka by steeping strips of lemon zest in regular vodka. Taste the vodka regularly and remove the lemon strips when it suits your taste. Or, infuse white wine with zest for apéritifs.
- Add a strip of zest to your favorite cocktail.

## Getting the most juice...

- The juiciest lemons tend to be those with thin skins. If the lemon skin is smooth rather than textured, that's a tip-off that the skin is thin. And small to medium lemons are generally thinner skinned than large ones.
- Juicers or reamers will get the maximum juice from lemons, especially two-part juicers: The reamer and strainer are a single piece that sits on top of a container that catches the juice and has a lip for pouring.
- If you squeeze the fruit using only your hands, first roll the lemon on the counter, then microwave for 30 seconds. You'll get more juice.
- One lemon yields 3 to 4 tablespoons of juice.
- Don't waste a drop: extra juice freezes well for up to 3 months.

## ...and seven ideas for using it

- Use lemon juice as you would a pinch of salt: It works wonders as a flavor enhancer.
- Don't be afraid to add a tablespoon or two of lemon juice to a stew or braise at the end of cooking to bring all the flavors together.
- Drizzle juice over cooked vegetables just before serving to bring out their flavor.
- Deglaze your pan with lemon juice and stock to make a tasty sauce or glaze for fish or vegetables.
- Make lemon butter: Mix lemon juice, zest, and minced garlic into softened butter, chill, and cut into slices to top grilled meats, fish, and vegetables.
- Make a simple seafood marinade by mixing olive oil, lemon juice, and chopped dill or fennel.
- Instead of reaching for the vinegar bottle, grab a lemon and replace the vinegar in salad dressing with lemon juice.

# Spaghetti with Garlic, Hot Pepper & Pecorino

*Serves four.*

Kosher salt

3 tablespoons extra-virgin olive oil

4 cloves garlic, halved and smashed

Heaping ¼ teaspoon crushed red pepper flakes

2 teaspoons chopped fresh rosemary

¾ pound dried spaghetti

¾ cup freshly grated Pecorino Romano

Freshly ground black pepper

**This dish is a cross between two simple Italian classics that rely on a "sauce" of flavor-infused olive oil: garlic and red pepper flakes come from spaghetti aglio, olio, and peperoncino, while black pepper and Pecorino are borrowed from spaghetti pepe and cacio. Here, they form a tasty hybrid.**

Bring a large pot of well-salted water to a boil.

Meanwhile, heat the oil and garlic in a 10-inch straight-sided sauté pan over medium-low heat, stirring, until the garlic is fragrant and starts to brown all over, 4 to 5 minutes. Add the red pepper and rosemary, cook for 30 seconds, and remove from the heat.

Cook the spaghetti in the boiling water, stirring occasionally, until al dente. Reserve ½ cup of the pasta water and drain the pasta.

Return the sauté pan to medium heat and discard the garlic. Add the drained pasta and ¼ cup of the reserved pasta water. Cook for 1 to 2 minutes, tossing and stirring, to blend the flavors. If the pasta isn't tender, add the remainder of the cooking water and continue to cook and stir until done. Toss with half the Pecorino and ½ teaspoon black pepper. Season with salt and more pepper to taste.

Serve immediately, sprinkled with the remaining Pecorino and a few grinds of black pepper. —*Tony Rosenfeld*

## Pecorino, sweet and peppery

A sampling of Italian Pecorinos, clockwise from top center: Sardo d'Oro, Romano D.O.P., Sardo Moliterno, Toscano Brinata, and Toscano di Pienza.

Pecorino (derived from pecora, Italian for sheep) is a sheep's milk cheese that's been produced in central and southern Italy since well before the rise of the Roman Empire. Made with either pasteurized or unpasteurized milk, Pecorino can be aged anywhere from 20 days—resulting in a soft-textured, mild-flavored cheese with an edible rind—to up to a year for harder, more pungent cheeses. Its many varieties are grouped into four main government-protected regional categories (D.O.P.) subject to strict production rules: Toscano, made in Tuscany; Sardo, from the island of Sardinia; Siciliano, produced in Sicily; and Romano, mainly from the countryside around Rome.

The last, which is saltier than other Pecorinos, is primarily a grating cheese when aged. The mass-produced Pecorinos we're used to seeing in grocery stores are also Romanos, but they're a far cry from their artisanal cousins.

# Fettuccine with Arugula-Walnut Pesto

*Serves four to six.*

4 ounces arugula, washed and spun dry (about 3 lightly packed cups)

½ cup freshly grated Parmigiano-Reggiano; more for sprinkling

½ cup walnuts, toasted on a baking sheet in a 375°F oven until golden brown, 5 to 10 minutes

2 tablespoons fresh lemon juice

1 clove garlic, smashed and peeled

Kosher salt

½ cup extra-virgin olive oil

¼ cup walnut oil

1 pound dried fettuccine

**Walnut oil smooths out the peppery bite of the arugula, but you can substitute extra-virgin olive oil instead. Nut oils can turn rancid quickly, so store them in the fridge to prolong their shelf life. A Caesar salad, served with or after the pasta, is a good complement.**

Bring a large pot of well-salted water to a boil.

Meanwhile, put the arugula, Parmigiano, walnuts, lemon juice, garlic, and 1 teaspoon salt into a food processor and process until the mixture is finely ground, 30 to 60 seconds. In a measuring cup, combine the olive oil and walnut oil. With the food processor running, drizzle the oil through the feed tube and process the mixture until mostly smooth.

Cook the fettuccine in the boiling water just until al dente. Drain. In a medium bowl, toss the fettuccine with enough of the pesto to generously coat the pasta. Serve sprinkled with extra Parmigiano, if desired.

*—Julianna Grimes Bottcher*

# Bucatini in a Spicy Tomato Sauce with Crisped Pancetta

*Serves four.*

½ pound ¼-inch-thick slices pancetta (about 6), cut into ¼-inch dice

3 tablespoons extra-virgin olive oil

1 large red onion, halved and thinly sliced

¼ teaspoon crushed red pepper flakes

Kosher salt

One 28-ounce can peeled whole tomatoes, puréed in a blender

1 teaspoon dried oregano

Freshly ground black pepper

¾ pound dried bucatini (or thick spaghetti)

¾ cup freshly grated Pecorino Romano

**If you don't have pancetta, you can substitute bacon, which will give the dish a smokier flavor but will still be delicious. Parmigiano-Reggiano can also sub for the Pecorino.**

Bring a large pot of well-salted water to a boil.

Meanwhile, in a large skillet over medium heat, sauté the pancetta in the oil, stirring often, until it's crisp and browned, about 8 minutes, then transfer to a plate lined with paper towels. Raise the heat under the pan to medium high, add the onion and red pepper, season with salt, and cook, stirring often, until the onion is soft and translucent, 6 to 7 minutes. Add the puréed tomatoes to the skillet and cook to thicken the sauce slightly, about 5 minutes. Stir in the oregano and season generously with salt and pepper to taste. Remove the sauce from the heat until ready to serve.

Meanwhile, cook the bucatini in the boiling water just until al dente.

Drain the pasta and add to the sauce (reheat it if necessary) along with the pancetta and ½ cup of the pecorino. Toss well to combine. Serve immediately in warm bowls, topped with any sauce that may remain in the bottom of the pan and a sprinkling of the remaining Pecorino. —*Tony Rosenfeld*

# Rigatoni with Red Pepper & Parmigiano Cream Sauce

**The combination of roasted red peppers and cream makes this sauce rich and satisfying. You could stir in some sautéed cauliflower or Italian sausage to add a little more substance.**

Bring a large pot of well-salted water to a boil.

Meanwhile, heat the oil and garlic in a 10-inch straight-sided sauté pan over medium heat until the garlic sizzles steadily for about 1 minute and just starts to brown around the edges. Add the roasted red peppers, thyme, and red pepper flakes and cook, stirring, for a couple of minutes to heat through. Add the broth and vinegar. Raise the heat to medium high and bring to a boil. Remove from the heat, let cool for a couple of minutes, then transfer to a blender or food processor and purée.

Return the puréed pepper mixture to the sauté pan. Stir in the cream and ¾ cup of the Parmigiano and bring to a boil. Remove from the heat and season with salt and black pepper to taste.

Meanwhile, cook the rigatoni in the boiling water, stirring occasionally, until it's just al dente. Drain and add to the sauté pan. Cook over medium heat for 1 to 2 minutes, tossing and stirring, to blend the flavors and slightly thicken the sauce. Season with salt and pepper to taste.

Serve immediately, sprinkled with the remaining cheese and a few grinds of black pepper. *—Tony Rosenfeld*

*Serves four.*

Kosher salt

2 tablespoons extra-virgin olive oil

1 clove garlic, chopped

One 12-ounce jar roasted red peppers, drained and thinly sliced (about 1 cup)

2 teaspoons chopped fresh thyme

¼ teaspoon crushed red pepper flakes

¾ cup homemade or canned low-salt chicken broth

1 tablespoon sherry vinegar

2 tablespoons heavy cream

1 cup freshly grated Parmigiano-Reggiano

Freshly ground black pepper

¾ pound dried rigatoni or penne rigate

# Rigatoni with Spicy Tomato-Vodka Sauce

*Serves four.*

2 cloves garlic, minced

¾ teaspoon crushed red pepper flakes; more to taste

2 tablespoons extra-virgin olive oil

One 28-ounce can diced tomatoes

3 tablespoons vodka

½ cup freshly grated Parmigiano-Reggiano

¼ cup chopped fresh flat-leaf parsley

3 tablespoons heavy cream

½ teaspoon kosher salt

½ teaspoon freshly ground black pepper

¾ pound dried rigatoni (about 4 cups)

**Alcohol unlocks certain flavor compounds in tomato, and vodka, unlike wine, can do it without contributing any other flavors to the dish. The result is a very tomatoey sauce that gets its backbone from a healthy dose of spicy red pepper flakes. If you're not a fan of spicy foods, you can use less crushed red pepper flakes.**

Bring a large pot of well-salted water to a boil.

Meanwhile, in a large saucepan over medium-high heat, heat the garlic and red pepper in the oil until they're fragrant and sizzle steadily for about 30 seconds. Add the tomatoes and their juices and the vodka, and bring to a boil. Reduce the heat to a steady simmer, cover with the lid slightly ajar, and cook to intensify the flavors and reduce the sauce slightly (by about one-quarter), 10 to 15 minutes.

Purée the tomatoes using a hand blender or in a regular blender. If you used a regular blender to purée, return the sauce to the saucepan. Stir in ¼ cup of the Parmigiano, the parsley, cream, salt, black pepper, and more red pepper, if you like. Simmer to incorporate the cream and reduce the sauce slightly, about 5 minutes. Reduce the heat to low, cover, and keep warm.

Meanwhile, cook the pasta, stirring occasionally, just until al dente. Drain well and return the pasta to its pot. Add the sauce, set the pot over medium heat, and cook, stirring, to let the pasta absorb some of the sauce, about 1 minute. Serve immediately with a sprinkled with the remaining ¼ cup Parmigiano. *—Tony Rosenfeld*

# Fettuccine Primavera

*Serves six.*

Kosher salt

1 pound dried fettuccine

2 tablespoons unsalted butter, cut into chunks

2 cloves garlic, minced

3 cups very thinly sliced mixed spring vegetables, such as asparagus (leave tips whole), baby carrots, baby leeks, baby turnips, baby zucchini, spring onions, and sugar snap peas

1 cup whole, shelled fresh, or thawed frozen peas, baby lima beans (preferably peeled), or fava beans; or a mix of all

1 cup heavy cream

1 tablespoon thinly sliced lemon zest (remove zest with a vegetable peeler and thinly slice)

2 cups loosely packed pea shoots, watercress sprigs, or baby arugula

½ cup freshly grated Parmigiano-Reggiano

½ cup roughly chopped mixed fresh herbs such as basil, chervil, chives, mint, parsley, and tarragon

¼ teaspoon crushed red pepper flakes

Freshly ground black pepper

¼ cup pine nuts, toasted in a dry skillet over medium-low heat, stirring frequently, until fragrant and slightly colored, about 5 minutes

**This quintessential springtime pasta includes lots of fresh vegetables and herbs. The specific vegetables and herbs used are up to you; choose what looks best at the market.**

Bring a large pot of well-salted water to a boil and cook the fettuccine, stirring occasionally, just until al dente. (While the pasta is cooking, scoop out 1½ cups of pasta cooking water.)

Meanwhile, melt the butter in a 10-inch straight-sided sauté pan over medium heat. Add the garlic and cook until softened and fragrant but not browned, about 1 minute. Add 1 cup of the reserved water. Add the sliced vegetables and peas or lima beans (if using fresh). Cover and simmer until the vegetables are just tender, about 3 minutes. Add the cream and lemon zest along with any fava beans or thawed, frozen peas or lima beans (if using). Bring to a simmer.

Drain the fettuccine and return it to its cooking pot. Toss with the sauce, pea shoots (or watercress or arugula), Parmigiano, all but 1 tablespoon of the herbs, and the red pepper. Season to taste with salt and black pepper. If necessary, adjust the consistency of the sauce with the remaining ½ cup pasta water; the sauce should generously coat the vegetables and pasta. Serve immediately, sprinkled with the remaining fresh herbs and the pine nuts.
*—Allison Ehri*

# Fregola with Grill-Marinated Red Peppers & Zucchini

*Serves six to eight.*

2 red bell peppers, cored and each cut into four pieces

1¼ pounds zucchini (4 small), trimmed and quartered lengthwise

5 tablespoons Rosemary-Garlic Oil (see page 14)

Kosher salt and freshly ground black pepper

1 tablespoon red-wine vinegar

3 tablespoons chopped fresh mint, plus 3 tablespoons torn leaves

2 teaspoons chopped fresh thyme

¾ pound fregola

**Grill-marinating is an Italian technique in which vegetables, such as the zucchini and peppers in this dish, are first grilled, then bathed in a vinaigrette, which gives them a pleasing tang. Fregola, sometimes referred to as Sardinian couscous, is a tiny toasted pasta.**

Heat a gas grill to medium or prepare a medium-hot charcoal fire. In a large bowl, toss the peppers and zucchini with 2 tablespoons of the oil, 1 teaspoon salt, and ½ teaspoon pepper. Arrange the vegetables on the grill and cook, covered if using a gas grill, until they have nice grill marks, about 3 minutes for zucchini and 5 minutes for peppers. Flip and cook until the other sides are well browned, too, another 3 to 5 minutes. Continue cooking and flipping occasionally until the zucchini is crisp-tender and the peppers are completely tender with very charred skins, 8 to 10 minutes total for zucchini and 12 to 15 minutes total for peppers. Transfer to a large cutting board to cool.

Scrape the charred skins off the peppers. Coarsely chop the vegetables and transfer to a large serving bowl. Toss with 2 tablespoons of the oil, the vinegar, chopped mint, and thyme. Season with salt and pepper to taste and let sit for up to 2 hours at room temperature.

Up to 1 hour before serving, bring a large pot of well-salted water to a boil. Add the fregola and cook, stirring occasionally, just until al dente.

Drain the fregola and toss with the vegetables. Drizzle with the remaining 1 tablespoon oil and season to taste with salt and pepper. Sprinkle with the torn mint and set out on the table for serving. —*Tony Rosenfeld*

## Buy fregola, or make your own toasted pasta

Fregola, also known as succu or Sardinian couscous, is made from coarsely ground semolina and water. Compared to the more familiar North African style of couscous, which is very small and light, fregola is larger and more toothsome, and it has a deliciously nutty flavor because it's toasted.

Unless you have a good Italian specialty store in your area, fregola can be hard to find, though you can order it from many online sources. You can also make a good substitute using acini di pepe, a tiny spherical pasta that's often added to soup. It's available in many supermarkets. Israeli couscous and orzo or other tiny pasta shapes are also options.

To mimic the nutty flavor of fregola, toast the pasta or Israeli couscous in a large, dry skillet over medium-low heat, tossing occasionally, until it browns a bit, about 10 minutes. If using Israeli couscous, rinse it with cold water for 10 seconds after boiling to prevent overcooking.

# Spaghetti with Pine Nuts, Tomatoes & Garlic Breadcrumbs

*Serves four.*

½ cup extra-virgin olive oil

2 cloves garlic, minced

2½ cups fresh coarse breadcrumbs

Kosher salt and freshly ground black pepper

½ cup pine nuts, toasted in a dry skillet over medium-low heat, stirring frequently, until fragrant and slightly colored, about 5 minutes

¾ pound dried spaghetti

¼ cup raisins

¼ teaspoon crushed red pepper flakes

1 pint cherry tomatoes, halved

6 tablespoons chopped fresh flat-leaf parsley

**When you toast pine nuts, watch them carefully because they burn easily. After adding pasta to boiling water, be sure to stir it often so that the pasta doesn't stick together. Also, don't add oil to the water or the pasta won't absorb its sauce as well.**

Bring a large pot of well-salted water to a boil.

Meanwhile, heat 2 tablespoons of the oil and half the garlic in a heavy, 10-inch skillet over medium-high heat until the garlic is fragrant but not brown, about 30 seconds. Reduce the heat to medium, toss in the breadcrumbs, season with salt and pepper, and cook, stirring often, until the crumbs brown and turn crisp, 6 to 10 minutes. Transfer to a medium bowl and stir in the pine nuts.

Cook the pasta in the boiling water just until al dente.

Meanwhile, add another 2 tablespoons of the oil to the skillet and cook the remaining garlic, the raisins, and red pepper until the garlic is fragrant but not browned, about 30 seconds. Add the tomatoes, season generously with salt and black pepper, and sauté for 5 minutes so they start to soften and lose their shape. Fold in all but 2 tablespoons of the parsley.

Drain the pasta, put it in a large serving bowl, and toss with the tomato mixture, half of the breadcrumbs, and 2 tablespoons of the oil. Taste for salt and black pepper. Drizzle each serving with ½ tablespoon of the remaining oil and sprinkle with the remaining breadcrumbs and parsley. Serve immediately.

*—Tony Rosenfeld*

# Penne with Tomatoes, Artichokes & Black Olives

*Serves four.*

**Kosher salt**

**2 tablespoons extra-virgin olive oil**

**3 cloves garlic, minced**

**One 14-ounce can artichoke bottoms (or hearts), drained, rinsed, and thinly sliced**

**¼ teaspoon crushed red pepper flakes**

**Two 15.5-ounce cans diced tomatoes**

**½ cup pitted Kalamata olives, drained and halved**

**Freshly ground black pepper**

**¾ pound dried penne rigate**

**⅓ cup freshly grated Parmigiano-Reggiano**

**3 ounces very thinly sliced prosciutto (preferably imported), cut into thin strips (about ¾ cup)**

**Laying strips of prosciutto on top of the pasta just before serving heats the ham without ruining its delicate texture and flavor.**

Bring a large pot of well-salted water to a boil.

Meanwhile, heat the oil and garlic in a 12-inch skillet over medium-low heat, stirring occasionally, until the garlic becomes fragrant and starts to brown all over, about 4 minutes. Raise the heat to medium high, add the artichokes and red pepper, and cook, stirring occasionally, until the artichokes start to brown, about 3 minutes. Add the tomatoes and their juices and bring to a boil. Reduce the heat to a simmer, cover, and cook for 10 minutes.

Stir in the olives and season generously with salt and black pepper to taste. Cover and keep warm over low heat.

Meanwhile, cook the penne in the boiling water, stirring occasionally, just until al dente. Drain and return the pasta to its cooking pot. Add the sauce and about half the Parmigiano. Cook over medium-high heat for 1 to 2 minutes, tossing and stirring, to blend the flavors. Season with salt and black pepper to taste.

Serve immediately, scattering the prosciutto and remaining Parmigiano over each serving. *—Tony Rosenfeld*

**tip :** A quick, neat way to pit an olive is to use a chef's knife or a small skillet or saucepan. The action is the same for both tools: Apply pressure with the bottom of the pan or the side of the knife until the olive splits, exposing the pit enough that it can be plucked away by hand.

# Farfalle in a Broth of Wild Mushrooms & Browned Shallots

**If shiitake or oyster mushrooms aren't available, you can substitute other kinds; just be sure to slice them very thinly.**

Bring a large pot of well-salted water to a boil.

Remove the stems from the shiitake and oyster mushrooms and thinly slice the caps. Heat 2 tablespoons of the oil in a large skillet over medium-high heat for 1 minute. Add the mushrooms, season with salt and pepper, and cook, tossing occasionally, until soft, 2 to 3 minutes. Transfer to a plate.

Cook the pasta in the boiling water just until al dente.

Meanwhile, add the remaining 2 tablespoons oil and the shallots to the skillet. Season with salt and cook for 2 minutes, stirring occasionally. Reduce the heat to medium low and cook until the shallots brown and soften, 2 to 4 minutes (don't let them burn). Raise the heat to high, add the sherry, and cook, scraping the bottom of the pan, until it is almost completely boiled off, about 30 seconds. Add the broth. After 2 minutes, return the mushrooms to the pan, reduce the heat to medium, and cook for another 2 minutes. Sprinkle in the thyme and Tabasco and taste for salt and pepper.

Drain the pasta and return to its cooking pot. Pour the broth and mushrooms over the pasta and stir well. Serve immediately in bowls with a generous sprinkling of the Parmigiano. *—Tony Rosenfeld*

*Serves four.*

6 ounces fresh shiitake mushrooms

¼ pound fresh oyster mushrooms

¼ cup extra-virgin olive oil

Kosher salt and freshly ground black pepper

¾ pound dried farfalle

4 shallots (about 3 ounces total), sliced crosswise into ¼- to ⅛-inch-thick rings

¼ cup dry sherry

3 cups homemade or canned low-salt chicken broth

2 teaspoons fresh thyme leaves, chopped

¼ teaspoon Tabasco; more to taste

¼ cup freshly grated Parmigiano-Reggiano

# Penne with Eggplant, Tomato & Basil

*Serves four.*

1/4 cup plus 2 tablespoons extra-virgin olive oil; more for drizzling

1 medium eggplant (1 pound), cut into 1/4-inch dice (about 6 cups)

Kosher salt

1 small red onion, thinly sliced

1/4 teaspoon crushed red pepper flakes; more to taste

1 1/4 pounds tomatoes, seeded and cut into 1/2-inch dice (about 2 1/3 cups)

3 medium cloves garlic, finely chopped

1 cup roughly chopped fresh basil

3/4 pound dried penne rigate

1/2 cup coarsely grated Parmigiano-Reggiano or ricotta salata

**Eggplant, tomatoes, and basil combine for a simplified version of ratatouille that stands up to hearty penne. Ricotta salata is a slightly salty, dry sheep's milk cheese that marries particularly well with the robust flavors of the dish.**

Bring a large pot of well-salted water to a boil.

Meanwhile, heat 1/4 cup of the oil in a 12-inch skillet over high heat until shimmering hot. Add the eggplant and a generous pinch of salt. Reduce the heat to medium high and cook, stirring occasionally, until the eggplant is tender and light golden brown, about 6 minutes. Transfer to a plate. Reduce the heat to medium, return the pan to the stove, and add the remaining 2 tablespoons oil, the onion, red pepper, and a pinch of salt. Cook until the onion is tender and golden brown, about 6 minutes. Add the tomatoes and another pinch of salt, and cook until the tomatoes start to break down and form a sauce, about 3 minutes. Add the garlic and cook for 1 minute. Return the eggplant to the pan, add the basil, and cook for 1 minute more to let the flavors meld. Taste the sauce and add salt if needed.

Meanwhile, cook the pasta in the boiling water just until al dente. Drain, reserving a small amount of the cooking water. Put the pasta in a large bowl and toss with the eggplant mixture. If it needs a little more moisture, add a splash of the pasta water. Taste and add salt if needed. Put the pasta on a platter or divide among shallow bowls and finish with a drizzle of oil. Sprinkle the Parmigiano or ricotta salata on top and serve immediately. *—Tasha DeSerio*

When a recipe calls for seeded and diced fresh tomatoes, there are a few ways to go about it. Here are two of our favorite methods, with some pros and cons of each.

## Method 1
### Best for round tomatoes

Core the tomato and cut it in half crosswise with a serrated knife to expose the seed chamber. Gently squeeze out the seeds, using a finger or a small table knife to help empty the chambers. Lay the seeded tomato halves, cut side down, on a cutting board. Holding the serrated knife parallel to the board, cut each half horizontally into slices that are as thick as you want your dice to be. Next, cut each stack of tomato slices into strips as wide as you want your dice, then slice these strips crosswise into dice.

**Pros:** You use the whole tomato; good for beefsteaks, which have a lot of delicious inner flesh.

**Cons:** Takes a little more time; the stacks can be awkward to slice.

Use a small table knife or a fingertip to flick out the seeds.

Cut the tomato into strips, then slice crosswise into dice, as you'd cut an onion.

## Method 2
### Best for plum tomatoes

Cut a thin slice from the bottom to create a flat surface on which to stand the tomato. Cut wide strips from the top, curving down to the bottom, to separate the flesh from the inner seed core. Cut all the flesh away in this manner, leaving the seedy core of the tomato; discard the core. Cut each strip of flesh lengthwise as wide as you want your dice to be, then cut these strips crosswise into dice.

**Pros:** Fast; good for tomatoes with big seed chambers and less inner flesh, such as plum tomatoes.

**Cons:** You don't use the whole tomato.

Cut the flesh away from the seeds in wide, petal-like strips.

Cut the strips lengthwise, then crosswise into dice.

# Pasta with Mushrooms, Peas, Prosciutto & Sour Cream

See photo on page 97.

*Serves two to three.*

¼ pound thinly sliced prosciutto

½ cup sour cream

2 teaspoons all-purpose flour

Kosher salt

1 tablespoon extra-virgin olive oil

1 tablespoon unsalted butter

1 pound mixed fresh mushrooms, cleaned, trimmed, and sliced ¼ inch thick

2 cloves garlic, minced

¼ cup chopped fresh flat-leaf parsley

Freshly ground black pepper

½ pound dried corkscrew-shaped pasta (cellentani or cavatappi)

1 cup homemade or canned low-salt chicken broth

½ cup frozen peas

**To speed the making of this dish along, put the pasta water on while you make the mushroom sauté. When sautéing mushrooms, stir them less often than you might want to for the best browning and the fullest flavor. The browned bits that stick to the pan contribute a ton of flavor when the pan gets deglazed.**

Cut the sliced prosciutto crosswise into thin pieces about ⅛ inch wide. Stir together the sour cream and flour.

Bring a large pot of well-salted water to a boil.

Meanwhile, heat the oil and butter together in a 12-inch sauté pan or skillet over medium heat until the butter foams. Add the mushrooms and garlic. Sprinkle with ½ teaspoon salt and stir with a wooden spoon until the mushrooms start to release their moisture and begin to shrink, 2 to 3 minutes. Increase the heat to medium high so that you hear a steady sizzle; stir occasionally. In about 5 minutes, when the liquid evaporates and the mushrooms start to brown, give just an occasional sweep with the spoon (about once a minute) to allow them to brown nicely, cooking them another 2 to 4 minutes. Resist the inclination to stir too often. Turn off the heat and toss the mushrooms with 2 tablespoons of the parsley. Season with pepper to taste. Transfer the mushrooms to a plate.

Cook the pasta in the boiling water just until al dente.

Meanwhile, return the mushroom pan to medium-high heat. Pour in the broth and scrape the bottom of the pan with a wooden spoon to stir any browned bits into the broth. Boil until reduced to about ¾ cup, 2 to 3 minutes. Reduce the heat to a very gentle simmer and whisk in the sour cream. Stir in the peas and maintain a gentle simmer.

Drain the pasta and return it to its cooking pot.

Stir the mushrooms and prosciutto into the sauce and let heat briefly, about half a minute. Toss the sauce and the remaining 2 tablespoons parsley into the pasta. Season to taste with pepper and serve in warmed pasta bowls.

*—Lynne Sampson*

# Baked Pasta with Cream & Parmigiano-Reggiano

**This dish is essentially a baked version of fettuccine alfredo; you can't help but notice the similarity when you take the first bite.**

Heat the oven to 500°F.

Bring a large pot of well-salted water to a boil.

In a large bowl, combine the cream with all but 2 tablespoons of the cheese, ¼ teaspoon kosher salt, and white pepper to taste.

Place the pasta in the boiling water and undercook it slightly so that it's a bit toothier than al dente, 1 to 2 minutes less than the package directions. Drain well.

Add the pasta to the cream mixture and toss to coat. Divide among four individual shallow ceramic gratin dishes (6 to 8 inches wide). Sprinkle with the remaining cheese and dot with the butter. Bake until the sauce is bubbly and hot and the edges begin to brown, about 10 minutes. Don't overbake or the sauce may separate. Let rest for 3 to 5 minutes before serving.

—*Joanne Killeen & George Germon*

*Serves four.*

1¼ cups heavy cream

3 ounces Parmigiano-Reggiano, freshly grated (1 generous cup)

Kosher salt and freshly ground white pepper

8 ounces dried ziti

2 tablespoons unsalted butter, cut into small pieces

# Deconstructed Pesto Pasta

*Serves four to six.*

Kosher salt

½ cup pine nuts

1 pound dried fusilli or radiatore
pasta

6 tablespoons extra-virgin
olive oil

8 cloves garlic, very thinly sliced

Freshly ground black pepper

4 ounces Pecorino Romano,
coarsely grated (about 1 cup);
more for serving

2 cups packed sweet basil
leaves or your favorite basil
variety, cut into ¼-inch-wide
strips (to yield about 1½ cups)

**What happens with you simply toss the ingredients for pesto right into
your pasta instead of blending them into a paste first? Each bite packs
a bigger punch of bright, elemental flavors—and you don't have to clean
your food processor.**

Bring a large pot of well-salted water to a boil.

Meanwhile, toast the pine nuts in a 10-inch skillet over medium-low heat,
stirring frequently, until golden in places, about 5 minutes. Pour onto a plate
and set aside to cool.

Cook the pasta in the boiling water just until al dente.

Meanwhile, gently heat the oil and garlic over low heat in the same skillet
used for the nuts, stirring frequently, until the garlic starts to turn golden,
4 to 8 minutes. Remove from the heat and stir in ¾ teaspoon salt and
¼ teaspoon pepper.

Drain the pasta, reserving ½ cup of the cooking water. Return the pasta to
the pot. Pour the garlic and oil over it and toss. Pour the reserved pasta water
into the skillet, swirl it around, and pour it over the pasta. Toss well. Add the
pine nuts and cheese and toss again until thoroughly mixed.

Transfer to a serving bowl and let cool for 5 minutes. Then, just before
serving, toss in the basil. Pass extra cheese around with a grater for those
who want more. *—Jessica Bard*

Basil is such an appealing herb, it's no wonder it's a favorite among gardeners. The most common plants are a sweet variety that's often labeled "Genovese." Here are seven varieties to look for at your nursery or farmers' market.

## Purple Ruffles

This variety's large, shiny maroon leaves have distinctive frilly edges. The flavor is on the delicate side, with soft notes of licorice, sweet cinnamon, and mint. It's happy to be an ornamental plant, but the leaves can also be used in place of sweet basil.

## Dwarf Bush

This compact bushy plant, also known as Spicy Globe or Greek basil, has dainty leaves and grows well in a pot on a sunny kitchen windowsill. The leaves have a pungent peppery aroma with citrus and mint notes and make a beautiful garnish on fish or salads.

## Cinnamon

Native to Mexico, this variety has vivid green leaves with reddish purple stems. Sweetly fragrant with a bright, spicy, cinnamon flavor, it's especially good with bean salads and spicy vegetable dishes.

## Sweet Genovese

This familiar variety has large, satiny green leaves and is very fragrant. Its flavor is delicious in pasta sauces and tomato salads.

## Dark Opal

More mildly flavored than sweet basil, this variety has dark purple, almost black, leaves with subtle notes of cinnamon, anise, mint, and clove. Use the leaves, torn or sliced, in salads or other uncooked summer dishes.

## Miniature Purple

This compact plant has tiny purple and green leaves on slender purple stems. Fragrant and flavorful, the leaves are delicious sprinkled on pizza and salads.

## Thai

The small, pointy green leaves of this variety are sometimes mottled with purple, and the plants have purple-red stems. Its heady, sweet peppery aroma has strong notes of anise and licorice. Use this variety in Southeast Asian dishes.

# Butternut Squash Ravioli with Rosemary Oil

*Serves six.*

½ pound butternut squash, peeled, seeded, and cut into ½-inch dice (1½ cups)

⅔ cup water

¼ cup extra-virgin olive oil

Kosher salt and freshly ground black pepper

1 clove garlic, minced

1½ teaspoons minced fresh rosemary

¼ cup heavy cream

¼ cup freshly grated Parmigiano-Reggiano; more for serving

36 square or round wonton wrappers

**Who has time to make homemade ravioli? You do! This recipe uses wonton wrappers, which taste great and are a breeze to work with. It makes enough ravioli for six servings, but you can freeze what you don't plan to use before cooking it. Leave the uncooked ravioli on a wire rack and freeze until firm before transferring to a freezer bag.**

Put the squash, water, 1 tablespoon of the oil, and a scant ½ teaspoon salt in a large, deep sauté pan. Turn the heat to high until the water simmers; cover and steam the squash until it's just tender and the water has just evaporated, 5 to 6 minutes; check often. Stir in the garlic and ½ teaspoon of the rosemary; sauté until fragrant, about 1 minute. Transfer to a food processor and add the cream, Parmigiano, and a few grinds of pepper. Process, scraping the bowl as needed, until the mixture is mostly smooth.

While the squash cools slightly, wash the sauté pan and fill it with water and 1 tablespoon salt; bring to a simmer over medium-high heat. With a large wire rack and a small bowl of water close by, lay six wonton wrappers on a clean, dry countertop. Drop a rounded teaspoon of the filling in the center of each wrapper. Brush the edges of each wrapper with a little water. Fold each wrapper to create a triangle or half-moon, pushing out any air bubbles and pressing the edges to seal completely. Transfer the ravioli to the rack; repeat the process with the remaining wrappers and filling, making sure the countertop is dry after each batch.

Heat the remaining 3 tablespoons oil and 1 teaspoon rosemary in a small skillet or saucepan over medium heat. When the rosemary starts to sizzle, take the pan off the heat.

Drop half of the ravioli into the simmering water. Cook until the wrappers over the filling starts to wrinkle and the ravioli turn translucent, 3 to 4 minutes. With a large slotted spoon, transfer six ravioli to each of three warm pasta plates. Repeat to cook the remaining ravioli. Drizzle each portion of the ravioli with 2 teaspoons of the pasta water and 1 teaspoon of the rosemary oil, sprinkle with a little Parmigiano, and serve immediately. —*Pam Anderson*

# Beef & Pork Ragù Lasagne

*Serves eight to ten.*

## For the ragù:

6 tablespoons (¾ stick) unsalted butter

¼ cup extra-virgin olive oil

2 medium ribs celery, finely chopped (1⅓ cups)

2 medium carrots, peeled and finely chopped (⅔ cup)

2 small yellow onions, finely chopped (1⅓ cups)

1 pound boneless beef brisket or chuck, finely diced or ground (2 cups)

1 pound boneless pork shoulder, finely diced or ground (1½ cups)

8 ounces pancetta, finely diced (1¼ cups)

2 cups dry red wine

½ cup canned tomato purée

¼ cup tomato paste diluted in ½ cup water

2 cups homemade or canned low-salt beef or chicken broth; more as needed

1 cup whole milk

Kosher salt and freshly ground black pepper

## To assemble:

1 tablespoon unsalted butter, cut into small cubes, plus more for the pan

¾ pound fresh lasagne noodles (store-bought or homemade) or 1 pound dried noodles, cooked according to package instructions

Double recipe of Basic Cream Sauce (see page 133)

1 cup freshly grated Parmigiano-Reggiano

**Lasagne can be a laborious undertaking, particularly when it involves a long-simmered ragù, and a cream sauce (see page 133) in place of ricotta cheese. But this rich version is worth the effort, and preparing the components ahead of time makes it more manageable. You can cook the ragù up to four days ahead and refrigerate it, or freeze it for up to one month. Reheat it gently until the sauce is warm enough to spread for assembling the lasagne.**

**Make the ragù:** In a 5- to 6-quart Dutch oven, melt the butter with the oil over medium heat. Add the celery, carrots, and onions and cook, stirring occasionally, until softened and lightly golden, about 15 minutes. Add the beef, pork, and pancetta and cook, breaking up the meats with a spoon and stirring often, until they lose their redness, 5 to 8 minutes. Stir in the wine, tomato purée, and tomato paste and simmer vigorously until the liquid is almost evaporated, 15 to 20 minutes. Add the broth and milk, cover with the lid askew, reduce the heat to low, and simmer gently until you have a rich, concentrated sauce, about 2½ hours. Check every 30 minutes to see if more liquid is needed, adding more broth if necessary to prevent scorching. Season to taste with salt and pepper, if needed. Let cool. Skim off the fat from the top, if desired. You should have about 6 cups ragù.

**Assemble the lasagne:** Position a rack in the center of the oven and heat the oven to 350°F. Choose a baking dish that's about 9x12 inches and 3 inches deep, or about 10x14 inches and 2 inches deep. Butter the baking dish. Spread ½ cup of ragù in a sparse layer on the bottom of the dish. Then cover with a slightly overlapping layer of cooked noodles, cutting them as needed to fill the gaps. Spread one-third of the remaining ragù (about 1½ cups) over the first layer of noodles. Drizzle on one-third of the Basic Cream Sauce (about 1 cup) and spread it with a rubber spatula or the back of a spoon. Sprinkle with ⅓ cup of the Parmigiano. Add a new layer of noodles, overlapping them slightly.

Repeat the layers until all of the filling ingredients are used, to make a total of three layers (you may not need all the pasta). Dot the top with the butter cubes.

Put the baking dish on a baking sheet and bake until heated through and bubbling at the edges, 45 to 50 minutes. Remove from the oven and let rest for 10 to 15 minutes before serving. *—Joyce Goldstein*

## How to cook and layer fresh lasagne noodles

Prepare a large bowl of ice water. Slip the noodles, two or three at a time, into a big pot of boiling salted water and cook them until they're tender and pale, 3 to 5 minutes (thinner noodles will cook more quickly). To make sure they're done, taste a small piece. If it's still tough, it needs a little more cooking (fresh pasta is not cooked al dente like dried pasta). Carefully scoop the noodles out with a large wire skimmer and slide them into the ice water to stop the cooking. When they're cool, layer them between clean dish towels until you're ready to assemble the lasagne.

### How to cook

An ice bath halts the cooking. Fresh pasta noodles can overcook easily, so have a bowl of ice water ready to cool them quickly.

Towels prevent sticking. Layering the noodles between towels dries them and keeps them separate. They'll keep this way for up to 2 hours.

### How to assemble

If one noodle doesn't cover the whole dish, cut a second noodle to fit, overlapping it slightly with the previous noodle.

Spread the ragù over each layer of noodles, followed by the cream sauce and a sprinkle of Parmigiano.

# Spinach & Ricotta Lasagne

*Serves eight to ten.*

## For the filling:

1½ pounds (about 3 cups) whole-milk ricotta

2 pounds fresh spinach or two 10-ounce packages frozen chopped spinach, thawed

¼ cup (½ stick) unsalted butter

½ medium yellow onion, finely chopped (about ½ cup)

3 medium cloves garlic, minced

½ cup freshly grated Parmigiano-Reggiano

2 large eggs, lightly beaten

1 teaspoon kosher salt

½ teaspoon freshly ground black pepper

Pinch freshly grated nutmeg

## To assemble:

1 recipe Quick Tomato Sauce (see page 133)

¾ pound fresh lasagne noodles, or 1 pound dried noodles, cooked according to package instructions

1 recipe Basic Cream Sauce (see page 133)

1 cup freshly grated Parmigiano-Reggiano

1 tablespoon unsalted butter, cut into small cubes

You can make the spinach and ricotta filling up to 4 hours ahead and store it in the refrigerator in an airtight container. The assembled lasagne will keep for at least a day in the fridge or four months tightly wrapped in the freezer. Thaw in the fridge and bring it to room temperature before baking.

**Make the filling:** Drain the ricotta in a fine sieve set over a bowl for 1 hour, or longer if the ricotta is very wet.

If using fresh spinach, stem and rinse it well; don't dry the leaves. In a 12-inch skillet over medium-high heat, cook the spinach until wilted, 3 to 5 minutes. Drain well, squeeze out the excess moisture, and chop finely. If using thawed frozen spinach, squeeze it dry.

Melt the butter in a 10- or 12-inch skillet over medium-low heat, add the onion, and cook until soft and translucent, 5 to 8 minutes. Add the garlic and cook for about 1 minute. Add the spinach and toss for 1 or 2 minutes to coat it with the butter. Transfer to a bowl and let cool to room temperature, then add the ricotta, Parmigiano, eggs, salt, pepper, and nutmeg. Mix well. You should have about 4½ cups.

**Assemble the lasagne:** Position a rack in the center of the oven and heat the oven to 350°F. Choose a baking dish that's about 9x12 inches and 3 inches deep or about 10x14 inches and 2 inches deep. Spread ½ cup of the Quick Tomato Sauce in a sparse layer on the bottom of the baking dish. Cover the sauce with a slightly overlapping layer of cooked noodles, cutting them as needed to fill the gaps. With a rubber spatula, spread one-third of the filling (about 1½ cups) over the first layer of noodles. Then spread one-third of the remaining sauce (about 1⅓ cups) and one-third (½ cup) of the Basic

Cream Sauce over the filling. Sprinkle ⅓ cup of the Parmigiano on top. Add a new layer of noodles, overlapping them slightly, and repeat the layers as instructed above, using all of the filling and ending with the Parmigiano, to make a total of three layers (you may not need all the pasta). Dot the top with the butter cubes.

Put the baking dish on a baking sheet and bake until heated through and bubbling at the edges, 45 to 50 minutes. Remove from the oven and let rest for 10 to 15 minutes before serving. *—Joyce Goldstein*

## Basic Cream Sauce (Besciamella)

*Yields about 1½ cups.*

**If using this recipe for the Beef & Pork Ragú Lasagne on page 130, remember to double it, and use a 3-quart saucepan.**

3 tablespoons unsalted butter

3 tablespoons all-purpose flour

1¾ cups whole milk, heated

½ teaspoon kosher salt

⅛ teaspoon freshly ground black pepper

Small pinch freshly grated nutmeg

In a 2-quart saucepan, melt the butter over medium-low heat. Add the flour and cook, whisking constantly for 2 to 3 minutes. Do not let the mixture brown. Slowly whisk in the hot milk and bring just to a simmer, whisking frequently. Reduce the heat to low and cook, whisking often, until the sauce has thickened to a creamy, gravy-like consistency and no longer tastes of raw flour, 6 to 8 minutes for a single batch, 10 to 12 minutes for a double batch. Remove from the heat and whisk in the salt, pepper, and nutmeg. If not using right away, transfer to a bowl and press a piece of plastic wrap directly on the surface of the sauce to keep a skin from forming. Plan to use the sauce within 30 minutes because it thickens if it's left to sit for too long. If that should happen, add a little warm milk and whisk well to thin it.

## Quick Tomato Sauce

*Yields about 4½ cups.*

**This sauce will keep in an airtight container in the refrigerator for about 5 days or you can freeze it for up to 3 months.**

3 tablespoons extra-virgin olive oil

1 medium carrot, finely chopped

1 medium rib celery, finely chopped

½ medium yellow onion, finely chopped

¼ cup chopped fresh flat-leaf parsley

5 large fresh basil leaves, chopped

Kosher salt and freshly ground black pepper

½ cup dry white wine

One 28-ounce can plus one 14-ounce can plum tomatoes with juice, coarsely chopped

In a 3- or 4-quart saucepan, heat the oil over medium heat. Add the carrot, celery, onion, parsley, basil, a generous pinch of salt, and a couple grinds of pepper. Cook until the vegetables are pale gold, stirring a few times, 10 to 12 minutes. Add the wine and cook until it evaporates, about 5 minutes. Add the tomatoes with their juices, stir well, and simmer gently to blend the flavors and reduce the sauce to about 4½ cups, 15 to 20 minutes (adjust the heat as necessary to maintain a gentle simmer). Season to taste with salt and pepper. If you want a smoother texture, pass the sauce through a food mill or purée in a food processor.

# 5 Poultry

p160

p166

Smoked Paprika & Fennel Seed
Roast Turkey with Onion Gravy
(recipe on page 175)

# Grilled Chicken with Tomato, Lime & Cilantro Salsa

*Serves four as a main course, six to eight as a "small plate."*

2 cups seeded, diced ripe tomatoes (2 to 3 medium tomatoes)

½ cup finely chopped fresh cilantro

4 scallions (white and green parts), thinly sliced

2 tablespoons fresh lime juice

3 tablespoons extra-virgin olive oil

1½ to 2 teaspoons granulated sugar

Finely grated zest of 1 lime (about 1 teaspoon)

Kosher salt and freshly ground black pepper

2 teaspoons minced chipotle (from a can of chipotles in adobo sauce)

4 boneless, skinless chicken breast halves (1½ to 2 pounds total)

**This dish is also delicious served cold or at room temperature over salad greens, rather than right off the grill, and it's easy to make it ahead: Grill the chicken, let it cool for 20 minutes, refrigerate (for up to 8 hours), and slice just before serving with the salsa. The salsa ingredients may be prepared up to 2 hours ahead, but mix them together at the last minute for the freshest flavor.**

Prepare a medium-hot grill fire.

In a medium bowl, combine the tomatoes, cilantro, scallions, lime juice, 1 tablespoon of the oil, 1½ teaspoons of the sugar, and the lime zest. If your tomatoes aren't perfectly ripe and sweet, add the remaining ½ teaspoon sugar. Season with ½ teaspoon salt and ¼ teaspoon pepper, or to taste.

In another medium bowl, mix the chipotle, the remaining 2 tablespoons oil, ½ teaspoon salt, and ¼ teaspoon pepper.

Trim any excess fat from the chicken. If the tenders are still attached, remove them and save for another use. Use the flat side of a meat mallet to pound each chicken breast to an even ½-inch thickness. Add the chicken to the chipotle mixture and toss well to coat.

When the grill is ready, lay the chicken on the hot grates and cook, covered, until it has grill marks and the edges turn opaque, 2 to 3 minutes. Flip the breasts and continue to cook until the chicken is cooked through, 2 to 3 minutes more. Transfer to a clean cutting board and let rest for 5 minutes.

Cut each breast crosswise on the diagonal into ½-inch-thick slices. Arrange on a platter and top with the salsa. *—Jessica Bard*

## Smoky-sweet heat in a can

Whenever you want to add a hit of hot, smoky flavor to your cooking, reach for a can of chipotle chiles en adobo. Chipotles are dried, smoked jalapeños and adobo is a tangy, slightly sweet red sauce. Put them together in a can and they become a versatile pantry staple. You can use just the chipotles for intense smoky chile heat or just the sauce if you want a sour-sweet flavor and a slightly less fiery smoky heat.

Any Mexican or Latin food market will have them, and many supermarkets carry chipotles en adobo in their Mexican food sections.

**How to use:** The chipotles are soft and ready to go straight from the can. They can be quite spicy, but you can temper the heat a bit by scraping out the seeds. The size of chipotles often varies, so if a recipe calls for two chipotles and you choose the biggest one, you might want to use just one.

**How to store:** Transfer unused chiles and sauce to an airtight container—preferably glass, as the sauce tends to stain plastic—and refrigerate for about a month. Or try freezing individual chiles in an ice cube tray, then transfer the cubes to a zip-top freezer bag. Frozen, they'll keep for about three months.

# Grilled Chicken Breasts with Green-Olive Relish

*Serves four.*

4 boneless, skinless chicken breast halves, trimmed of excess fat

About ¾ cup extra-virgin olive oil

Kosher salt and freshly ground black pepper

½ pound green olives (about 1½ cups), such as Lucques or Picholine, rinsed, pitted, and coarsely chopped

¼ cup blanched almonds, lightly toasted on a baking sheet in a 375°F, 5 to 10 minutes, and roughly chopped

2 tablespoons capers, rinsed and coarsely chopped

2 tablespoons roughly chopped fresh flat-leaf parsley

2½ teaspoons finely grated lemon zest

1½ teaspoons chopped fresh thyme

1 small clove garlic, mashed to a paste with a pinch of salt (see box far right)

**This savory-citrusy relish would be delicious on sautéed chicken as well as grilled. Serve it either way with boiled or roasted new potatoes tossed with olive oil and parsley or, for something lighter, an escarole salad with chunky garlic croutons.**

Prepare a hot grill fire.

Put one chicken breast on one side of a large piece of plastic wrap. Drizzle about 1 teaspoon oil on the breast and loosely fold half of the wrap over the chicken. (There should be enough room to allow the chicken to expand when you pound it.) Using a meat mallet or heavy sauté pan, pound the chicken until it's about ½ inch thick. Discard the wrap and repeat the process with the remaining breasts. Season the chicken with salt and pepper on both sides, and coat with 2 tablespoons of the oil. Let sit at room temperature while you prepare the other ingredients.

In a medium bowl, combine the olives, almonds, capers, parsley, lemon zest, thyme, garlic, and ½ cup of the oil.

Lay the chicken on the grill and cook, undisturbed, until it has grill marks, 2 to 3 minutes. Flip the chicken and continue to grill until it's cooked through, 2 to 3 minutes more. Transfer to a clean cutting board and let rest for 2 to 3 minutes.

Cut each breast on the diagonal into ½-inch-thick slices and arrange them on a platter. Spoon the relish on top or to the side of the chicken and serve immediately. —*Tasha DeSerio*

## Make a garlic paste for easy blending

When we want to add raw garlic to a dressing or a dip, we often mash it to a paste first, rather than just mincing it. Raw garlic is a potent ingredient, and it can overwhelm when you get too much of it in a bite. Garlic paste basically dissolves into whatever you add it to, so as long as you don't use too much, its flavor won't knock you out.

To make garlic paste, begin by finely chopping the garlic. Sprinkle the chopped garlic with a big pinch of kosher salt—the salt is an abrasive that speeds the mashing, and it keeps the garlic from sticking to the knife. Next, hold the knife nearly parallel to the cutting board and scrape the side of the cutting edge of over the garlic to mash the garlic against the board. Use the knife to scrape the garlic back into a pile and repeat the mashing until the garlic becomes a fine paste.

# Grilled Mustard-Rosemary Chicken for a Crowd

*Serves eight.*

3½ to 4 pounds boneless, skinless chicken breasts or thighs (or a mix), trimmed of excess fat

Kosher salt and coarsely ground black pepper

⅓ cup Dijon mustard

⅓ cup mayonnaise

½ teaspoon chopped fresh rosemary

This is wonderfully versatile recipe. Serve the tangy-herby chicken as part of a cookout, serve the extras the next day cold for lunch, or use the leftover chicken as a delicious ingredient base for salads. For a variation, you can add other chopped fresh herbs or spices or a little pesto or hot sauce to the mustard-mayonnaise mixture.

Heat a gas grill to medium high. Remove the tenderloins from the chicken breasts for more even cooking; reserve for another use. Put the chicken in a large bowl and season with 1½ teaspoons salt and lots of coarsely ground pepper. Add the mustard, mayonnaise, and rosemary and mix thoroughly to combine and to coat the chicken well. Lay the chicken on the grill, watching out for flare-ups. Cover the grill. Grill on one side until golden brown grill marks form, 2 to 3 minutes. Rotate the chicken 90 degrees and grill for another 2 to 3 minutes (to get a crosshatch of grill marks); flip and repeat on the other side, grilling for another 4 to 5 minutes (for a total cooking time of 8 to 10 minutes) until cooked through. The chicken should be firm and golden brown all over. Arrange on a platter to serve family-style. *—Susie Middleton*

# Roasted Chicken Thighs, Yukon Gold Potatoes & Lemons with Cilantro Gremolata

**In this one-pan dish, the well-seasoned chicken thighs release flavorful juices that mingle with the potatoes on the baking sheet. Serve this with sautéed green beans sprinkled with some of the gremolata.**

Heat the oven to 425°F.

Stir together the butter, 2 teaspoons of the ginger, 2 teaspoons of the lemon zest, half the garlic, the coriander, the cumin, ½ teaspoon salt, and ¼ teaspoon pepper in a small bowl. In another small bowl, stir together the cilantro, the remaining ginger, lemon zest, and garlic to make the gremolata garnish. Set aside.

Smear the butter mixture under the skin of the chicken thighs. Arrange the chicken skin side up on one end of a large rimmed baking sheet. Sprinkle lightly with salt. At the other end of the baking sheet, toss the potatoes and lemon wedges with ½ teaspoon salt and ¼ teaspoon pepper and spread into a single layer. Roast for 20 minutes. Baste the chicken with the pan juices using a brush, and flip the potatoes and lemon with a metal spatula (they may be a little stuck and need loosening). Continue to roast, basting the chicken and flipping the potatoes every 10 minutes, until the chicken and potatoes look crisp and deeply golden, about 30 minutes more.

Stir the potatoes and lemon, transfer to a serving bowl with a slotted spoon, and gently stir in half of the cilantro gremolata. Baste the chicken, transfer with tongs to a serving platter, sprinkle with the remaining gremolata, and serve hot. —*Lori Longbotham*

*Serves four.*

- 3 tablespoons unsalted butter, softened
- 1 tablespoon peeled and minced fresh ginger
- 1 tablespoon finely grated lemon zest
- 2 cloves garlic, minced
- 1½ teaspoons ground coriander
- 1½ teaspoons ground cumin
- Kosher salt and freshly ground black pepper
- 2 tablespoons coarsely chopped fresh cilantro
- 8 bone-in, skin-on chicken thighs (about 6 ounces each), trimmed of excess fat and skin
- 2 medium Yukon Gold potatoes (12 ounces total), each cut into 8 wedges
- 1 lemon, ends trimmed and quartered

# Salad of Roast Chicken & Spring Vegetables with Lemony Dressing

*Serves six.*

6 medium bone-in, skin-on chicken breast halves, trimmed of excess fat and skin

About ½ cup extra-virgin olive oil

Kosher salt and freshly ground black pepper

1 tablespoon fresh thyme leaves

1 pound asparagus, trimmed

1 pound trimmed baby carrots (or larger carrots, peeled, halved crosswise, and thick halves split lengthwise)

¼ cup fresh lemon juice; more if needed

1 teaspoon finely grated lemon zest

¼ teaspoon Dijon mustard

6 cups salad greens (a nice mix is bibb lettuce torn into pieces with some sliced radicchio added for color)

1 medium fennel bulb, trimmed, cut in half lengthwise, cored, and sliced crosswise as finely as possible

½ cup fresh flat-leaf parsley leaves

½ cup fresh mint leaves (torn into bite-size pieces if large)

⅓ cup pine nuts, toasted in a dry skillet over medium-low heat, stirring frequently, until fragrant and slightly colored, about 5 minutes

Thin shavings Parmigiano-Reggiano (use a vegetable peeler)

**In this main-dish salad, fresh greens and herbs cradle succulent slices of roasted chicken breast, carrots, and asparagus. The chicken and vegetables should be served slightly warm but not hot, so there's no rush to the table with this dish.**

Position racks in the top and bottom thirds of the oven. Heat the oven to 400°F.

Arrange the chicken in a shallow, flameproof roasting pan, rub each breast with oil, and season both sides generously with salt and pepper. Sprinkle the thyme on top of the chicken breasts. Roast skin side up on the upper rack until the juices run clear (an instant-read thermometer should register 165°F), 35 to 45 minutes.

Meanwhile, put the asparagus in a medium baking dish (9x13 inches, or one in which they'll fit in a single, uncrowded layer). Drizzle on enough oil to coat, season with salt and pepper, and toss. Arrange in a single layer. In a separate dish, do the same with the carrots. Roast the vegetables on the lower rack along with the chicken until they're tender, 12 to 16 minutes for the asparagus and 20 to 30 minutes for the carrots. The carrots can be roasted very deeply, but take care not to over-roast the asparagus or they'll turn mushy. When the vegetables are done, set them aside.

When the chicken is done, transfer the breasts to a platter and tent with foil. Pour any juices and fat from the roasting pan into a small bowl (don't worry if there isn't much). Put the pan on a burner over medium heat. Add 3 tablespoons of the lemon juice to the pan and, using a wooden spoon or metal spatula, quickly scrape up all the browned juices, dissolving them in the lemon. Pour this into the bowl with the cooking juices. Once the chicken has rested for about 10 minutes, uncover and add any accumulated juices to the bowl. Whisk in the lemon zest, mustard, and enough olive oil to balance the acidity of the lemon juice. Season to taste with salt and pepper. You should have about ½ cup dressing.

When the chicken is cool enough to handle but still quite warm, slide your fingers between the meat and the bones and pull the meat and skin away in one piece (the tender may come off in a separate piece). Cut each breast (and tender) into about 6 slices on the diagonal, keeping them intact so you can fan them out on the salad later.

Put the greens, fennel, and herb sprigs in a large bowl. Toss with the remaining 1 tablespoon lemon juice and about 2 tablespoons of oil, adding more if needed to lightly coat the salad. Season with salt and pepper to taste.

On six large plates or in six large shallow bowls, arrange a bed of the greens. On each plate lay a fan of chicken meat on one side, a few spears of asparagus on another side, and some carrots on another. Drizzle about a tablespoon of the dressing over the meat and vegetables. Sprinkle with the pine nuts and top with a few Parmigiano shavings. Serve immediately.
—*Martha Holmberg*

# Burnished Chicken Thighs with Roasted Sweet Potatoes, Parsnips & Shallots

*Serves four.*

3 tablespoons extra-virgin olive oil

3 tablespoons whole-grain Dijon mustard

1½ tablespoons balsamic vinegar

½ teaspoon kosher salt; more as needed

½ teaspoon freshly ground black pepper

8 bone-in, skin-on chicken thighs (about 6 ounces each), trimmed of excess fat and skin

1 medium-large sweet potato (12 ounces), peeled and cut into ½-inch pieces

4 medium parsnips (6 ounces total), peeled and cut into ½-inch pieces

4 small shallots, lobes separated, peeled and halved through the root end

3 strips bacon

¼ cup coarsely chopped fresh flat-leaf parsley

**Chicken and sweet potatoes isn't a common combination, but it's one you'll fall in love with after eating this dish. The potatoes get earthy complexity from the parsnips and shallots, and the whole dish is lifted by the punchy accents of whole-grain mustard, salty bacon, and fresh parsley. Adding a pinch of caraway seeds to the vegetables before roasting delivers one more interesting twist.**

Stir together the oil, mustard, vinegar, ¼ teaspoon of the salt, and ¼ teaspoon of the pepper in a large bowl. Add the chicken and toss to coat. Cover with plastic wrap and marinate in the refrigerator, turning occasionally, for at least 1 hour and up to 8 hours.

Heat the oven to 425°F.

Arrange the chicken skin side up on one end of a large rimmed baking sheet and drizzle with any remaining marinade. At the other end of the baking sheet, toss together the sweet potato, parsnips, shallots, and the remaining ¼ teaspoon each salt and pepper. Spread into a single layer. Sprinkle the chicken and vegetables lightly with a little more salt and roast for 20 minutes. Baste the chicken with the pan juices using a brush and stir the vegetables. Continue to roast, basting and stirring every 10 minutes, until the chicken is burnished—deeply browned—and the vegetables are tender, about 30 minutes more.

Meanwhile, cook the bacon over medium heat in a large skillet until crisp, 5 to 8 minutes, then drain on paper towels. When the bacon is cool enough to handle, crumble it and toss with the parsley.

When the chicken is done, stir the vegetables and transfer them to a serving bowl with a slotted spoon. Toss with half of the bacon mixture. Baste the chicken and transfer with tongs to a serving platter. Sprinkle with the remaining bacon mixture and serve hot. *—Lori Longbotham*

**tip:** As with any tender, fresh herb, be sure to use a sharp chef's knife when you chop parsley. The sharper your knife, the less the leaves will bruise and wilt. Some cooks like to use a nifty tool called a mezzaluna, which means half-moon in Italian. It consists of a single blade or two parallel blades shaped like a half-moon and is made for repeated rocking back and forth. It's perfect for chopping piles of herbs.

# Paprika Chicken with Kielbasa

*Serves six.*

6 bone-in, skin-on chicken
  thighs (about 2 pounds)

Kosher salt and freshly ground
  black pepper

4 to 5 tablespoons olive oil

1 pound kielbasa, cut on the
  diagonal into 12 chunks

1 medium onion, cut into small
  dice

2 medium garlic cloves, chopped

2 medium green bell peppers,
  seeded and cut into medium
  dice

2 tablespoons sweet Hungarian
  paprika

1 teaspoon sweet smoked
  Spanish paprika (pimentón)

One 28-ounce can diced
  tomatoes

1 cup homemade or canned low-
  salt chicken broth

½ cup sour cream

3 tablespoons chopped fresh
  flat-leaf parsley

**This is a riff on a traditional Hungarian dish, chicken paprikás. The additions of kielbasa and pimentón contribute a lovely smoky flavor. You can make this dish up to three days ahead without adding the sour cream. Reheat over medium heat and stir in the sour cream as directed.**

Season the chicken on both sides with ¾ teaspoon salt and ½ teaspoon pepper. Heat 2 tablespoons of the oil in a 6-quart Dutch oven over medium-high heat until shimmering hot. Sear the chicken on both sides until nicely golden brown, about 8 minutes total. Transfer the chicken to a plate and sear the cut ends of the kielbasa until golden brown, about 2 minutes total. Transfer to the plate with the chicken. Pour off and discard the fat from the pan.

Add 2 more tablespoons of the oil to the pan, reduce the heat to medium, and cook the onion, stirring occasionally, until it begins to soften, 3 to 4 minutes. Add the garlic and cook until fragrant and the onion is completely soft and golden, 2 to 3 minutes more. Push the onion and garlic to one side of the pan and add another tablespoon of oil if the pan looks dry. Add the peppers and cook, stirring once or twice, until beginning to brown, 4 to 5 minutes.

Remove the pan from the heat, add both of the paprikas, and stir together with all the vegetables for 30 seconds. Return the pan to the heat and add the tomatoes, broth, and ¼ teaspoon pepper. Immerse the chicken in the sauce and scatter the kielbasa on top. Cover and simmer over medium-low heat until the thighs are cooked through (cut into a thigh near the bone to check for doneness), 25 to 30 minutes. Remove the skin from the chicken if you like. Stir in the sour cream, season with salt to taste, and serve sprinkled with parsley. *—Allison Ehri*

**tip:** Look for paprika packaged in a tin with a tight-fitting lid and store it away from light and heat. Heating it in a little oil or butter helps bring out the flavor, but because of the high natural sugar content, it burns easily, so keep the heat low and the time over the flame short. It's usually best to add it off the heat at the end of sautéing, before adding liquids.

# Chicken Thighs with Braised Fennel, Scallions & Olives

*Serves four.*

5 tablespoons extra-virgin
  olive oil

2 medium fennel bulbs (about
  12 ounces each), trimmed,
  quartered lengthwise, cored,
  and sliced lengthwise into
  ¼-inch-thick slices

Kosher salt

1 bunch scallions (about 8),
  trimmed and cut into 2-inch
  pieces

1 cup pitted Kalamata olives

½ cup all-purpose flour

8 boneless, skinless chicken
  thighs (about 1¾ pounds)

Freshly ground black pepper

½ cup dry white wine

½ cup homemade or canned
  low-salt chicken broth

**This dish uses an ingenious cooking method in which you layer the chicken, fennel, and scallions and roast everything together so all the flavors marry into a delicious whole. A handful of Kalamata olives adds a pungent contrast to the sweet-mellow vegetables and mild chicken.**

Position a rack in the center of the oven and heat the oven to 425°F.

Heat 2 tablespoons of the oil in a 12-inch heavy skillet over high heat. Add the fennel, sprinkle with salt, and cook, stirring occasionally, until nicely browned in places, about 5 minutes—don't stir too often or it won't brown. Remove the skillet from the heat. Transfer the fennel to a 9x13-inch baking pan, spreading it evenly. Layer the scallions on top of the fennel, sprinkle with ½ teaspoon salt, and scatter the olives over the scallions.

Put the flour in a shallow dish. Trim any excess fat from the chicken and season it with 1 teaspoon salt and ½ teaspoon pepper. Dredge the chicken in the flour.

Heat the remaining 3 tablespoons oil in the skillet over high heat. Turn on the exhaust fan. When the oil is very hot, add the chicken (it may be a tight fit, but the chicken will shrink as it cooks) and sear until the first side is well browned, 3 to 4 minutes. Reduce the heat to medium-high, flip the chicken using tongs, and cook until the second side is well browned, about another 3 minutes.

Arrange the thighs on top of the vegetables. Carefully pour the wine into the skillet and cook over medium-high heat, scraping up the browned bits from the bottom of the pan with a wooden spoon, until the wine reduces by half, about 1 minute. Add the broth and bring to a simmer. Pour the wine mixture over the chicken and bake until the chicken is cooked through and the fennel is tender, 15 to 20 minutes.

*—Julianna Grimes Bottcher*

Here's a flavor guide to some of the olives you might come across, either at the olive bar or elsewhere in the store.

### 1. Gaeta (aka Gyeta)

Medium Italian olives cured in either salt or brine. Brine-cured Gaetas (shown here) have a tangy yet mild flavor.

### 2. Manzanilla (aka Manzanillo or Spanish)

Widely known as the "martini olive." Usually sold pitted and often stuffed with pimento, they have a meaty texture and a briny flavor.

### 3. Niçoise

Tiny French olives that are brown to black in color. They have an intensely savory flavor and are often sold in an herbal marinade.

### 4. California (aka Mission or black)

Medium to large with a meaty texture; usually sold canned. Their lye curing process leaves them with a very mild to bland flavor.

### 5. Picholine

Medium French green olives with a slender almond shape. A soak in lime and wood ash before brining adds to their complex, sweet, slightly floral flavor.

### 6. Cerignola

Black or green, very large, oval, pointy-ended Italian olives with a high flesh-to-pit ratio. Both colors have a delicate, sweet buttery flavor, but the blacks are quite mild and the greens are slightly tangy. They are often dyed bright red or green.

### 7. Oil-cured (aka dry-cured or salt-cured)

Medium black and slightly shriveled, a result of being cured in salt and then rubbed with oil. Less meaty than brine-cured olives, they have a concentrated, pleasantly bitter flavor.

### 8. Kalamata (aka Calamata)

Medium Greek olives with a toothsome texture. Juicy, fruity, and nutty with bright acidic flavor from the vinegar brine in which they're cured. Often sold already pitted, making them convenient for using in recipes.

# Braised Chicken Legs with Red Wine, Tomato, Anchovies & Rosemary

*Serves four.*

6 oil-packed anchovy fillets, rinsed and patted dry

2 medium cloves garlic, thinly sliced

1 tablespoon chopped fresh rosemary, plus 1 teaspoon whole rosemary leaves

1 cup homemade or canned low-salt chicken broth

4 medium bone-in, skin-on chicken thighs (1½ to 1¾ pounds), trimmed of excess fat and skin

4 chicken drumsticks (1¼ to 1½ pounds), trimmed of excess fat and skin

Kosher salt and freshly ground black pepper

2 tablespoons vegetable oil

1 cup dry red wine

6 plum (Roma) tomatoes, peeled, quartered, and seeded

1 tablespoon red-wine vinegar

**The anchovies in this dish are the secret ingredient. Once everything's cooked together, you won't taste "anchovy," you'll just taste a rich, robust tomato-rosemary sauce that flavors the moist chicken legs and is luscious with wide egg noodles or even mashed potatoes.**

Position a rack in the center of the oven and heat the oven to 350°F.

Put the anchovies, garlic, and chopped rosemary in a food processor and process until finely chopped, scraping the sides of the bowl as needed. Add the broth and process again until well blended, about 30 seconds.

Season the chicken pieces generously with salt and pepper. In a straight-sided 10- or 11-inch ovenproof sauté pan with a lid, heat the oil over medium-high heat until very hot. Arrange the chicken pieces skin side down in the pan (it'll be crowded), cover with a splatter screen, if you have one, and cook until deeply browned, about 5 minutes. Turn the pieces over and cook until the other sides are deeply browned, 3 to 5 minutes more. Transfer to a plate. Pour out and discard all the fat from the pan.

Return the pan to medium-high heat, carefully add the wine, and bring to a boil, scraping up the browned bits from the bottom of the pan with a wooden spoon. Pour in the broth mixture. Return the chicken pieces to the pan, along with any accumulated juices on the plate. Add the tomatoes and cover. Transfer the pan to the oven and braise until the chicken is fork-tender and the drumstick meat starts to come away from the bone, 45 to 50 minutes.

With a slotted spoon, transfer the chicken and tomato pieces to a large serving dish and keep warm by covering the dish loosely with foil. Tilt the sauté pan and skim off as much fat as possible from the sauce. Bring the sauce to a boil over medium-high heat. Reduce the heat to medium low and simmer until the sauce is slightly reduced and full-flavored, about 5 minutes. Add the vinegar and whole rosemary leaves. Season to taste with salt and pepper. Pour the sauce over the chicken and serve.

*—Jennifer McLagan*

# Braised Italian Chicken with Green Beans, Tomatoes & Olives

Cutting boneless chicken thighs into chunks means you can have this savory stew made in minutes yet still have the moist, flavorful meat of a longer-cooking dish. Because the green beans are incorporated right into the braise, all you'll need for a complete dinner is some crusty bread or a scoop of creamy polenta.

Season the chicken with 1 teaspoon salt and ½ teaspoon black pepper. Spread the flour on a plate, and lightly dredge the chicken in the flour. Heat 2 tablespoons of the oil in a large Dutch oven or casserole over medium-high heat until the oil is shimmering hot. Cook the chicken in two to three batches (to avoid crowding the pot) until well browned on both sides, 2 to 3 minutes per side. Transfer each batch to a plate as it finishes and, if the pot looks dry between batches, add the remaining 1 tablespoon oil.

Return the chicken to the pot, add the green beans, garlic, ½ teaspoon salt, and ½ teaspoon black pepper, and cook, stirring, for 2 minutes. Add the wine and cook until it almost completely evaporates, 1 to 2 minutes. Add the tomatoes and their juices, rosemary, and red pepper. Bring to a boil, then lower the heat to a steady simmer. Cover, leaving the lid slightly askew, and cook, stirring occasionally for 15 minutes.

Add the olives and continue simmering with the lid askew until the chicken and green beans are very tender, about 5 minutes more. Season with salt and pepper to taste. Serve immediately. *—Tony Rosenfeld*

*Serves four.*

- 2 pounds boneless, skinless chicken thighs, trimmed of excess fat and each cut into 3 uniform pieces
- Kosher salt and freshly ground black pepper
- ½ cup all-purpose flour
- 2 to 3 tablespoons extra-virgin olive oil
- ¾ pound green beans, trimmed and halved
- 3 cloves garlic, smashed and peeled
- ⅓ cup dry red wine
- One 14.5-ounce can diced tomatoes
- 1 teaspoon chopped fresh rosemary
- ½ teaspoon crushed red pepper flakes
- ⅓ cup pitted and quartered Kalamata olives

# Braised Chicken Legs with White Wine, Bacon, Cipolline Onions & Mushrooms

*Serves four.*

8 small cipolline onions (or 4 large cipolline, halved)

4 bone-in, skin-on medium chicken thighs (1½ to 1¾ pounds total), trimmed of excess fat and skin

4 chicken drumsticks (1¼ to 1½ pounds total), trimmed of excess fat and skin

Kosher salt and freshly ground black pepper

2 tablespoons vegetable oil

8 medium cremini mushrooms, trimmed and halved

3 strips bacon, cut crosswise into ¼-inch-wide strips

1 medium carrot, peeled and sliced into ¼-inch-thick rounds

1 cup dry white wine

3 large thyme sprigs

1 cup homemade or canned low-salt chicken broth

2 teaspoons fresh thyme leaves

**Cipollines are small, disk-shaped onions that are especially sweet and tasty for braising and roasting. If you can't find them, small shallots would be a good substitute. The sauce in this dish is exquisite, so serve something to catch it all, like a mound of mashed potatoes or creamy polenta.**

Position a rack in the center of the oven and heat the oven to 350°F.

Bring a 2-quart saucepan of water to a boil. Drop in the onions and blanch for 1 minute. Drain in a colander, then shower with cold water to stop the cooking. Peel the onions, leaving enough of the root end intact so that they will remain whole while cooking.

Season the chicken pieces generously with salt and pepper. In a 10- or 11-inch straight-sided ovenproof sauté pan with a lid, heat the oil over medium-high heat until very hot. Arrange the chicken skin side down in the pan (it'll be crowded), cover with a splatter screen, if you have one, and cook until deeply browned, about 5 minutes. Turn the pieces over and cook until the other sides are deeply browned, 3 to 5 minutes more. Transfer to a plate. Pour out and discard all the fat from the pan.

Put the pan over medium heat. Add the peeled onions, mushrooms, bacon, and carrot and cook until the bacon is crisp and the vegetables are browned, 8 to 10 minutes. Add the wine and thyme sprigs and bring to a boil, scraping the browned bits from the bottom of the pan with a wooden spoon. Boil until the wine has reduced to ½ cup, about 5 minutes. Add the broth and bring to a boil.

Return the chicken to the pan, along with any accumulated juices, and cover. Transfer to the oven and braise until fork-tender and the drumstick meat starts to come away from the bone, 45 to 50 minutes.

With a slotted spoon, transfer the chicken, onions, bacon, carrots, and mushrooms to a serving dish and keep warm by covering the dish loosely with foil. Discard the thyme sprigs. Tilt the sauté pan and skim off as much fat as possible from the sauce. Bring the sauce to a boil over medium-high heat, reduce the heat to medium low, and simmer until the sauce is slightly thickened, skimming off any skin that forms on top, about 5 minutes. Season to taste with pepper (the sauce should be nicely salted at this point). Pour the sauce over the chicken, sprinkle with the thyme leaves, and serve. *—Jennifer McLagan*

# Chicken Tikka Masala

*Serves six to eight.*

One 2-inch-long hot green chile (preferably serrano), stemmed but not seeded, chopped

One 1-inch piece fresh ginger, peeled and chopped

One 28-ounce can whole tomatoes

½ cup (1 stick) unsalted butter

Roasted Tandoori Chicken (see page 155), meat removed from bones in large pieces; try not to shred (about 5 cups)

2 teaspoons sweet paprika

2 tablespoons cumin seeds, toasted in a dry skillet over medium-low heat until fragrant and slightly darkened, 2 to 4 minutes, then ground in a spice grinder

1 cup heavy cream

Kosher salt

2 teaspoons garam masala

¾ cup coarsely chopped fresh cilantro

**This Indian restaurant favorite is even more delicious when you make it at home. The chicken is first roasted tandoori-style (marinated in yogurt and spices), then finished in a fragrant creamy tomato sauce. Don't be tempted to skip the toasting and grinding of the cumin seeds, which will make the different between a good tikka masala and a phenomenal one.**

In a food processor, pulse the chile and ginger together until very finely chopped. Add the tomatoes with their juice and process until puréed. Set aside.

Melt 6 tablespoons of the butter in a 6- to 8-quart Dutch oven over medium heat. When the foam subsides, add about a third of the chicken pieces and cook, stirring frequently, until it absorbs some of the butter and begins to brown, 3 to 4 minutes. With a slotted spoon, transfer the chicken to a plate. Repeat with the remaining two batches of chicken.

Add the remaining 2 tablespoons butter to the pan. When it's melted, add the paprika and 4 teaspoons of the cumin and stir until the spices just begin to darken, 10 to 15 seconds. Immediately add the tomato mixture. Simmer vigorously, uncovered, stirring frequently, until the sauce has thickened slightly, 6 to 8 minutes. Add the cream and 1 teaspoon salt and stir well. Add the chicken and stir gently to mix. Reduce the heat to medium low and simmer, uncovered, stirring occasionally, for 10 minutes.

Stir in the garam masala and remaining cumin. Remove from the heat, cover, and allow to rest for 15 minutes. Taste and add more salt if necessary. Transfer to a serving bowl, garnish with cilantro, and serve. —*Suneeta Vaswani*

**tip:** Chicken tikka masala employs the unusual step of cooking the chicken twice—first by roasting it tandoori-style, then by sautéing large pieces of the roasted thigh meat in butter. This second step infuses the chicken with flavor and slightly crisps the edges of the meat.

# Roasted Tandoori Chicken

Restaurants use food coloring to give this style of chicken its traditional red color, but this ingredient is optional. The roasting method keeps the chicken moist and works best if you're using the chicken in the Chicken Tikka Masala recipe at left. If you want to serve tandoori chicken as its own dish, use the grilling method below, which is more flavorful.

**Marinate the chicken:** Remove the skin and trim any excess fat from the chicken. With a sharp chef's knife, cut three or four long, diagonal slits on each thigh against the grain, almost to the bone.

In a large, shallow bowl, mix together the yogurt, lemon juice, ginger, garlic, coriander, cumin, garam masala, salt, and cayenne. Stir in the food coloring, if using. Add the chicken, turning to coat and making sure that the marinade gets into all of the slits in the chicken. Cover and marinate in the refrigerator for at least 2 hours and up to 12 hours.

**To roast the chicken:** Position a rack in the center of the oven and heat the oven to 375°F. Line a large rimmed baking sheet with foil. Transfer the chicken from the marinade to the baking sheet, spacing the thighs evenly. Discard any remaining marinade. Roast until the juices run clear when the chicken is pierced and an instant-read thermometer in a meaty party of a thigh registers 170°F, about 45 minutes.

Squeeze the lemon halves over the chicken. Let it cool before using in the Chicken Tikka Masala recipe. Refrigerate if making ahead.

**To grill the chicken for a stand-alone dish:** You'll need ¼ cup melted unsalted butter, plus 1 extra lemon, cut into wedges, and 1 small sweet onion, cut into rings, for garnish.

Heat a gas grill to medium high. Oil the grill liberally. Remove the chicken from the marinade and lay it on the grill. Discard the marinade. Cover and cook until grill marks appear, 5 to 7 minutes. Using tongs, flip the chicken and continue to cook until the second side has grill marks, about 5 minutes more.

Reduce the heat to low and cook, covered, flipping occasionally, until it is no longer pink near the bone (cut into a thigh to check), 10 to 15 minutes for small thighs, 15 to 20 minutes for large. Transfer the chicken to a platter and let it rest for 5 minutes, then brush with the melted butter and squeeze the lemon halves on top. Garnish with the lemon wedges and the sliced onion and serve. *—Suneeta Vaswani*

*Serves six.*

12 bone-in, skin-on chicken thighs

1 cup plain nonfat yogurt

⅓ cup fresh lemon juice (from about 2 medium lemons)

1 tablespoon peeled and finely chopped fresh ginger

1 tablespoon finely chopped garlic

2 teaspoons ground coriander

2 teaspoons ground cumin

2 teaspoons garam masala

1½ teaspoons kosher salt

½ teaspoon cayenne

Few drops of red and yellow food coloring (optional)

1 lemon, halved

# Braised Chicken Legs with Cider, Apples & Mustard

*Serves four.*

4 bone-in, skin-on medium chicken thighs (1½ to 1¾ pounds total), trimmed of excess fat and skin

4 chicken drumsticks (1¼ to 1½ pounds total), trimmed of excess fat and skin

Kosher salt and freshly ground black pepper

2 tablespoons vegetable oil

2 medium apples such as Rome, Spy, or Mutsu, peeled, cored, and cut into 6 wedges each

2 cups dry hard apple cider

¼ cup Dijon mustard

3 large fresh marjoram sprigs

¼ cup heavy cream

1 tablespoon chopped fresh marjoram

**Use dry hard cider (which is alcoholic) for this recipe, not fresh sweet cider. There are some excellent American hard ciders now, and ciders from Brittany or Normandy are consistently good. The alcohol content in a cider is lower than in wine, so it's a nice beverage to serve with dinner, as well as to cook with.**

Position a rack in the center of the oven and heat the oven to 350°F.

Season the chicken pieces generously with salt and pepper. In a 10- or 11-inch straight-sided ovenproof sauté pan with a lid, heat the oil over medium-high heat until very hot. Arrange the chicken skin side down in the pan (it'll be crowded), cover with a splatter screen, if you have one, and cook until deeply browned, about 5 minutes. Turn the pieces over and cook until the other sides are deeply browned, 3 to 5 minutes more. Transfer to a plate. Pour out and discard all but 1 tablespoon of the fat from the pan. Set the pan aside to cool for a few minutes.

Return the pan to medium-high heat, add the apple wedges, and cook, turning once, until both cut sides are golden brown, about 2 minutes per side. Transfer to a different plate. Carefully pour the cider into the pan and bring to a boil, scraping the browned bits from the bottom of the pan with a wooden spoon.

Whisk the mustard into the cider. Return the chicken to the pan, along with any accumulated juices. Add the marjoram sprigs and cover. Transfer the pan to the oven and braise for 10 minutes.

Add the apples and continue to braise until the chicken is fork-tender and the drumstick meat starts to come away from the bone, 35 to 40 minutes more.

With a slotted spoon, transfer the chicken and apples to a large serving dish and keep warm by covering the dish loosely with foil. Discard the marjoram sprigs. Tilt the sauté pan and skim off as much fat as possible from the sauce. Bring the sauce to a boil over medium-high heat and whisk in the cream. Reduce the heat to medium low and simmer until the sauce is slightly thickened, about 5 minutes. Season to taste with salt and pepper. Pour the sauce over the chicken, sprinkle with the chopped marjoram, and serve.

*—Jennifer McLagan*

# Braised Chicken Legs with Carrot Juice, Dates & Spices

*Serves four.*

4 bone-in, skin-on medium chicken thighs (1½ to 1¾ pounds total), trimmed of excess fat and skin

4 chicken drumsticks (1¼ to 1½ pounds total), trimmed of excess fat and skin

Kosher salt and freshly ground black pepper

2 tablespoons vegetable oil

1 large red onion, thinly sliced (about 3 cups)

1 teaspoon ground ginger

1 teaspoon ground cinnamon

½ teaspoon ground cumin

1¼ cups carrot juice

¾ cup homemade or canned low-salt chicken broth

½ pound (10 to 12) Medjool dates, pitted and halved lengthwise (or 6 whole pitted prunes or dried apricots)

2 tablespoons fresh lemon juice

2 tablespoons chopped fresh cilantro

**If you have never cooked with carrot juice you may be surprised by the fresh sweetness it brings to this dish. Warm spices and dates create a Moroccan flavor palate that's both exotic and comforting. Serve the chicken and sauce over couscous or rice.**

Position a rack in the center of the oven and heat the oven to 350°F.

Season the chicken pieces generously with salt and pepper. In a 10- or 11-inch straight-sided ovenproof sauté pan with a lid, heat the oil over medium-high heat until very hot. Arrange the chicken skin side down in the pan (it'll be crowded), cover with a splatter screen, if you have one, and cook until deeply browned, about 5 minutes. Turn the pieces over and cook until the other sides are deeply browned, 3 to 5 minutes more. Transfer to a plate.

Pour out and discard all but 1 tablespoon of the fat in the pan. Put the pan over medium heat. Add the onion and cook, stirring frequently, until it's soft and begins to color, 6 to 8 minutes. Add the ginger, cinnamon, and cumin and stir into the onions for about 1 minute. Pour in the carrot juice and broth and bring to a boil, scraping the browned bits from the bottom of the pan with a wooden spoon. Return the chicken to the pan, along with any accumulated juices. If using prunes or apricots in place of the dates, add them now. Cover, transfer to the oven, and braise for 15 minutes.

Add the dates, if using, and continue to braise until the chicken is fork-tender and the drumstick meat starts to come away from the bone, 30 to 35 minutes more.

With a slotted spoon, transfer the chicken and dried fruit to a serving dish and keep warm by covering the dish loosely with foil. Tilt the sauté pan and skim off as much fat as possible from the sauce. Bring the sauce to a boil over medium-high heat, reduce the heat to medium low, and simmer until the sauce is slightly thickened, about 5 minutes. Add the lemon juice and season to taste with salt and pepper. Pour the sauce over the chicken, sprinkle with the chopped cilantro, and serve. —*Jennifer McLagan*

# Chicken "Stroganoff" with Mushrooms, Sherry & Sage

*Serves three to four.*

- 4 teaspoons extra-virgin olive oil
- One 8-ounce package sliced cremini (baby bella) mushrooms
- Kosher salt
- 1 shallot, finely chopped
- 2 tablespoons finely chopped fresh sage
- Freshly ground black pepper
- 1¾ pounds boneless, skinless chicken thighs (5 or 6), trimmed of excess fat and cut into 1½- to 2-inch pieces
- 1 tablespoon finely chopped garlic (about 2 large cloves)
- ⅓ cup dry sherry
- 1 whole jarred roasted red pepper, cut into thin strips (about ½ cup)
- ½ cup sour cream
- 1 plum tomato, cored, seeded, and cut into medium dice

The flavors of this warming dish are both deep, with sage and roasted red pepper, and delicate with mild chicken and sliced mushrooms. A generous dose of dry sherry pulls everything together in a lovely variation on traditional beef stroganoff. Cremini mushrooms are young portabellas; they have a slightly fuller flavor than regular button mushrooms, but buttons are fine as a substitute.

In a 10-inch straight-sided sauté pan, heat 2 teaspoons of the oil over medium-high heat. Add the mushrooms, season generously with salt, and cook undisturbed until well browned on one side, 1 to 3 minutes. Add half of the shallot and ½ tablespoon of the sage to the pan and continue to cook, stirring, until the mushrooms are well browned all over, another 3 to 5 minutes. Season generously with pepper and transfer to a bowl. Leave the pan off the heat.

Generously season the chicken with salt and pepper. Return the pan to medium-high heat, add the remaining 2 teaspoons oil, and swirl to coat the pan. Add the chicken and cook undisturbed for 1 minute. Add ½ tablespoon of the garlic, ½ tablespoon of the sage, and the remaining shallot and continue to cook, stirring, until the chicken is no longer pink on the outside, 2 to 4 minutes. Add the mushrooms, sherry, and roasted pepper and cook to reduce the sherry slightly, about 2 minutes. Lower the heat to medium and stir in the sour cream, tomato, and the remaining garlic. Partially cover the pan and simmer until the chicken is cooked through, 15 to 20 minutes. If the sauce seems overly thick, thin it with a little water. Season to taste with more salt and pepper. Serve sprinkled with the remaining sage. *—Joanne McAllister Smart*

# Chicken Stir-Fry with Spicy Sichuan Sauce

**Stir-frying is fast and fun, but it does go quickly, so have all your ingredients, including the sauce, prepped before you start cooking.**

Season the chicken with ¼ teaspoon salt and a dash of white pepper. Heat a 12-inch skillet or stir-fry pan over high heat for 2 minutes. Add 1 tablespoon of the oil, swirl to coat the pan evenly, and heat until the oil just barely begins to smoke, about 30 seconds—only a light haze is necessary. Add the chicken. Let it sear for about 15 seconds, then begin to stir occasionally (every 10 seconds or so) until its raw appearance is gone but the center is slightly undercooked, 1 to 2 minutes. Transfer to a bowl.

Add the remaining 1 tablespoon oil to the pan and swirl to coat evenly. Add the broccoli, peppers, snap peas, and water and cook, stirring constantly, for 1 minute. Add the scallion, ginger, and garlic and cook, stirring constantly, until the vegetables are crisp-tender, 1 to 4 minutes. If the bottom of the pan looks like it's starting to burn, add more water, 1 tablespoon at a time. Stir the chicken back into the pan and cook for another 30 seconds to reheat and to blend the flavors.

Whisk the sauce to recombine it, then pour into the stir-fry, stirring well to coat evenly, and cook until it thickens, 15 to 20 seconds. Transfer the stir-fry to a bowl and serve immediately. *—Robert Danhi*

## Spicy Sichuan Sauce

*Yields about ⅔ cup.*

**Many supermarkets now carry Asian chile paste, but for a better selection, try an Asian grocery store.**

1½ teaspoons cornstarch

1½ teaspoons soy sauce

¼ cup homemade or low-salt chicken broth

2 tablespoons dry sherry

1 tablespoon Asian chile paste

1 tablespoon sliced scallion (white and green parts)

1 tablespoon honey

1 tablespoon hoisin sauce

½ teaspoon peeled and minced fresh ginger

½ teaspoon minced garlic

In a 1-cup liquid measuring cup, combine the cornstarch and soy sauce, whisking to blend, then whisk in the remaining ingredients.

*Serves three to four.*

1 pound boneless, skinless chicken breasts, cut crosswise into 2 or 3 even pieces; turn each piece and cut into ¼-inch strips across the grain

Kosher salt and freshly ground white pepper

2 tablespoons vegetable oil

1 small broccoli crown, cut into ¾-inch florets (about 1⅓ cups)

1 medium bell pepper, seeded and cut into 2x⅓-inch strips (about 1⅓ cups)

1⅓ cups sugar snap peas, stems snapped off and strings removed

1 tablespoon water; more as needed

2 tablespoons very thinly sliced scallion (white and green parts)

2 teaspoons peeled and minced fresh ginger

2 teaspoons minced garlic

1 recipe Spicy Sichuan Sauce (see recipe at left)

# Chicken Thighs Roasted with Rosemary, Red Onions & Red Potatoes

*Serves four.*

2 navel oranges

3 tablespoons extra-virgin olive oil

1 teaspoon kosher salt; more as needed

½ teaspoon crushed red pepper flakes

8 baby red-skinned potatoes (12 ounces total), halved

2 medium red onions, sliced into ½-inch-thick circles

Two 5-inch sprigs fresh rosemary, plus ¾ teaspoon minced

8 chicken thighs (about 6 ounces each), trimmed of excess fat and skin

**If you're adventurous, try this with the full half-teaspoon of red pepper flakes—the heat is a wonderful contrast to the sweetness of the orange—but feel free to use less.**

Heat the oven to 425°F. Finely grate 1 teaspoon orange zest. Stir together the zest, oil, 1 teaspoon salt, and red pepper in a small bowl.

On one end of a large rimmed baking sheet, toss 1 tablespoon of the oil mixture with the potatoes, onions, and 1 sprig rosemary; separate the onions into rings and spread the onions and potatoes into a single layer as much as possible. At the other end of the baking sheet, arrange the chicken, skin side up, and brush the tops with the remaining oil mixture. Tuck the remaining rosemary sprig between a couple of thighs and sprinkle the chicken and vegetables lightly with salt.

Roast for 20 minutes. Baste the chicken with the pan drippings using a brush and stir the potatoes and onions. Continue to roast, basting and stirring every 10 minutes, until the chicken skin looks crisp and golden and the potatoes are lightly browned in spots, about 30 minutes more.

Meanwhile, peel the oranges with a sharp knife, making sure you've removed the white pith and membrane. Slice the flesh crosswise into roughly ½-inch-thick circles, then chop into roughly ½-inch pieces, discarding any thick center membranes. Transfer to a small bowl and stir in ¼ teaspoon of the minced rosemary.

When the chicken is done, remove the rosemary sprigs from the pan and discard. Stir the potatoes and onions, transfer with a slotted spoon to a serving bowl, and stir in the remaining ½ teaspoon minced rosemary. Baste the chicken and transfer with tongs to a serving platter, top with the orange mixture, and serve hot. —*Lori Longbotham*

## Getting it browned, keeping it moist

Truly great roasted chicken and potatoes should be beautifully browned and crisp outside yet moist and tender inside. Here's how to make that happen:

• **Use dark meat.** It's richer than white meat, so it stays moist and juicy even if you cook it a little longer than might be ideal.

• **Don't crowd the pan.** An 11x17-inch heavy-duty rimmed baking sheet is the perfect size for the recipes here and on pages 141 and 144. If you don't have a large one, use two smaller baking sheets.

• **Baste the chicken and stir the potatoes often.** For the best browning and crisping, bake them on opposite sides of the baking sheet, and baste and stir from time to time to incorporate the flavorful browned bits from the baking sheet.

# Yogurt-Marinated Butterflied Chicken

*Serves four.*

One 3½- to 4-pound chicken, trimmed of excess fat and skin

Kosher salt

½ cup fresh lemon juice (from 2 large lemons)

½ cup fresh lime juice (from 2 to 3 large limes)

2 cups plain whole-milk yogurt (about 1 pound)

2 teaspoons coriander seeds, crushed

8 medium cloves garlic, cut into slivers

One 2-inch knob fresh ginger, peeled and finely grated

**Butterflying is a technique every cook should learn to do. A butterflied chicken or game hen not only looks impressive, but the flat shape allows for more even heat distribution during cooking, so it cooks faster and stays juicier. And more skin is exposed to the dry air of the oven, so it gets golden and crisp all over. In this recipe, the marinade forms a delicious crust.**

Butterfly the chicken as directed on page 167.

Sprinkle both sides of the chicken evenly with 1½ tablespoons salt. Put the chicken in a 9x13-inch Pyrex or other large nonreactive baking dish or a large zip-top plastic bag. Add the lemon and lime juice and turn to coat the chicken well. Cover and set aside at room temperature for 30 minutes.

Meanwhile, combine the yogurt, coriander, garlic, and ginger in a large, shallow, nonreactive bowl and stir until the mixture is smooth and all of the seasonings are distributed evenly. Drain the excess citrus juice off the chicken but don't pat the chicken dry. Put the chicken in the yogurt marinade, coating the chicken on all sides and working the yogurt mixture under the breast and thigh skin as much as possible. Cover tightly and refrigerate for 2 to 4 hours. If necessary, turn the chicken occasionally so that all of the surfaces are coated evenly with the marinade.

Position a rack in the center of the oven and heat the oven to 375°F. Just before cooking, remove the chicken from the marinade and discard the marinade. Don't wipe off the marinade that coats the chicken because it will keep the meat moist and form a delicious crust as it roasts. Set the chicken skin side up on a broiler pan or on a rack set inside a rimmed baking sheet. Sprinkle with salt. Tuck the wingtips under the breast. Roast until the juices run clear and the thigh registers 175° to 180°F, 45 to 55 minutes. Let the chicken rest for 10 minutes before cutting it into quarters and serving.

*—Elizabeth Karmel*

**tip :** A butterflied chicken is a lot easier to carve than a whole one. Just use your kitchen shears (or a sharp chef's knife) to cut the chicken into halves or quarters.

# Grilled Beer-Brined Butterflied Chicken

*Serves four.*

One 3½- to 4-pound chicken, trimmed of excess fat and skin

¾ cup plus ½ teaspoon kosher salt

¾ cup plus ½ teaspoon packed dark brown sugar

1 tablespoon plus ¼ teaspoon freshly ground coarse black pepper

6 bay leaves, crumbled

4 cups very hot water

Two 12-ounce cans or bottles cold lager beer (like Budweiser®)

4 cups ice cubes

1 teaspoon smoked sweet Spanish paprika (pimentón)

½ teaspoon ground cumin

¼ teaspoon celery salt

¼ teaspoon chili powder

Large pinch dried oregano, crushed

Pinch cayenne

2 tablespoons extra-virgin olive oil

**Brining the chicken before grilling makes it juicier and more flavorful. Though not difficult to do—it's just a matter of soaking the chicken in a solution of salt and sugar—you'll want to start a couple of hours before grilling.**

Butterfly the chicken as shown below right.

In a large bowl, combine the ¾ cup salt, ¾ cup brown sugar, 1 tablespoon pepper, and bay leaves. Add the hot water and stir to dissolve the salt and sugar. Add the beer and stir well to remove the carbonation. Add about 4 cups ice cubes to cool the brine rapidly. When the ice has melted and the brine is cool, put the chicken in the brine, adding cold water if needed to cover. Refrigerate, covered, for 2 to 4 hours.

In a small bowl, mix together the remaining ½ teaspoon salt, ½ teaspoon brown sugar, and ¼ teaspoon pepper, the paprika, cumin, celery salt, chili powder, oregano, and cayenne.

Remove the chicken from the brine and let it air dry for 10 minutes. Meanwhile, build a charcoal fire or heat a gas grill with all burners on high. For a charcoal grill, when the charcoal is covered with a white-gray ash, divide it into two piles and set a drip pan between the coals. For a gas grill, turn the burners that will be directly underneath the chicken off and the other burners to medium. (If your grill has only two burners, turn one off and set the other one at medium. You may need to rotate the chicken periodically so that both sides brown.)

When ready to cook, if the chicken is still very wet, blot it dry with paper towels. Brush or rub both sides of the chicken with the oil and sprinkle with the spice mixture. Tuck the wingtips under the breast. Set the chicken, skin side up, in the center of the grill (or not directly over the heat). Cover and cook until the juices run clear and a meat thermometer inserted in the thickest part of the thigh registers 175° to 180°F, 40 to 50 minutes. Let the chicken rest for 10 minutes before cutting it into quarters and serving. *—Elizabeth Karmel*

**tip:** Tuck the wingtips under the breast. This makes for a more compact package and keeps the wings from moving around during cooking.

## Two easy steps to butterflied chicken

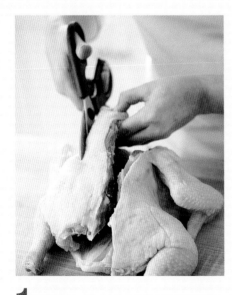

1 Using poultry shears, cut along each side of the backbone to remove it.

2 Flip the chicken over, press firmly on the center of the breast, and break the breastbone.

# Herb-Roasted Chicken with Lemons

*Serves four.*

2 large lemons

1 tablespoon olive oil

One 4½-pound chicken (if there are giblets, save for another use)

Kosher salt and freshly ground black pepper

1 large sprig fresh thyme

1 sprig fresh rosemary

2 large cloves garlic, crushed and peeled

2 tablespoons unsalted butter, melted

2 teaspoons dried herbes de Provence

¼ to ⅓ cup sweet vermouth

1 cup homemade or canned low-salt chicken broth

½ teaspoon cornstarch

**This herb-crusted chicken is roasted with wedges of lemon, which prop it up in the pan and also add a wonderful flavor to the pan juices. After roasting, the wedges develop a bitterness that isn't for everyone, but if you appreciate that bitter note, go ahead and serve them alongside the chicken as a garnish.**

Heat the oven to 425°F.

Cut the lemons in half crosswise and squeeze 2 tablespoons juice from one half; set the juice aside in a dish. Reserve the squeezed half for the chicken cavity. Cut each of the 3 remaining halves in half again for a total of 6 pieces.

Coat the bottom of a small flameproof roasting pan with the oil.

Wash and pat the chicken dry. Remove any excess fat and skin. Season the chicken inside and out with salt and pepper. Put the squeezed lemon half inside the chicken along with the thyme, rosemary, and garlic cloves. Truss the bird by crossing the legs, tying them lightly with string, and tucking the wings behind the back. Brush the chicken all over with the melted butter. Sprinkle with the herbes de Provence. Set the chicken on its side in the roasting pan, using the 6 lemon pieces, flesh side down, to support it.

Roast the chicken for 20 minutes, then turn the bird on its other side, turning the lemon pieces as well to their other flesh side. Roast for another 20 minutes. Turn the bird on its back and turn the lemons skin side down. Reduce the oven temperature to 350°F. Add ¼ cup of the vermouth to the pan, stir to mix with the pan juices, then baste the chicken. Roast the chicken until an instant-read thermometer inserted into the thickest part of the thigh reads 170°F, about 40 minutes more.

Transfer the chicken to a carving board, placing it breast side down. Tent with foil and let rest for 10 to 15 minutes. Discard the roasted lemons (or save to serve). Tip the roasting pan and spoon out and discard as much fat as you can, leaving behind the juices. Set the pan over medium-high heat. Add the broth and deglaze the pan by scraping up the browned bits from the bottom of the pan with a wooden spoon. Bring to a boil and reduce to ⅔ cup, about 3 minutes.

Mix the cornstarch and 1 tablespoon of the reserved lemon juice in a dish. Whisk this into the pan mixture. Return to a boil for about 2 minutes to thicken, then remove the pan from the heat.

Remove the trussing string from the chicken and carve the chicken. (Discard the herbs, lemon, and garlic from the cavity.) Add any juices from the chicken to the sauce. Taste the sauce and adjust the seasoning with salt, pepper, and the remaining lemon juice and vermouth. The balance of flavors will depend on the acidity of the lemons and your taste. Serve the chicken with the sauce. *—Jennifer McLagan*

## Herbes de Provence: Flavors of the South of France

Fresh thyme, summer savory, basil, marjoram, rosemary, and lavender thrive in the Mediterranean climate of Provence, a region of southern France. These herbs are the backbone of herbes de Provence, a mélange of dried herbs that may also include bay, sage, and sometimes cracked fennel seed (even though fennel isn't an herb).

The use of herbes de Provence isn't limited to the Mediterranean region, however; it's a kitchen staple throughout France, probably because its flavor is so versatile. It goes smashingly with everything from roasted lamb and potatoes to zucchini, eggplant, and tomatoes. Herbes de Provence is best added to dishes before or during cooking.

If your market doesn't carry herbes de Provence in its spice section, you can make your own by mixing together: 1 tablespoon dried thyme, 1 tablespoon dried summer savory, 1 tablespoon dried marjoram, 1 tablespoon dried basil, 2 teaspoons dried rosemary, 1 teaspoon dried sage, 1 teaspoon cracked fennel seeds, 1/2 teaspoon dried lavender (optional).

# Cranberry-Honey-Glazed Chicken

*Serves four to six.*

## For the cranberry-honey glaze:

1 cup fresh or frozen cranberries, picked through and rinsed

½ cup honey

¼ cup rice vinegar

2 tablespoons chopped fresh thyme leaves (reserve the stems for the chicken cavity)

## For the chicken:

One 5-pound chicken

3 tablespoons unsalted butter, melted

Kosher salt and freshly ground black pepper

1 large shallot, halved

Fresh Cranberry Relish (see recipe below)

## Fresh Cranberry Relish

*Serves four to six.*

You can make this relish a day ahead; just keep it refrigerated and give it a good stir before serving.

12 ounces (3 cups) fresh or frozen cranberries, picked through and rinsed

½ cup granulated sugar

¼ cup rice vinegar

1 tablespoon finely grated orange zest

Combine the cranberries, sugar, vinegar, and orange zest in the bowl of a food processor and pulse until finely chopped. Transfer to a bowl, cover, and refrigerate at least 1 hour to develop the flavors.

This tangy-sweet roast chicken is brushed with a cranberry-honey glaze during the last half hour of roasting. The sugar in the honey and the red color from the cranberries help the chicken brown to a beautiful burnished glow, and the slightly sweet skin is a nice complement to the juicy chicken meat. Serve with the uncooked cranberry relish below left—it's fresh tasting and a breeze to make. Rice vinegar adds tang and keeps the relish from being cloying. This dish is an ingenious option for Thanksgiving dinner for a small group because it's so festive, but much more manageable in size than a turkey.

**Make the cranberry-honey glaze:** Combine the cranberries, honey, and vinegar in a small saucepan and bring to a boil, then turn down the heat to medium and simmer until the cranberries pop and are very soft, 4 to 5 minutes. Remove from the heat and pour the mixture into a fine sieve set over a bowl. Use a rubber spatula to force most of the pulp through the sieve, leaving the skins and seeds behind (be sure to get the pulp clinging to the bottom of the sieve). Add the chopped thyme and stir until the glaze is well combined. Set aside to cool and thicken.

**Prepare the chicken:** Position a rack in the lowest part of the oven and heat the oven to 425°F. Set a V-rack in a foil-lined medium or large roasting pan. Trim any excess fat and skin from the chicken and clean out the cavity. Tuck the wingtips behind the neck and set the chicken on a tray or cutting board. Put the shallot and reserved thyme stems in the cavity of the chicken, then brush it all over with half the melted butter. Generously season all over with salt and pepper, including the cavity. Tie the legs loosely if you want and set the chicken, breast side up, on the rack in the pan.

Roast on the bottom oven rack for 20 minutes. Baste with the remaining melted butter and roast another 10 minutes. Stir the glaze to loosen it, then brush the chicken with about half of it. Don't worry if some of the glaze slides off the chicken. Roast for 10 minutes, then brush with the remaining glaze. Continue roasting until an instant-read thermometer inserted in the thickest part of the thigh reads 170°F and the juices run clear, 30 to 35 minutes more. The skin should be a caramelized reddish brown. If any parts of the chicken begin to get too brown before the chicken is done, tent it with foil.

Remove the pan from the oven and tilt the chicken to allow the juices in the cavity to drain into the pan. (As long as the thighs have reached 170°F, it's fine if these juices are pink.) Transfer the chicken to a cutting board or platter and let it rest for 5 to 10 minutes. Carve and serve with the cranberry relish.

*—Tom Douglas*

# Dried Apricot & Date Stuffed Turkey Breast with Marsala Glaze

*Serves four, or two with leftovers.*

## For the stuffing:

1 tablespoon unsalted butter

⅓ cup finely chopped onion

⅓ cup coarsely chopped pitted dried dates

¼ cup coarsely chopped dried apricots

3 tablespoons toasted, skinned, and chopped hazelnuts (see below, far right)

2 tablespoons chopped fresh flat-leaf parsley

2 teaspoons chopped fresh sage

Kosher salt and freshly ground black pepper

## For the turkey breast:

1 boneless, skinless or skin-on turkey breast half (1¾ to 2 pounds)

Kosher salt and freshly ground black pepper

2 strips thick-sliced bacon

1½ tablespoons extra-virgin olive oil

1½ cups sweet Marsala wine

**The sweetness of the dried fruit in this stuffing makes a harmonious combo with the turkey. Tying a couple of strips of bacon onto the stuffed turkey breast with kitchen twine adds some much needed fat to the lean white meat and helps keep it moist. The breast roasts in just 40 minutes and, instead of gravy, a simple Marsala wine reduction is easy and quite delicious. This dish is delicious any time, but for Thanksgiving, if you're having only a couple of people over, it's a perfect solution: It feels special, keeps with the turkey tradition, and cooks quickly.**

**Make the stuffing:** Melt the butter in a 10-inch skillet over medium heat. Add the onion and cook, stirring frequently, until soft and lightly browned, about 4 minutes. Set aside to cool. Put the dates and apricots in the bowl of a food processor and pulse until finely chopped. Add the hazelnuts, parsley, sage, and reserved onions and pulse a few more times until everything is minced and well combined. Transfer to a small bowl and season to taste with salt and pepper.

**Prepare the turkey breast:** Heat the oven to 350°F. Put the turkey breast on a cutting board and, holding your knife parallel to the work surface, slice open the turkey breast horizontally, working from the thicker side of the lobe to the thinner side and not cutting all the way through. Open the turkey breast like a book and season generously with salt and pepper.

Spread the stuffing evenly over half the opened turkey breast, leaving a little border around the outer edges. Fold the other half of the turkey breast over the stuffing, enclosing the stuffing as much as possible. Lay the bacon lengthwise on top of the turkey breast and tie the breast crosswise with kitchen string in four or five places to hold it all together.

Season the turkey on both sides with salt and pepper. Heat the oil in a 12-inch ovenproof skillet over medium-high heat. Beginning with the bacon side down, sear the turkey breast on both sides until nicely browned, 3 to 4 minutes per side. Transfer the skillet to the oven (the turkey should be bacon side up) and roast for 20 minutes. Remove the pan from the oven, flip the turkey breast, return to the oven, and roast until an instant-read thermometer inserted into the center of the breast reads 165°F, 20 to 30 minutes more. Remove the pan from the oven, transfer the turkey to a large plate and let it rest, loosely covered with foil, for about 10 minutes.

**Make the Marsala glaze:** Pour off the fat from the skillet and discard any lumps of stuffing that may have fallen out of the turkey and burned. Put the skillet over medium-high heat, pour the Marsala in the skillet, and bring it to a boil, stirring with a wooden spatula to scrape up any browned bits on the

bottom of the pan. Add to the pan any juices that have collected around the turkey while resting on the plate. Continue boiling until the Marsala is reduced to ¼ cup, 5 to 7 minutes. Season with salt and pepper to taste.

Remove the strings from the turkey. Cut the turkey crosswise into ½-inch-thick slices and arrange the slices on a serving platter. Pour the Marsala glaze into a small bowl and pass with the turkey. —*Tom Douglas*

## How to toast and skin hazelnuts

You'll need 3 tablespoons toasted, skinned, chopped hazelnuts for the turkey breast stuffing, so start with a scant ¼ cup whole nuts to be sure you have enough. Heat the oven to 375°F and toast the whole nuts on a baking sheet until fragrant and lightly browned, 5 to 10 minutes. Hazelnuts have thin, papery skins, which can burn, so watch carefully. After roasting, remove as much of the skin as you can by rubbing the warm nuts in a clean dishtowel.

# Roasted Cornish Game Hens with Pesto & Goat Cheese

*Serves six.*

6 tablespoons homemade or prepared basil pesto

⅓ cup fresh goat cheese (about 2½ ounces), at room temperature

3 large Cornish game hens (1½ to 2 pounds each), giblets removed

1½ tablespoons extra-virgin olive oil

Kosher salt and freshly ground black pepper

**This is a perfect dinner party dish: easy, do-ahead, and elegant. A half a hen looks attractive on the plate and makes a nice portion, with each person getting both dark and light meat. The simple step of inserting the pesto-goat cheese stuffing under the skin adds delightful flavor to the mild game hen.**

Position a rack in the center of the oven and heat the oven to 425°F. Arrange a large wire rack over a large rimmed baking sheet or shallow roasting pan. In a small bowl, combine the pesto and goat cheese, mashing it with a fork until evenly mixed.

Place a hen, breast side down, on a cutting board. Remove the backbone by cutting along both sides with poultry shears. Flip the hen and flatten it by pressing down on the breastbone with your palms. With a chef's knife, split the hen in two along the breastbone. Extend the wings on each side, and chop off the last two joints. Remove and discard any large deposits of fat or excess skin. Repeat with the remaining hens.

With your fingers, loosen the skin over the breast and leg. Insert a heaping tablespoon of the pesto mixture under the skin and work it so it evenly covers the breast and leg meat. Smooth the skin back to its original position and repeat with the remaining hens. The hens may be prepared up to this point and refrigerated for several hours.

Arrange the hens on the large wire rack. They should not overlap. Brush the surface of the hens with the oil and sprinkle with salt and pepper. Roast the hens, rotating the pan about halfway through, until they're nicely browned and the juices run clear when a thigh is pricked with a skewer or toothpick, about 30 minutes. Cover loosely with foil and allow to rest for about 5 minutes before serving. *—Molly Stevens*

# Smoked Paprika & Fennel Seed Roast Turkey with Onion Gravy

This roast turkey may be one of the most succulent and unusual you've ever tasted. A flavored butter, fragrant with smoked paprika and toasted ground fennel seed, is rubbed under the skin of the turkey to keep the breast moist and juicy. The turkey roasts on a bed of onions, which brown very slowly, bathing in the pan drippings and becoming wonderfully soft and fragrant—the perfect foundation for a rich, flavorful gravy that's robust and chunky with shreds of sweet, caramelized onion. Be sure to use a flameproof roasting pan so it can go directly over the burner when it's time to make the gravy.

**Make the paprika-fennel butter:** Put the butter in a small bowl. Add the fennel seeds, paprika, thyme, salt, and pepper, and mix until well blended. Set aside at room temperature (refrigerate if making ahead).

**Prepare the turkey:** Position a rack in the lowest part of the oven and heat the oven to 350°F. Brush a large flameproof roasting pan lightly with 1 tablespoon of the melted butter. Make a bed of the onions in the center of the pan.

Trim off the wingtips at the first joint and, if already loose, trim the tail from the turkey. Remove the giblets (discard the liver) and neck and set them aside with the wingtips and tail for making the broth for the onion gravy. Rinse the turkey and pat it dry with paper towels.

Set the turkey on a work surface and loosen the skin over the breasts by sliding your hands under the skin. Rub all of the paprika-fennel butter under the skin, smearing it over the breast. Brush the turkey skin all over with the

*Serves ten to twelve, or six to eight with leftovers.*

**For the smoked paprika and fennel seed butter:**

6 tablespoons (¾ stick) unsalted butter, softened

1 tablespoon fennel seeds, toasted (see page 59)

1 tablespoon sweet pimentón (Spanish smoked paprika)

1 tablespoon chopped fresh thyme (save the stems for the turkey cavity)

½ teaspoon kosher salt

¼ teaspoon freshly ground black pepper

**For the turkey:**

¼ cup (½ stick) unsalted butter, melted

1 large onion, thinly sliced

One 11- to 12-pound turkey, trimmed of excess fat

Fennel Salt (see page 176)

6 cloves garlic, peeled

Zest of 1 lemon, removed in long strips with a vegetable peeler

4 large sprigs fresh thyme, plus the stems from the chopped thyme above

**For the onion gravy:**

7 tablespoons all-purpose flour

4½ to 5 cups hot turkey broth (see page 177)

## Fennel Salt

*Yields about 5 tablespoons.*

This simple mixture makes a wonderful "finishing salt"—a flavored salt you can sprinkle on meat or fish after it's cooked and sliced so you get a bit of seasoning with every bite. But it's also a great seasoning to sprinkle on a turkey or chicken before roasting.

3 tablespoons kosher or sea salt

1 tablespoon fennel seeds, toasted (see page 59) and ground

1 tablespoon freshly ground black pepper

Combine the salt, fennel, and pepper in a small bowl. Reserve 2 tablespoons of the mixture for sprinkling on the turkey and transfer the rest to a couple of small, shallow dishes for passing at the table.

remaining 3 tablespoons melted butter. Sprinkle 2 tablespoons of the Fennel Salt all over the skin of the turkey (sprinkle a little inside the cavity, too). Place the garlic cloves, lemon zest, and thyme sprigs inside the cavity. If you like, tuck the legs into the tail flap (or tie them together loosely if there is no flap).

Set the turkey, breast side up, on top of the onions in the roasting pan (there is no need for a rack). Roast for 1 hour and then baste the turkey with the drippings that have collected in the pan and rotate the pan. Continue to roast, basting every 20 minutes, until an instant-read thermometer inserted in the thickest part of both thighs reads 170°F, 1½ to 2 hours more. (If the turkey is browning too much, tent it with foil.) Set the turkey on a large platter to rest, tented with foil, for about 20 minutes while you make the gravy.

**Make the gravy:** Set the roasting pan with the onions and juices over medium-high heat (it may need to straddle two burners, depending on your stove). With a wooden spoon, stir up any browned bits stuck to the bottom of the pan and continue stirring for a few minutes, allowing the onions to brown a little more. Sprinkle the flour evenly over the onions and juices and stir until the flour is well combined, 1 to 2 minutes. Start adding the broth, 1 ladleful at a time, whisking out the lumps before you add more broth. Continue to add broth gradually, whisking each time until smooth, until you've added about 4½ cups of broth. Add any juices that have collected on the platter around the turkey. Lower the heat to medium or medium low and gently simmer the gravy, whisking occasionally, until it's full-flavored and thickened, 8 to 10 minutes. If it seems too thick, add the remaining ½ cup broth. Season with salt and pepper to taste. Keep warm until ready to serve, then transfer to a gravy boat.

Carve the turkey. Pass the gravy boat and the remaining fennel salt at the table. —*Tom Douglas*

**tip:** The turkey roasts on a bed of onions, which brown very slowly, bathing in the pan drippings and becoming wonderfully soft and fragrant—the perfect foundation for a rich, flavorful gravy that's chunky with shreds of sweet, caramelized onion. Stir flour into the roasting pan with the onions and drippings, then add turkey broth a ladleful at a time for a rich onion gravy.

# Turkey Broth

*Yields 5 to 6 cups.*

**Use all the "extra bits" of the turkey—the neck, tail, wingtips, and giblets—to make a turkey-enriched chicken broth, which is the foundation of the gravy. Make the broth while the turkey is roasting or a day ahead if you like.**

2 teaspoons vegetable oil

Turkey neck, wingtips, tail, and giblets (excluding the liver)

½ cup dry white wine

8 cups homemade or low-salt canned chicken broth

½ medium onion, coarsely chopped

½ medium carrot, coarsely chopped

½ medium rib celery, coarsely chopped

8 black peppercorns

2 sprigs fresh parsley

1 bay leaf

Heat the oil in a 3- or 4-quart saucepan over medium-high heat. Add the turkey parts and brown them well on all sides, 8 to 10 minutes. Pour in the wine and use a wooden spoon to scrape up any browned bits from the bottom of the pan. Add the broth, onion, carrot, celery, peppercorns, parsley, and bay leaf and bring to a boil over high heat. Reduce the heat to medium low or low and simmer the broth gently for 1 hour, skimming off the scum occasionally with a skimmer or a large slotted spoon. Strain the broth through a sieve and discard the solids. Let the broth cool and spoon off the fat.

## Spanish paprika adds smoke and spice

Ground from dried chiles, paprika plays an honored role in both Hungarian and Spanish cuisines. Each country has a distinctive style of paprika, both of which are generally better than the generic paprika found in supermarkets.

Spanish paprika or pimentón comes from western Spain's La Vera valley. It differs from Hungarian paprika in that the chiles are dried over smoldering oak logs, giving them a smoky flavor. It comes in three heat levels: dulce, agridulce, and picante (sweet, bittersweet, and hot). It's a key ingredient in paella, chorizo, and many tapas dishes. In the United States, pimentón isn't as commonly available as Hungarian paprika, but it's well worth seeking out. Add a little pimentón to scrambled eggs, black-bean chili, or roasted potatoes. It's delicious wherever you'd like a smoky flavor, but remember that smokiness can easily overwhelm a dish, so start experimenting by using only ¼ to ½ teaspoon.

# 6
# Beef, Veal, Lamb & Pork

p216

p208

Spicy Korean-Style Pork Medallions with
Asian Slaw (recipe on page 220)

# Filet Steaks with an Irish Whisky & Cream Pan Sauce

*Serves four.*

**Four 1- to 1¼-inch-thick pieces beef tenderloin (about 7½ ounces each)**

**Kosher salt and freshly ground black pepper**

**1 tablespoon vegetable oil (if not using a cast-iron pan)**

**1 tablespoon unsalted butter**

**3 tablespoons finely chopped shallot (from 1 large shallot)**

**¼ cup Irish whisky, such as Jameson®, or brandy**

**½ cup homemade or canned low-salt beef or chicken broth**

**½ teaspoon Worcestershire sauce**

**2 teaspoons Dijon mustard**

**½ cup heavy cream**

**½ to 1 teaspoon fresh lemon juice**

This is a take on Steak Diane, the famous tableside dish served for eons in fancy French and "Continental" restaurants. Instead of the traditional pounded steaks for Steak Diane, this recipe uses 1-inch-thick butter-tender beef filet; its somewhat subtle flavor can use the boost of a zesty sauce.

Season each steak generously with salt and pepper. Heat a heavy (preferably cast-iron) skillet that's large enough to hold the steaks in a single layer over high heat until quite hot. (Add the oil if not using cast iron.) Test the level of heat by touching the edge of one steak to the pan surface; it will sizzle briskly when ready. Immediately arrange the steaks in the skillet and sear one side for 2 minutes. Sneak a peek to see if the first side is nicely browned. If not, continue to sear that side for another minute or so. Flip the steaks and sear the other side for 2 to 3 minutes. Reduce the heat to medium high, cook for another 2 minutes, flip, and cook until an instant-read thermometer inserted in the center of the meat reads 120°F for rare or 125°F for medium rare, another 1 to 2 minutes. Transfer the steaks to a warm platter and let them rest, covered loosely with foil, while you make the sauce.

To make the pan sauce, return the unwashed pan to medium heat. Add the butter and let it melt. Add the shallot and cook, stirring, until fragrant and just tender, 1 to 2 minutes. Add the whisky or brandy and stir with a wooden spoon, scraping up any browned bits stuck to the bottom of the pan. Add the broth and Worcestershire, raise the heat to medium high, and bring to a boil. Whisk in the mustard, then the cream. Continue to cook at a boil, stirring, until reduced to a saucy consistency, 3 to 5 minutes. Taste the sauce and season with salt, pepper, and lemon juice. Serve the steaks with the sauce. *—Bruce Aidells*

## Is it Prime, Choice, or Select?

All meat processed in this country is done so under the inspection of the U.S. Department of Agriculture. If a meat packer chooses, the USDA will also grade the meat for quality. The top grades are Prime, Choice, and Select. Because it's expensive to do so, not all packers choose to have their meat graded. If a steak isn't labeled, chances are that if it were graded by the USDA, it would be stamped Select. Unfortunately, Prime beef, which has the best marbling, texture, and flavor, rarely reaches the markets where you and I shop, instead going straight to restaurants or overseas. Your best quality guarantee? Buy steak labeled Choice, though bear in mind that within this designation there's great variation in quality. Taste and compare the offerings from different markets and stick with what you like. *—Bruce Aidells*

## Filet steak (aka filet mignon)

Filet steak, which is cut from the tenderloin, is exceedingly tender. Ask for center-cut filets, rather than ones from the tail or head; 6 to 8 ounces per person is a good serving. Filet has a bit less flavor than other cuts, but it's perfectly suited for the sauté pan, especially because its tender texture is an excellent match for a rich pan sauce. Serve this cut rare or medium rare; when cooked past that, its flavor can become livery.

# New York Strip Steak with Sweet Pepper-Chorizo Butter

*Serves four.*

## For the sweet pepper-chorizo butter:

2 cloves garlic, peeled

¼ cup diced ready-to-eat chorizo

¼ cup jarred roasted red peppers

1 tablespoon chopped fresh flat-leaf parsley

½ cup (1 stick) unsalted butter, softened

2 teaspoons sweet Hungarian paprika

¼ teaspoon Worcestershire sauce

Kosher salt and freshly ground black pepper

## For the steak:

Two 1¼- to 1½-inch-thick New York strip steaks (¾ to 1 pound each)

Kosher salt and freshly ground black pepper

1 tablespoon canola or vegetable oil (if not using a cast-iron pan)

Chorizo is a spicy, cured sausage often used in Spanish cooking. Be sure to buy the ready-to-eat kind found in many supermarket delis, as you won't be cooking the sausage any. For an even bolder flavor, replace the paprika with pimentón (smoked Spanish paprika) and the red peppers with jarred Spanish piquillo (medium-size, fleshy red peppers that you can buy fire-roasted). This recipe makes more flavored butter than you'll need; freeze the rest for another steak.

**Make the flavored butter:** Chop the garlic in a food processor. Scrape down the bowl and add the chorizo, roasted peppers, and parsley. Pulse a few times to finely chop. Add the butter, paprika, Worcestershire, ¼ teaspoon salt, and ½ teaspoon pepper; pulse to blend. Scrape the flavored butter onto a large sheet of plastic wrap. Using the plastic, shape the butter into a rough block or log, wrap well, and refrigerate until firm. (You can refrigerate the butter for up to a week or freeze up to two months.)

**Cook the steaks:** Take the steaks out of the refrigerator, season both sides with salt and pepper, and let sit at room temperature for at least 15 or up to 30 minutes. Turn on your exhaust fan. Have ready a warm platter.

Heat a heavy (preferably cast-iron) skillet that's large enough to hold the steaks in a single layer over high heat until quite hot (add the oil if not using cast iron). Test the heat level by touching the edge of one steak to the pan surface; it will sizzle briskly when ready. Immediately arrange the steaks in the skillet and sear one side for 3 minutes. Sneak a peek to see if each steak is nicely browned. If not, continue to sear that side for another minute or so. Flip the steak and sear the other side for 2 to 3 minutes. Reduce the heat to medium high, cook another 3 minutes, flip, and cook until an instant-read thermometer at the center of the meat reads 120°F for rare, 125°F for medium rare, and 130°F for medium, another 1 to 3 minutes. Transfer the steaks to the warm platter, cover loosely with foil, and let rest for 5 minutes.

Cut each steak in half and portion onto warm plates. Top each steak with some of the flavored butter (it may crumble a bit when you slice it; that's fine) and serve immediately. *—Bruce Aidells*

## New York strip (aka top loin, New York steak, shell steak, strip steak, sirloin strip, Kansas City steak)

The official name for this steak is top loin, and it comes from the middle back, called the short loin, which is located on the exterior surface of the spinal column. Confusingly, it goes by as many as 20 names. (In California, it's called New York steak. In New York, it's often called shell steak or strip steak or sirloin strip—despite its not coming from the sirloin.) Whatever it's called, this steak is tender and well flavored and you will pay accordingly. It takes especially well to dry rubs and compound butters. For evenly seared steaks, buy one or two large, thick steaks (rather than several thin ones) and cut them into servings after cooking, especially if you like meat rare or medium rare.

# Star Anise & Rosemary Rib-Eye Steak

*Serves four to six.*

1 tablespoon chopped fresh
rosemary

1 teaspoon ground star anise
or ½ teaspoon Chinese five-
spice powder

Kosher salt and freshly ground
black pepper

2 teaspoons olive oil; more as
needed

One 1½- to 2-inch-thick
boneless rib-eye steak
(1½ to 2 pounds)

**This recipe combines the decidedly Eastern flavor of star anise with a very Western herb: fresh rosemary. Unusual, yes, but this inspired pairing works deliciously well with rib-eye's robust flavor.**

In a small bowl, combine the rosemary and star anise with 2 teaspoons salt and 1 teaspoon pepper. Coat the steak on both sides with the oil and rub the seasoning mix all over both sides, too. Set aside for half an hour at room temperature or, for even more flavor, wrap the steak in plastic wrap and refrigerate for at least 2 hours and up to 24 hours. (If refrigerating the steak, let it sit at room temperature for at least 15 minutes before cooking it.)

Turn on your exhaust fan. Have ready a warm platter. Heat a heavy (preferably cast-iron) skillet that's large enough to hold the steak over high heat until quite hot. (If not using cast iron, add the oil to the pan and heat over medium-high heat.) Test the heat level by touching the steak to the pan surface; it will sizzle briskly when ready. Immediately place the steak in the skillet and sear one side for 3 minutes. Sneak a peek to see if the steak is nicely browned. If not, continue to sear that side for another minute or so. Flip the steak and sear the other side for 3 minutes. Reduce the heat to medium high if using cast-iron (medium if using another heavy pan) and cook for another 4 to 6 minutes. Flip and cook until an instant-read thermometer inserted in the center of the meat reads 120°F for rare, 125°F for medium rare, and 130°F for medium, another 4 to 8 minutes, depending on thickness. Transfer the steak to the warm platter and let rest, covered loosely with foil, for 5 to 7 minutes.

To serve, slice the steak into ½-inch-thick strips or cut the meat into four smaller pieces. Serve immediately. *—Bruce Aidells*

## Rib-eye steak (aka Delmonico, beauty steak, market steak, Spencer steak)

A rib-eye is a brilliant steak for pan-searing. It's cut from the prime rib area of the upper back and is the most flavorful and fattiest of the common steaks. Rib-eye comes boneless or bone-in; both are great, though bone-in offers a bit more flavor. Butchers often cut this steak too thin, so that a single steak will weigh a pound or less. It's better to buy it thick, preferably at least 1½ inches, because it cooks better. The deep, beefy flavor of rib-eye holds up well to most dry rubs or wet marinades and is especially well suited to strong flavors like soy, garlic, ginger, and chiles.

# Seared Rib-Eye Steaks with Edamame & Garlic

*Serves two.*

⅓ cup extra-virgin olive oil

10 large cloves garlic, peeled and halved lengthwise

Kosher salt

Two 1-inch-thick boneless rib-eye steaks (6 to 8 ounces each)

Coarsely cracked black peppercorns

2 cups frozen shelled edamame

Pinch cayenne; more to taste

1 tablespoon finely chopped fresh flat-leaf parsley (optional)

Lemon wedges, for serving

**Look for frozen edamame, or soybeans, in the frozen foods section of the supermarket, or blanched edamame in the fresh produce section. If you can't find them, try tossing drained canned cannellini beans with the garlic oil instead.**

In a 1-quart saucepan over medium heat, warm the oil with the garlic and a pinch of salt. When the oil starts to bubble gently, reduce the heat to maintain a steady simmer. Cook the garlic, stirring occasionally, until it is light golden brown and perfectly tender when pierced with a fork, about 15 minutes; remove from the heat. Meanwhile, bring a medium pot of water (about 5 cups) to a boil.

Generously season the steaks on both sides with salt and pepper. Heat a large sauté pan over medium-high heat until hot. Add 2 tablespoons of the garlic oil and the steaks. Don't disturb the steaks until they have a nice brown crust, about 3 minutes. Turn and cook the other side until the steaks are done to your liking, about 3 minutes more for medium rare. Transfer the steaks to a plate and let them rest for about 5 minutes.

While the steaks rest, add 1 teaspoon salt and the edamame to the boiling water. Return to a boil and cook, uncovered, until they are tender, 3 to 4 minutes. Drain and transfer to a medium bowl. Add 2 tablespoons of the garlic oil, the cayenne, and parsley, if using. Toss to combine. Taste and add salt if necessary.

Holding your knife at an angle, cut the steaks into ½-inch-thick slices and transfer to dinner plates. Remove the garlic from the remaining oil and scatter it over the beef. Serve with the edamame and the lemon wedges on the side.
—*Tasha DeSerio*

## Edamame aren't just for snacking

Lean, green, and high in protein, edamame—Japanese for "beans on a branch"—are a type of soybean that's picked when young, plump, and tender (as opposed to field soybeans, which are harvested when mature and dry). Edamame have a sweet, nutty flavor that goes especially well with beer—in Japan, edamame are often served as a bar snack.

Because they're popular in Japan, edamame pods can be found fresh there. But here, it's more common to find frozen parcooked edamame, either shelled or still in the pod. Some markets also carry fully cooked shelled edamame in the produce sections. Parcooked edamame require just a quick warm-up to be ready to eat.

To prepare edamame for snacking out of hand, heat the frozen pods in boiling water until hot or in a dry skillet over high heat until thawed and slightly charred. Sprinkle the pods with kosher or sea salt. As your guests shell the edamame, the salt will stick to their fingers and season the beans.

Edamame aren't just a snack, though; they go well with other foods. Think of them as an alternative to fava beans or lima beans. Here's a great destination for them: "soyccotash": Sauté shelled edamame in butter with a mix of fresh vegetables and herbs, like sweet onion, fresh corn, summer squash, bell pepper, tomatoes, fresh marjoram, and a little jalapeño or serrano for kick.

# Grilled Steak Kebab Pitas with Ginger & Garlic Dressing

*Serves four as a main course, six to eight as a "small plate."*

½ cup extra-virgin olive oil; more for brushing

1 tablespoon peeled and finely grated ginger

1 tablespoon green Tabasco or other jalapeño hot sauce

2 teaspoons cider vinegar

1 small to medium clove garlic, finely grated or minced

Kosher salt and freshly ground black pepper

1½ to 1¾ pounds 1-inch-thick boneless beef strip steaks (2 to 3 steaks), trimmed and cut into 1-inch cubes

6 to 8 bamboo skewers (at least 8 inches long), soaked in water for at least 20 minutes

1 large red bell pepper, cored and cut into 1¼- to 1½-inch squares

6 to 8 pita breads, preferably pocketless

2 cups shredded lettuce, preferably a crisp variety like iceberg or romaine

**Warmed, tender pita breads are delicious landing pads for juicy grilled chunks of steak and a gingery dressing. Bell pepper adds color and crunch; you could add mushrooms for an earthier note, if you like.**

Prepare a medium-hot grill fire.

In a 1-cup liquid measuring cup, whisk the ½ cup oil with the ginger, Tabasco, vinegar, garlic, ¼ teaspoon salt, and ¼ teaspoon pepper.

Thread four cubes of meat onto each skewer, inserting a red pepper square between the cubes. (You may not need all the skewers.) Brush the kebabs with oil and sprinkle lightly with salt and pepper.

Just before grilling, lightly oil the grill grates. Set the kebabs on the grill and cook, with the lid closed, turning every 2 minutes, 4 to 6 minutes total for medium rare. Warm the pitas on the grill.

To serve, slide each kebab off its skewer into a pita. Top each with some of the lettuce. Whisk the dressing to recombine and drizzle over the meat and vegetables. *—Jessica Bard*

# Spicy Thai Beef Curry

**This quick-to-make curry has a modest kick, but you can pump up the heat by using the full two teaspoons of curry paste. Fragrant jasmine rice is a good accompaniment.**

Heat the oil in a 10-inch straight-sided sauté pan over medium-high heat. Season the sirloin tips with salt and pepper and sear the meat in batches until nicely browned on two sides, 1 to 2 minutes per side. Transfer to a plate.

Reduce the heat to medium. Add the shallots to the pan and cook until just tender and lightly browned, 2 to 4 minutes. Add the ginger and cook, stirring, until fragrant, about 1 minute. Add the curry paste and cook, stirring, about 30 seconds. Stir in ¼ cup of the broth, scraping up any browned bits that are stuck to the bottom of the pan. Add ⅓ cup of the coconut milk, stirring until the curry paste has blended in completely. Stir in the remaining coconut milk and broth. Add the fish sauce. Increase the heat to medium high. Return the beef to the pan (along with any juices), stir, and simmer until the meat is just cooked through, 8 to 12 minutes.

Take the pan off the heat. Remove the meat and transfer to a cutting board. Stir the sugar snap peas into the sauce and cover the pan. Let the meat rest for 1 minute, then slice it thinly across the grain; return it to the pan along with the lime zest. If necessary, return the pan to medium heat until the peas are thawed and heated through.

Portion the curry into four warm bowls, sprinkle with the cilantro, and serve with the lime wedges. *—Joanne McAllister Smart*

*Serves four.*

1 tablespoon vegetable oil

1½ pounds beef sirloin tips

Kosher salt and freshly ground black pepper

½ cup thinly sliced shallots (about 2 medium-large)

¼ cup peeled and finely chopped fresh ginger

1 to 2 teaspoons Thai red curry paste

½ cup canned low-salt chicken broth

One 13.5-ounce can unsweetened coconut milk

1 tablespoon fish sauce

1½ cups frozen sugar snap peas

1 large lime, zest finely grated and fruit cut into wedges

⅓ cup chopped fresh cilantro

# Cottage Pie with Beef & Carrots

*Serves six to eight.*

## For the beef stew:

1¾ cups canned low-salt beef broth (one 14-ounce can)

½ ounce dried porcini mushrooms

2 to 3 tablespoons olive or vegetable oil

2½ pounds thin-cut beef chuck steaks, preferably top blade (or flat iron), ½ to ¾ inch thick, trimmed of any excess fat or gristle

Kosher salt and freshly ground black pepper

3 medium carrots, peeled and cut into ½-inch dice (about 1⅓ cups)

2 ribs celery, cut into ½-inch dice (about 1 cup)

2 small onions, cut into ½-inch dice (about 2 cups)

1½ teaspoons fresh thyme leaves (or ½ teaspoon dried)

2 tablespoons tomato paste

3 tablespoons all-purpose flour

¾ cup dry white wine or dry vermouth

## For the topping:

2 pounds russet potatoes (3 to 4 medium), peeled and cut into 1½- to 2-inch chunks

Kosher salt

5 tablespoons unsalted butter (at room temperature, cut into 3 pieces) plus 2 teaspoons (cold, cut into small bits); more for the baking dish

½ cup milk, light cream, or half-and-half, warmed

Freshly ground black pepper

Cottage pie originated as a way to use up leftover beef stew, but why wait for leftovers? Here's how to make the ultimate comfort meal from scratch. To streamline the preparation, make the beef stew several days ahead and keep, covered, in the refrigerator; just reheat before proceeding with the recipe. You can also fully assemble the pie one day ahead: Dot the top with the two teaspoons butter, cool the pie, cover with plastic, and refrigerate until ready to bake.

**Make the beef stew:** Position a rack in the center of the oven and heat the oven to 350°F.

Pour the broth into a small saucepan and add the mushrooms. Bring to a simmer over medium-high heat. Remove from the heat, cover, and let steep for at least 15 minutes.

Meanwhile, heat 2 tablespoons of the oil in a heavy stew pot or shallow 5-quart Dutch oven over medium-high heat. Pat the steaks dry, season lightly with salt and pepper, and put only as many in the pan as will fit without crowding. Sear the steaks, flipping once, until nicely browned, 3 to 4 minutes per side. Set aside on a platter and repeat with the remaining steaks.

Lower the heat to medium and, if the pan looks dry, add the remaining 1 tablespoon oil. Add the carrots, celery, onions, and thyme. Season with salt and pepper and cook, stirring occasionally, until the vegetables begin to soften, about 7 minutes. Stir in the tomato paste and cook for a few minutes. Add the flour, stirring to blend, and cook for another minute. Add the wine, bring to a simmer, and reduce the heat to low.

With a slotted spoon, scoop the mushrooms from the broth and transfer to a cutting board. Coarsely chop the mushrooms and add them to the vegetables. Slowly add the broth, being careful to hold back the last few tablespoons, which may contain grit from the mushrooms.

Cut the steaks into ½- to ¾-inch cubes and add to the pot, along with any juices. Cover tightly and transfer to the oven. Cook, stirring once or twice, until the meat is tender, about 1 hour. Season to taste with salt and pepper. Set the stew in a warm place and increase the oven temperature to 375°F. (Or, if making ahead, let cool, then cover and refrigerate.)

**Make the topping:** About 30 minutes before the stew is ready, put the potatoes in a large saucepan and cover by an inch with cold water. Add 1 teaspoon salt. Bring to a simmer over medium heat, partially cover, and simmer until the potatoes are easily pierced with a skewer, about 20 minutes. Drain and return the potatoes to the saucepan. Put the pan over low heat and

shake or stir the potatoes until a floury film forms on the bottom of the pot, 1 to 2 minutes. Using a ricer, food mill, or potato masher, mash the potatoes. Stir in the 5 tablespoons softened butter with a broad wooden spoon. Once the butter is thoroughly absorbed, add the milk or cream in three parts, stirring vigorously between additions. Season to taste with salt and pepper.

**Assemble and bake:** Lightly butter a shallow 3-quart baking dish. Spoon the stew into the baking dish. Spread the potatoes on top in an even layer— you don't need to spread them all the way to the edge. Dot the top with the remaining 2 teaspoons cold butter. Bake at 375°F until the stew is bubbling around the sides and the top is lightly browned, 35 to 45 minutes (45 to 55 minutes if the pie has been refrigerated). *—Molly Stevens*

# Beef & Black Bean Chili with Chipotle & Avocado

*Serves four.*

Three 15-ounce cans black
  beans, rinsed and drained

One 14.5-ounce can diced
  tomatoes

1 medium chipotle plus
  2 tablespoons adobo sauce
  (from a can of chipotles in
  adobo sauce)

2 tablespoons extra-virgin
  olive oil

1 pound 85% lean ground beef

Kosher salt

1 large red onion, finely diced

1½ tablespoons chili powder

2 teaspoons ground cumin

Juice of 1 lime

½ cup chopped fresh cilantro

Freshly ground black pepper

1 ripe avocado, pitted, peeled,
  and cut into medium dice

**This quick chili gets its thick, long-cooked texture from puréeing some of the black beans and the tomatoes to blend with the other ingredients. Lime-spiked avocado chunks are a cooling topping and, for some crunch, coarsely crumble about three handfuls of tortilla chips in a zip-top bag, and use them as an additional chili topping.**

Put one-third of the beans into the bowl of a food processor, along with the tomatoes and their juices, chipotle, and adobo sauce. Process until smooth and set aside.

Heat the oil in a 5- to 6-quart Dutch oven or similar heavy pot over medium-high heat until it's shimmering hot, about 2 minutes. Add the beef, season with ½ teaspoon salt, and cook, using a wooden spoon to break up the meat, until it loses its raw color, about 3 minutes. Transfer the beef to a large plate using a slotted spoon. Add half of the onion and ¼ teaspoon salt, and cook, stirring, until it begins to brown and soften, about 3 minutes. Reduce the heat to medium. Add the chili powder and cumin and cook for 20 seconds. Add the remaining black beans, the puréed bean mixture, and the beef and simmer for 10 minutes, stirring frequently. Add half of the lime juice, half of the cilantro, and salt and pepper to taste. If the chili is thicker than you like, it may be thinned with water.

Meanwhile, in a small bowl, mix the remaining lime juice and onion with the avocado. Season generously with salt and pepper. Serve the chili topped with the avocado mixture and remaining cilantro. —*Tony Rosenfeld*

# Asian-Glazed Braised Short Ribs

*Serves four to six.*

4 to 5 pounds meaty bone-in beef short ribs, preferably English style (see page 197)

1 tablespoon Chinese five-spice powder

2 teaspoons kosher salt; more as needed

2 teaspoons light or dark brown sugar

1 teaspoon coriander seeds, toasted (see page 59) and ground

½ teaspoon cumin seeds, toasted (see page 59) and ground

½ teaspoon coarsely ground black pepper

3 tablespoons peanut oil

2 large yellow onions, coarsely chopped

3 large cloves garlic, smashed and peeled

2 tablespoons peeled and coarsely chopped fresh ginger

One 12-ounce bottle lager beer, at room temperature; more if needed

1 cup homemade or canned low-salt beef or chicken broth; more if needed

2 tablespoons soy sauce

1 bay leaf

¼ cup honey

2 tablespoons fresh orange juice

2 tablespoons ketchup

1 teaspoon fish sauce

**These succulent ribs are first rubbed with an aromatic blend of spices the day before braising. The spices permeate the beef, adding a heady, exotic element to the flavor of the whole dish. Just before serving, they're painted with a sweet glaze and run under the broiler until sizzling.**

**Prepare the ribs a day ahead:** Trim any excess fat from the top of each rib down to the first layer of meat, but don't take off any of the silverskin or the tough-looking bits that hold the ribs together or onto the bone. Combine the five-spice powder, salt, brown sugar, coriander, cumin, and black pepper in a small bowl. Rub this mixture all over the ribs. Arrange the ribs in a single layer on a tray or baking dish, cover loosely with plastic, and refrigerate for 12 to 24 hours.

**Cook the ribs:** Place a rack in the lower third of the oven and heat the oven to 300°F. Pat the ribs dry with a paper towel, but don't rub off the spices. Heat 2 tablespoons of the oil in a 5- to 6-quart Dutch oven (or other heavy ovenproof pot with a lid) over medium heat until hot. Add only as many ribs as will fit without touching and brown them, turning with tongs until nicely browned on all sides, 3 to 4 minutes per side. Transfer to a platter and continue until all the ribs are browned.

Pour off and discard most of the fat from the pot. Add the remaining 1 tablespoon oil and return the pot to medium heat. Add the onions, season lightly with salt and pepper, and cook, stirring occasionally, until the onions soften and start to brown, 5 to 7 minutes. Add the garlic and ginger and cook, stirring, until fragrant, about 2 minutes more. Add the beer and bring to a full boil over high heat. Boil for 2 minutes, scraping the bottom of the pot with a wooden spoon to dislodge any caramelized bits. Pour in the broth and soy sauce, return to a boil, and reduce the heat to a simmer. Add the bay leaf. Return the ribs to the pot, preferably in a single layer, along with any juices. The ribs should be at least three-quarters submerged in the liquid. If necessary, add a bit more beer or broth.

Crumple a large sheet of parchment and smooth it out again. Arrange it over the pot, pressing it down so it nearly touches the ribs, allowing any overhang to extend up and over the edges of the pot. Put the lid in place and transfer the pot to the oven. Braise, turning the ribs with tongs every 45 minutes, until the meat is fork-tender and pulling away from the bone, about 2½ hours.

**Make the glaze:** While the ribs are braising, measure the honey in a 1-cup liquid measure, add the orange juice, ketchup, and fish sauce, and combine using a whisk or a fork.

Use tongs or a slotted spoon to carefully transfer the ribs (meaty side up) to a flameproof gratin dish or a shallow baking pan that is large enough

to accommodate them in a single layer. Don't worry if some bones slip out. Cover loosely with foil to keep warm.

Strain the braising liquid through a fine mesh sieve into a 4-cup measuring cup, pressing gently on the solids with a spoon to extract the liquid. When the fat has risen to the top, tilt the cup so you can spoon off as much fat as you can. You should have about 1 cup of thin but flavorful sauce. If necessary, simmer the sauce in a saucepan over medium-high heat until the flavor is concentrated to your liking. Season to taste. Keep warm.

Position a rack 6 inches from the broiler and heat the broiler to high. Generously brush the honey-orange juice glaze on the tops of the ribs. Slide the ribs under the broiler and broil until the surface of the ribs develops a shiny, almost caramelized glaze and you can hear them sizzle, about 4 minutes. Serve with the sauce on the side for dipping, or drizzle it over the ribs. *—Molly Stevens*

# Red Wine Marinated Braised Short Ribs

*Serves four to six.*

2 large cloves garlic, smashed and peeled

2 large sprigs fresh thyme

2 strips orange zest (about 1 inch wide, 3 to 4 inches long)

2 bay leaves

¼ teaspoon allspice berries, coarsely crushed in a mortar or with the side of a chef's knife

¼ teaspoon black peppercorns

4 whole cloves

One 750-ml. bottle hearty, dry red wine such as Zinfandel

4 to 5 pounds meaty bone-in beef short ribs, preferably English style (see below, far right)

1½ teaspoons kosher salt; more as needed

3 tablespoons extra-virgin olive oil

1 medium to large yellow onion, coarsely chopped

1 medium rib celery, coarsely chopped

1 medium carrot, peeled and coarsely chopped

Freshly ground black pepper

2 tablespoons tomato paste

2 cups homemade or canned low-salt beef or chicken broth

2 tablespoons red-wine vinegar; more to taste

**These fall-apart tender ribs get an extra boost of flavor from an overnight soak in a spiced wine marinade, which leaves the meat deeply infused with flavor. To make these ahead, braise the ribs, refrigerate, then finish the sauce once you've reheated the dish.**

**Marinate the ribs:** Make a sachet by wrapping the garlic, thyme, orange zest, bay leaves, allspice, peppercorns, and cloves in a 6-inch square of cheesecloth, pouch style. Tie the sachet closed with kitchen twine. Pour the wine into a medium saucepan, add the sachet, and bring to a boil. Reduce the heat and simmer gently for 10 minutes. Set the marinade aside to cool.

Meanwhile, trim away any excess fat from the top of each rib down to the first layer of meat, but don't remove the silverskin or tough-looking tissue that holds the ribs together or onto the bone. Put the ribs in a container wide enough to fit them in a snug single layer (a 9x13-inch dish works well), season with 1½ teaspoons salt, and pour over the cooled marinade and sachet. Cover with plastic wrap and refrigerate for 12 to 24 hours, turning the ribs once or twice.

**Cook the ribs:** Position a rack in the lower third of the oven and heat the oven to 300°F. Remove the ribs from the marinade, reserving the marinade and the sachet. Pat the ribs dry thoroughly with paper towels. Heat 2 tablespoons of the oil in a 5- to 6-quart Dutch oven (or other heavy ovenproof pot with a lid) over medium heat until hot. Add only as many ribs as will fit without touching and brown them, turning with tongs, until nicely browned on all sides, 3 to 4 minutes per side. Transfer to a platter and continue until all the ribs are browned.

Pour off and discard most of the fat from the pot. Add the remaining 1 tablespoon oil and return the pot to medium heat. Add the onion, celery, and carrot, season with salt and pepper, and cook, stirring occasionally, until browned in spots, about 8 minutes. Stir in the tomato paste and cook for 2 minutes, stirring. Add half of the reserved wine marinade, increase the heat to high, stir to scrape up any browned bits from the bottom of the pot, and bring to a boil. Continue to boil until the liquid is reduced by half, 2 to 4 minutes. Add the remaining marinade and reduce again by about half, another 3 to 5 minutes. Add the broth and vinegar and boil for 3 minutes.

Return the ribs to the pot, preferably in a single layer, along with any accumulated juices and the sachet. Crumple a large sheet of parchment and smooth it out again. Arrange it over the pot, pressing it down so it nearly touches the ribs, allowing any overhang to extend up and over the edges of the pot. Set the lid in place and transfer to the oven. Braise, turning the ribs with tongs every 45 minutes, until the meat is fork-tender and pulling away from the bone, about 2½ hours. Use tongs or a slotted spoon to carefully

transfer the ribs to a serving dish. Don't worry if some bones slip out. Cover loosely with foil to keep warm.

**Make the sauce:** Strain the braising liquid through a fine mesh sieve into a 4-cup measuring cup, pressing gently on the solids and sachet to extract the liquid. When the fat has risen to the top, tilt the measuring cup so that you can spoon off and discard as much of the fat as you can. You should have about 1 cup of sauce that's the consistency of a vinaigrette (only slightly thick). If the sauce seems thin and the flavor weak, transfer to a saucepan and simmer over medium-high heat until reduced to an intensity and consistency you like. Taste and season with salt and pepper. If the sauce needs more punch, add a splash of vinegar. Spoon the sauce over the ribs and serve. *—Molly Stevens*

## Buying short ribs: English vs. flanken

Short ribs are the meaty ends of the beef ribs from the hard-working chest and front shoulders of cattle. The meatiest short ribs with the best ratio of fat and bone come from the chuck—the labels might say beef chuck short ribs or arm short ribs. Look for well-marbled, meaty ribs, firmly attached to the bone, and without a huge amount of surface fat.

You may find short ribs cut two ways: English style, which are 2- to 4-inch segments with one section of rib bone, or flanken style, which are 1½- to 2-inch strips containing multiple bone segments. (The recipes in this book were tested with English-style ribs, but if you can only find the flanken-style ribs, they should work fine—they're practically interchangeable because the meat is the same texture.) Avoid boneless short ribs because meat cooked on the bone will provide the best flavor.

When trimming short ribs, remove only the thickest layers of external fat. Don't remove the internal layers of connective tissue or the ribs will begin to fall apart, and don't remove the silverskin or membrane that holds the meat to the bone.

# Short Rib Ragù

*Serves six.*

3 to 4 pounds meaty bone-in beef short ribs, preferably English style (see page 197)

Kosher salt and freshly ground black pepper

2 tablespoons extra-virgin olive oil

3 ounces thickly sliced pancetta (about three ¼-inch-thick slices) or 3 strips thick-cut bacon, cut into ½-inch squares

1 medium yellow onion, diced (about 1 heaping cup)

1 rib celery, diced (about ½ cup)

1 carrot, peeled and diced (about ½ cup)

½ cup sliced white mushrooms

3 large cloves garlic, coarsely chopped

2 tablespoons tomato paste

Pinch crushed red pepper flakes

½ cup dry white wine or dry vermouth

One 28-ounce can peeled whole tomatoes

These braised short ribs are transformed into a ragù that's fabulous over tube-shaped pasta and sprinkled with Parmesan (you might need to reserve some of the pasta cooking water for loosening the sauce). But you can also leave the ribs whole and serve them, along with their sauce, over mashed potatoes or polenta.

Position a rack in the lower third of the oven and heat the oven to 300°F.

**Cook the ribs:** Trim away any excess fat from the top of each rib down to the first layer of meat, but don't remove the silverskin or tough-looking tissue that holds the ribs together or onto the bone. Pat the ribs dry with paper towels and season them with salt and pepper. Heat the oil in a 5- to 6-quart Dutch oven (or other heavy ovenproof pot with a lid) over medium heat until hot. Add only as many ribs as will fit without touching, and brown them on all sides, turning with tongs until nicely browned, 3 to 4 minutes per side. Transfer to a platter and continue until all the ribs are browned.

Pour off and discard most of the fat from the pot. Return the pot to medium heat and add the pancetta or bacon. Cook, stirring occasionally, until the pancetta or bacon has rendered some of its fat but is not crisp, about 3 minutes. Add the onion, celery, carrot, mushrooms, and garlic and season with salt and pepper. Cook, stirring occasionally, until softened, about 8 minutes. Add the tomato paste and red pepper and cook for 2 minutes, stirring. Add the wine, increase the heat to medium high, stir to scrape up any browned bits from the bottom of the pot, and bring to a boil. Add the tomatoes and their juices and bring to a simmer.

Return the short ribs (and any juices) to the pot in a single layer, nestling them into the sauce. Crumple a large sheet of parchment and smooth it out again. Arrange it over the pot, pressing it down so it nearly touches the ribs, allowing any overhang to extend up and over the edges of the pot. Set the lid in place and transfer to the oven. Braise, turning the ribs with tongs every 45 minutes, until fork-tender and the meat is pulling away from the bone, about 2½ hours.

**Make the ragù:** Use tongs or a slotted spoon to carefully transfer the ribs to a shallow baking dish or wide bowl. Set aside until just cool enough to handle. Skim any visible surface fat from the braising liquid and bring to a gentle simmer over medium heat. If the tomatoes haven't broken up, break them up with a wooden spoon. If the sauce seems watery, increase the heat to medium high and simmer to thicken. If not, keep it warm. Taste for salt and pepper.

When the beef is cool enough to handle, remove the meat from the bones. Chop the meat into bite-size chunks or pull into large strips. Return the meat to the sauce and keep warm until ready to serve or, if making ahead, cool and refrigerate. —*Molly Stevens*

## Successful braised short ribs

Here are a few pointers for braising the best short ribs:

- **Choose a heavy pot** with a lid (ideally a Dutch oven) that will hold the ribs snugly. They can overlap (you can also position them on their sides), but don't stack them in a double layer.

- **Be sure the meat is thoroughly dried** before browning. Wet meat will stick to the pan and won't brown evenly.

- **Brown the ribs** over medium heat; it should take 3 to 4 minutes per side. If the ribs brown too quickly over heat that's too high, you could scorch the meat and the pan; brown the ribs too slowly and the meat will dry out.

- **Cover the pot** with a sheet of parchment before setting the lid in place. The parchment reduces the headspace in the pot, which helps produce a more concentrated sauce. Extending the parchment over the sides helps tighten the seal of the lid.

# Slow-Roasted Prime Rib

*Serves six to eight.*

One 3-bone beef rib roast
(about 6 pounds), preferably
from the small or loin end and
Prime grade

3 tablespoons fleur de sel or
other flaky sea salt

1½ tablespoons coarsely
cracked black peppercorns

1 tablespoon extra-virgin
olive oil

8 to 10 sprigs fresh rosemary

8 to 10 sprigs fresh thyme

10 medium cloves garlic,
smashed and peeled

3 tablespoons unsalted butter,
cut into ½-inch cubes

A prime rib roast, or standing rib roast, makes a spectacular choice for special-occasion entertaining. Cut from the back of the upper rib section of the steer, it usually comprises a total of seven ribs, which means it easily serves six people. Try to get a cut from the loin end—called the small end or first cut; it has a large rib eye, meaning more meat and less fat.

To make the roast as tender and succulent as can be, bring the beef to room temperature before cooking, roast it in a low oven, baste it often, and let it rest before carving.

Take the beef out of the refrigerator 2 hours before cooking so it can come to room temperature. After 30 minutes, season the meat on all sides with the fleur de sel and cracked pepper.

Position a rack in the center of the oven and heat the oven to 325°F.

Turn on the exhaust fan. Heat a 12-inch skillet over high heat for 1 minute. Swirl in the oil and, when the oil puts off its first wisp of smoke, place the beef in the pan and sear it on all the outer sides (not the cut sides) until well browned, 6 to 8 minutes total. Use a set of tongs to flip the beef; be careful of splattering oil. With two sets of tongs, transfer the beef, bone side down, to a roasting rack set in a small roasting pan. Arrange the rosemary, thyme, garlic, and butter evenly on top. Roast the beef, basting every 30 minutes with a bulb baster, until an instant-read thermometer inserted into the center reads 120° to 125°F for rare (about 2 hours), 130° to 135°F for medium-rare (about 2¼ hours), or 140° to 145°F for medium (about 2½ hours). Let the meat rest for at least 15 minutes before carving.

To serve, carve the roast as instructed at right and drizzle with the roasting juices, if you like. *—Suzanne Goin*

**tip:** Sear the rib roast in a skillet to give it a nice caramelized crust. Grab the bone side with a pair of tongs to help you flip it in the skillet.

## How to carve a beef rib roast

**1** Using a long, sharp slicing knife or chef's knife, cut the meat from the rib bones in one piece, following the contour of the bones

**2** Slice the meat across the grain into whatever thickness you prefer. If you like, cut between the bones to make individual ribs for gnawing on in the privacy of your kitchen.

# Osso Buco

*Serves six.*

Six 1¼-inch-thick veal shanks

Kosher salt and freshly ground
  black pepper

½ cup all-purpose flour for
  dredging

¼ cup extra-virgin olive oil

1 tablespoon unsalted butter

3 cups finely diced yellow
  onions (about 2 medium
  onions)

1 cup finely diced celery (about
  2 ribs)

¾ cup finely diced carrots
  (about 2 small carrots)

1 teaspoon dried oregano

¾ cup dry white wine

2 tablespoons tomato paste

One 28-ounce can Italian
  plum tomatoes, drained and
  chopped, juices reserved

1 cup homemade or canned
  low-salt chicken broth; more
  if needed

1 large sprig fresh thyme

1 bay leaf

1 tablespoon arrowroot mixed
  with 2 teaspoons broth or
  water (look for arrowroot
  in the spice section of your
  grocery store)

**For the gremolata:**

3 tablespoons finely chopped
  fresh flat-leaf parsley

2 large cloves garlic, minced

1 tablespoon finely grated
  lemon zest

2 anchovy fillets, minced

**This is the world's best make-ahead dish—it tastes amazing on the second day. The classic accompaniment is saffron risotto.**

Heat the oven to 350°F.

Tie the veal shanks around the middle with kitchen string (if they're not tied already) and season with salt and pepper. Put the flour in a dish. Dredge the shanks very lightly in flour, thoroughly shaking off the excess.

Have ready a roasting pan or baking dish large enough to hold the shanks in a single layer (9x13-inch works well). In a large, heavy skillet, heat 3 tablespoons of the oil over medium-high heat. Put three veal shanks in the pan and sear on both sides until nicely browned, 2 to 3 minutes per side. Move the shanks to the roasting pan. Repeat with the remaining three shanks.

Carefully pour off the fat in the pan and wipe it out with paper towels (it's fine if the browned bits remain in the pan bottom; just wipe away the used oil). Return the pan to medium heat and add the butter and remaining 1 tablespoon oil. When the butter is melted, add the onions, celery, carrots, oregano, and 1 teaspoon salt. Cook the vegetables, stirring occasionally, until soft and lightly browned, 15 to 20 minutes. Increase the heat to medium high, add the wine, and cook, scraping up any browned bits from the bottom of the pan with a wooden spoon, until the wine is reduced to about ¼ cup, about 3 minutes. Stir in the tomato paste. Add the tomatoes with their juices, the broth, thyme, bay leaf, ½ teaspoon salt, and a few grinds of pepper. Bring to a boil and pour the contents of the pan over the shanks. Cover tightly with heavy-duty aluminum foil.

Braise the veal until fork-tender, 1½ to 2 hours, checking the liquid occasionally. If it has cooked down, add enough broth to keep the level about halfway up the shanks. To check for doneness, pierce a shank with a fork. The meat should pull apart easily. Taste a morsel—it should feel soft and tender. Do not overcook or the veal will fall apart.

Gently brush most of the vegetable bits off the shanks. With a wide, flat metal spatula, carefully transfer the shanks to a dish. Strain the pan juices through a medium-mesh sieve into a saucepan, pressing hard on the solids with the spatula to extract as much sauce as you can. Bring the sauce to a simmer. Whisk in the arrowroot mixture and cook briefly to thicken. (If making the dish ahead, pour the sauce over the shanks. Let them cool a bit and then refrigerate for up to two days; reheat gently.)

**Make the gremolata:** Just before serving, combine the parsley, garlic, lemon zest, and anchovies. Add 2 tablespoons of the gremolata to the sauce (or sprinkle it over the reheated shanks if made ahead. Remove the strings from the shanks. Serve the osso buco topped with the sauce and a small sprinkling of the remaining gremolata. —*Perla Meyers*

## Flavorful and tender veal shanks

The intial step of searing is important in developing rich flavor in this dish. Sear the shanks to a deep golden brown. It takes only a few minutes on each side, so don't rush them and don't fiddle with them too much. You'll get the best crust if the shanks sit undisturbed as they're browning.

The beauty in this dish is the fork-tender texture of the meat. You'll know the meat is done when it starts to pull away from the bone and from the string tied around the shanks. If in doubt, taste a piece to check that it's succulent and tender.

# Roast Rack of Veal with a Lemon, Caper & Tarragon Crust

*Serves six.*

**One 6-rib trimmed (but not frenched) veal rack with the chine bone removed, 4 to 6 pounds after the chine is removed**

**Kosher salt and freshly ground black pepper**

**2 tablespoons vegetable oil**

**¼ medium red onion, roughly chopped (to yield about ½ cup)**

**¼ cup capers, drained and rinsed**

**¼ cup fresh lemon juice**

**2 tablespoons Dijon mustard**

**1 large egg**

**¾ cup coarse fresh breadcrumbs, preferably from a baguette or other firm white bread**

**⅓ cup roughly chopped fresh tarragon**

**¼ cup freshly grated Parmigiano-Reggiano (grated on the small holes of a box grater or on a rasp grater)**

**2 scallions (white and green parts), thinly sliced (about ½ cup)**

**Finely grated zest of 1 medium lemon**

**Rémoulade, for serving (see page 205)**

**Mild, tender rack of veal benefits from a crunchy crust made with the piquant flavors of capers, lemon, tarragon, and mustard. Save this cut for special occasions; though delicious, it's pricey and generally special order.**

Let the roast sit at room temperature for 30 minutes. Position a rack in the middle of the oven and heat the oven to 400°F. Put a roasting rack in a roasting pan or a heavy-duty rimmed baking sheet. (Line the pan with foil for easier clean-up, if you like.)

Season the veal liberally with salt and pepper on all sides. Turn on the exhaust fan. Heat the oil in a 12-inch skillet over medium-high heat. When the pan is very hot, brown the meat on all sides, including the ends, about 3 minutes per side. Transfer the meat to the roasting rack, meaty side up. Set aside to cool while you prepare the crust.

Purée the red onion, capers, lemon juice, mustard, and egg in a food processor. The mixture will be fairly loose.

In a small bowl, stir together the breadcrumbs, tarragon, Parmigiano, scallions, and lemon zest. When the veal is cool enough to touch, pour the onion purée over the meat, using a rubber spatula to spread it evenly. Some of the mixture will spill off the roast and into the pan—that's fine. Pat the breadcrumb mixture into the onion purée on the top and sides of the rack of veal, pressing slightly to help the crust adhere.

Roast the veal until an instant-read thermometer inserted into the thickest part of the meat reads 125° to 130°F for medium rare, 55 to 90 minutes, depending on the size of the rack. (To keep the crust from overbrowning, start checking on the roast after 30 minutes of cooking; when the crust is golden brown, tent it with a sheet of aluminum foil.)

Remove the veal from the oven and let rest for 10 minutes (it will continue to cook as it rests) before carving into single chops and serving with the rémoulade. Don't fret if some of the crust falls off the meat when you carve.

*—Gordon Hamersley*

# Rémoulade

*Yields about 1 cup.*

**If you're concerned about the uncooked egg yolk in this sauce, use a pasteurized egg.**

1 large egg yolk, preferably pasteurized

1 tablespoon white-wine vinegar

1 tablespoon Dijon mustard

Kosher salt and freshly ground black pepper

½ cup extra-virgin olive oil

½ cup vegetable oil

1 teaspoon finely snipped fresh chives

1 teaspoon capers, drained, rinsed, and chopped

¼ teaspoon minced fresh tarragon

In a medium bowl, whisk together the egg yolk, vinegar, mustard, 1 teaspoon salt, and several grinds of pepper until smooth. Very slowly whisk in the olive oil, followed by the vegetable oil. The mixture should be thick and emulsified like mayonnaise. Add the chives, capers, and tarragon. Season with more salt, pepper, and vinegar to taste. The rémoulade can be stored, covered, in the refrigerator for up to two days.

# Broiled Spice-Rubbed Lamb Chops

*Serves four to six.*

¼ cup plus 2 tablespoons
   extra-virgin olive oil

¼ cup fresh lime juice

12 lamb rib chops, preferably
   Australian (about 1¾ pounds
   total)

1 tablespoon ground cumin

2 teaspoons ground coriander

½ teaspoon ground cinnamon

¼ teaspoon ground cloves

¼ teaspoon ground cayenne

2 cloves garlic, minced

Kosher salt

**Australian lamb chops are generally small and tender, but any lamb rib chop will do, especially ones from locally raised lamb. Serve these fragrant, Indian-spiced chops with couscous tossed with chopped scallions and diced tomato; add a dollop of plain yogurt, if you like.**

In the oven, position a rack 4 inches from the broiler and heat the broiler to high.

Combine ¼ cup of the oil and the lime juice in a wide, shallow dish. Put the lamb chops in the oil mixture and marinate, turning once, for 10 minutes. Meanwhile, in a small bowl, combine the remaining 2 tablespoons oil, the cumin, coriander, cinnamon, cloves, cayenne, and garlic; stir well.

Remove the chops from the marinade and arrange them on a rack fitted over a foil-lined rimmed baking sheet. Sprinkle 2 teaspoons salt evenly all over both sides of the lamb. With a brush or your fingers, dab the spice mixture onto both sides of the chops. Broil, turning halfway through cooking, until the chops are nicely browned on both sides and cooked to your liking, 8 minutes total for medium. *–Julianna Grimes Bottcher*

# Leg of Lamb Stuffed with Spinach, Anchovies & Tarragon

**Don't be afraid of the anchovies. In fact, if you're serving guests who aren't anchovy fans, don't even mention them. As the anchovies cook, they melt away, leaving behind a full, savory flavor without anything "fishy" at all. You can stuff, roll, tie, and "poke" the lamb early on the day it's to be cooked. Refrigerate the rolled lamb, but take it out about a half-hour before roasting to bring it to room temperature.**

Heat the oven to 375°F.

Open the lamb leg and cut away any visible pockets of fat. Sprinkle the boned surface with salt and pepper. Set aside.

Cut 1 ounce (about 5) of the anchovies into about 50 pieces and set aside. Coarsely chop the remaining 3 ounces.

Drop the spinach into a large pot of boiling water, stir, and let cook for 1 minute. Drain in a colander and immediately refresh it under cold running water. Squeeze out the water and chop the spinach finely.

Combine the coarsely chopped anchovies with the tarragon and spinach. Spread the mixture over the boned surface of the lamb. Roll and fold the meat into a neat cylinder and tie it at 1-inch intervals closely and snugly with kitchen twine. Poke the point of a sharp paring knife into the exterior of the lamb; gently push the knife away from you to make a gaping hole. Push a garlic sliver and an anchovy piece into the hole. Repeat this process 1 inch away from the first hole; continue until the entire surface of the lamb is studded. Season the lamb with salt and pepper.

Put the leg on a rack in a roasting pan and roast until the internal temperature of the meat registers 125°F on a meat thermometer, about 1¼ hours. Allow the lamb to rest in a warm place for about 20 minutes before slicing. —*Paul Bertolli*

*Serves six to eight.*

One 6½-pound butterflied leg of lamb

Kosher salt and coarsely ground black pepper

4 ounces anchovy fillets, rinsed well (about 20)

½ pound fresh spinach leaves

2 tablespoons finely chopped fresh tarragon

4 large cloves garlic, cut into about 50 thin slivers

# Rack of Lamb with Herb & Olive Crust

*Serves six.*

⅓ cup pitted and very coarsely chopped Kalamata, Picholine, or Manzanilla olives, or a mix

¼ cup very coarsely chopped fresh flat-leaf parsley

1½ tablespoons fresh thyme leaves

2 cloves garlic, coarsely chopped

Pinch crushed red pepper flakes

1½ tablespoons mayonnaise

2 racks of lamb (7 to 8 ribs each), trimmed or frenched

Kosher salt and freshly ground black pepper

¾ cup fresh breadcrumbs

**A rack of lamb makes such a stunning presentation, and it's actually one of the easiest cuts of meat to roast.**

Position a rack in the center of the oven and heat the oven to 450°F.

Combine the olives, parsley, thyme, garlic, and red pepper in a mini food processor or a mortar. Process or pound with a pestle into a rough paste. Stir in the mayonnaise. Set aside.

Heat a large, heavy skillet over high heat. Season one rack with salt and pepper and set it in the hot skillet, meat side down. When the surface is nicely browned, about 2 minutes, turn the rack with tongs and brown the bottom for another 2 minutes. Remove and repeat with the second rack. If necessary, reduce the heat to medium high to keep the meat from scorching.

Spread the breadcrumbs in a pie plate. Coat the surface of the lamb with the olive paste, then roll the meat in the breadcrumbs, pressing the crumbs so they adhere. Arrange the racks, bone side down, in a roasting pan (you may need to interlock the bone ends to make them fit). Wrap the tips of the bones with a strip of foil so they don't burn.

Roast until an instant-read thermometer inserted in the thickest part of the meat reads 120° to 125°F for rare or 130° to 135°F for medium rare, 20 to 25 minutes. Let the racks rest for about 5 minutes. Cut down between the bones to carve into chops, then serve. *—Molly Stevens*

# Broiled Ham Steak with Sweet & Spicy Rosemary Glaze

While the ham broils, watch it closely to make sure that the glaze browns but doesn't burn. Don't limit yourself to orange marmalade either; any berry preserves, such as blackberry, would taste wonderful with the rosemary and mustard.

Arrange an oven rack so a broiler pan will be able to sit 2 to 3 inches away from the element and heat the broiler on high (or prepare a hot charcoal or gas grill fire).

Pat the ham steak dry with paper towels and put it in the broiler pan (or on a plate for transferring to the grill).

In a small saucepan, combine the marmalade, vinegar, rosemary, mustard, soy sauce, and red pepper. Bring to a simmer over medium heat and cook, whisking to combine, for 2 to 3 minutes. Keep warm. Brush one side of the ham with the glaze and broil (or grill) until the glaze is bubbling and browned, 4 to 5 minutes. Flip, brush on the remaining glaze, and cook the other side for another 4 to 5 minutes. Serve immediately. *—Molly Stevens*

*Serves two.*

One ¾- to 1-pound ham steak, ½ to ¾ inch thick

⅓ cup orange marmalade

1 tablespoon cider vinegar

1½ teaspoons chopped fresh rosemary

½ teaspoon dry mustard

½ teaspoon soy sauce

Pinch crushed red pepper flakes

# Hot Italian Sausage with Fresh-Corn Polenta

**Serves six.**

7 cups water

Kosher salt

2 cups yellow stone-ground cornmeal

3 cups fresh corn kernels (cut from 4 large or 6 small ears of corn)

¼ cup (½ stick) unsalted butter

½ cup freshly grated Parmigiano-Reggiano; more for shaving

12 links fresh hot Italian sausage

1 tablespoon extra-virgin olive oil

1 to 2 tablespoons roughly chopped fresh flat-leaf parsley

**While nothing compares with the tenderness and sweet flavor of fresh-picked corn, feel free to use frozen corn if you want to make this dish in the off-season. As a side dish, sauté some red peppers and slivered garlic, and finish with a few drops of balsamic vinegar.**

Bring the water to a boil in a heavy, 4-quart saucepan. Add 1 tablespoon salt and whisk in the cornmeal in a fine stream. Continue to whisk until the polenta begins to thicken, 1 to 3 minutes. Turn the heat to medium low, and cook, uncovered, stirring frequently with a wooden spoon. (If the polenta becomes too thick to stir, add hot water, a little at a time, until the polenta is soft but will still hold its shape.) After about 20 minutes (the polenta should be about three-quarters done), stir in the corn and continue to cook until the corn is tender and the polenta is tender and no longer gritty, 10 to 13 minutes more. Stir in the butter and grated Parmigiano. Taste the polenta and add more salt if necessary.

Meanwhile, using a small, sharp knife, pierce each sausage in 3 or 4 places. Heat the oil in a 12-inch skillet over medium heat until hot. Add the sausages and cook, turning occasionally, until they are cooked through and golden brown on all sides, 15 to 20 minutes. Transfer to a cutting board, cut them in half on the diagonal, and keep warm.

Spoon the polenta onto dinner plates and arrange the sausages on the polenta. Using a vegetable peeler, shave a few curls of Parmigiano on top, sprinkle with the parsley, and serve. —*Tasha DeSerio*

# Spicy Sausage, Escarole & White Bean Stew

**For a more mild-mannered dish, use a sweet Italian sausage, which will be beautiful with the beans and escarole. Toasted bread rubbed with garlic and drizzled with olive oil makes a nice accompaniment.**

Heat the oil in a heavy, 5- to 6-quart Dutch oven over medium heat. Add the onion and cook, stirring a few times, until tender, 5 to 6 minutes. Add the sausage, raise the heat to medium high, and cook, stirring and breaking up the sausage with a wooden spoon or spatula until lightly browned and broken into small (1-inch) pieces, 5 to 6 minutes. Add the garlic and cook for 1 minute, then stir in the beans. Add the escarole to the pot in batches; using tongs, toss with the sausage mixture to wilt the escarole and make room for more.

When all the escarole is in, add the broth, cover the pot, and cook until the beans are heated through and the escarole is tender, about 8 minutes. Season to taste with the vinegar and salt. Transfer to bowls, sprinkle each portion with some of the Parmigiano, and serve. *—Joanne McAllister Smart*

*Serves three to four.*

1 tablespoon extra-virgin olive oil

1 medium yellow onion, chopped

¾ pound hot Italian sausage, casings removed

2 medium cloves garlic, minced

Two 15-ounce cans cannellini beans, rinsed and drained

1 small head escarole, washed, lightly dried, and chopped into 1- to 2-inch pieces,

1 cup homemade or canned low-salt chicken broth

1½ teaspoons red-wine vinegar; more to taste

Kosher salt

¼ cup freshly grated Parmigiano-Reggiano

# Pork Scaloppine with Prosciutto, Sage & Caramelized Lemon

*Serves two to three.*

2 to 3 lemons

1 small pork tenderloin (about ¾ pound)

Kosher salt and freshly ground black pepper

18 medium or 12 large fresh sage leaves

6 slices prosciutto (preferably imported)

3 tablespoons all-purpose flour

3 tablespoons vegetable oil

2 tablespoons unsalted butter

⅓ cup sweet vermouth; more to taste

½ cup homemade or canned low-salt chicken broth

**Caramelizing the lemon slices softens their acidity and makes them edible, peel and all. Eating them is optional, but highly recommended. The lemon's tangy, slightly bitter flavor is a bright complement to the rich, salty prosciutto in this recipe.**

Trim a thick slice off each end of one of the lemons, then cut ⅛-inch-thick slices from the lemon center—you need 12 slices, so you may need a second lemon. Juice the ends and enough of the remaining lemons to obtain ¼ cup juice. Set the slices and juice aside.

Heat the oven to 200°F. Set a heatproof serving platter and a baking sheet lined with a paper towel in the oven.

Trim the pork tenderloin of any silverskin and excess fat, then cut it into 6 thick medallions of roughly equal weight. Place a piece of plastic wrap on the countertop. Put one pork piece on top of the plastic with one cut side up and cover with a second piece of plastic wrap. With a meat mallet (or heavy skillet), pound the meat into ¼-inch-thick scaloppine. Repeat with the other pieces. Sprinkle both sides lightly with salt and pepper. Top each scaloppine with two to three sage leaves and a prosciutto slice, folding any of the overlap underneath the scaloppine.

Put the flour in a shallow bowl. Dredge the scaloppine in the flour, shaking off the excess.

In a 12-inch skillet, heat 1½ tablespoons of the oil over medium-high heat. Cook three of the scaloppine, prosciutto side down first, until lightly browned and just cooked through, 1½ to 2 minutes per side. Transfer the scaloppine to the baking sheet in the oven. Add the remaining 1½ tablespoons oil and repeat with the three remaining scaloppine. Transfer them to the baking sheet and keep warm in the oven.

Remove the pan from the heat and pour off any remaining oil. Add 1 table-spoon of the butter and let it melt. Add the lemon slices in a single layer. Turn the heat to medium and cook the lemon slices until lightly browned on one side, 2 to 4 minutes. Turn the slices and add 2 tablespoons of the vermouth. Continue to cook until the vermouth cooks down to a glaze, 2 to 3 minutes. (The lemon slices will resemble bicycle wheels, with much of the flesh going into the sauce.) Transfer the lemon slices to the scaloppine in the oven, placing two slices on each one.

Pour the remaining (approximately 3 tablespoons) vermouth into the pan, bring to a boil over medium-high heat, and deglaze the pan by scraping up the browned bits from the bottom of the pan. Add the broth and lemon juice and boil until reduced to ¼ cup, 3 to 5 minutes. Remove from the heat and stir in the remaining 1 tablespoon butter. Taste the sauce for seasoning; if it's too acidic, add a touch more vermouth to the pan.

Transfer the scaloppine to the serving platter, spoon the sauce over, and serve immediately. *—Jennifer McLagan*

# Spinach & Mushroom-Stuffed Pork Tenderloin with Sherry Cream Sauce

*Serves four.*

5 tablespoons extra-virgin olive oil

3½ ounces fresh shiitake mushrooms, stemmed and caps thinly sliced (1½ cups)

Kosher salt and freshly ground black pepper

6 ounces baby spinach (5 lightly packed cups)

1 large pork tenderloin (about 1¼ pounds)

1 tablespoon lightly chopped fresh thyme leaves

¼ cup freshly grated Parmigiano-Reggiano

2 large shallots, finely diced (½ cup)

¾ cup homemade or canned low-salt chicken broth

2½ tablespoons sherry vinegar

2 tablespoons heavy cream

**While this recipe is fairly simple to make, the results are spectacular, perfect for a dinner party. The roast gets cut into slices that show a pretty spiral of meat and stuffing, and the light pan sauce adds a touch of elegance.**

Set a rack in the center of the oven and heat the oven to 450°F.

Heat 2 tablespoons of the oil in a heavy, ovenproof 12-inch skillet over medium-high heat until shimmering hot. Add the mushrooms, sprinkle with ½ teaspoon each of salt and pepper, and cook, stirring, until browned and tender, about 3 minutes. Stir in the spinach, sprinkle with salt, and cook, tossing well with tongs, until just wilted, about 2 minutes. Transfer the spinach mixture to a colander and set the skillet aside.

Trim the pork of any silverskin and excess fat. Butterfly the tenderloin by making a horizontal slice lengthwise through the tenderloin almost all the way to the other side. Open the meat flat, like a book. Cover with plastic wrap and, using a meat mallet or a small heavy skillet, lightly pound the pork so that it's ¼ inch thick. Rub the pork all over with 1 tablespoon of the oil, half of the thyme, and about ½ teaspoon each of salt and pepper. Squeeze any excess liquid from the spinach and mushrooms. Spread over the pork, leaving bare a 2-inch border along one long edge. Sprinkle on the Parmigiano. Starting with the long side that's covered with filling, roll the stuffed tenderloin toward the bare-border side so that it forms a cylinder, and secure it with four or five toothpicks or kitchen twine.

Wipe the skillet clean if necessary. Heat the remaining 2 tablespoons oil in the skillet over medium-high heat until shimmering hot. Sear the pork on all three non-seam sides until well browned, about 6 minutes total. Flip onto the seam side, then transfer the skillet to the oven. Cook until an instant-read thermometer inserted into the thickest part of the roast registers 140°F, 10 to 15 minutes.

Transfer the meat to a clean cutting board, tent with foil, and let rest for 10 minutes. Meanwhile, return the skillet to the stove over medium-high heat (be careful; the skillet's handle will be hot). Add the shallots, season with ¼ teaspoon salt, and cook, stirring, until they soften and brown, about 2 minutes. Add the broth, vinegar, and the remaining 1½ teaspoons thyme, and simmer briskly until the mixture reduces by a bit more than half, about 4 minutes. Stir in the cream and season with salt and pepper to taste.

Cut the pork into ½-inch-thick slices (a serrated blade works well) and serve with the sauce. —*Tony Rosenfeld*

# Yucatán Pork Tenderloin with Jícama, Avocado & Red Onion Salad

*Serves four to six.*

2 tablespoons minced garlic

2 tablespoons pure chile powder (preferably ancho)

1 tablespoon dried oregano (preferably Mexican)

1½ teaspoons ground cumin

Kosher salt and freshly ground black pepper

½ cup grapefruit juice, preferably fresh

2 small pork tenderloins (1 to 1¼ pounds each), trimmed of silverskin and excess fat

1 small jícama (about 1¼ pounds)

2 ripe Hass avocados

½ small red onion, peeled

2 tablespoons fresh lime juice

**The crunch of the jícama salad is the perfect complement to the buttery texture of the pork tenderloin. The meat is sweet but mild, so the spicy rub is a welcome accent.**

Position a rack in the center of the oven and heat the oven to 450°F.

In a small bowl, combine the garlic, chile powder, oregano, cumin, 1 teaspoon each salt and pepper, and enough of the grapefruit juice (about ¼ cup) to make a paste. Rub the paste all over the pork and set on a rack in a small roasting pan. Roast until the thickest part of each tenderloin registers 140° to 145°F on an instant-read thermometer, 25 to 30 minutes. Transfer to a clean cutting board to rest.

Meanwhile, peel the jícama and cut it into matchsticks about 4 inches long and ¼ inch thick. Cut the avocados in half, remove the pits and peel, and diagonally cut the flesh into thin slices. Slice the onion half as thinly as possible. In a large bowl, gently combine the jícama, avocado, and onion. Drizzle with the lime juice and remaining grapefruit juice and season to taste with salt and pepper.

Slice the pork and divide it equally on dinner plates. Serve with the jícama salad. *—Kate Hays*

# Grilled Spice-Rubbed Pork Tenderloin Steaks with Honey-Chipotle Barbecue Sauce

*Serves four to six.*

2 large pork tenderloins (2 to 2½ pounds total)

1 tablespoon chili powder

2 teaspoons ground cumin

2 teaspoons light brown sugar

2 teaspoons garlic powder

Kosher salt and freshly ground black pepper

½ cup honey

¼ cup cider vinegar

3 tablespoons tomato paste

1 chipotle, minced, plus 2 tablespoons adobo sauce (from a can of chipotles in adobo sauce)

1 teaspoon Dijon mustard

**These steaks are delicious with roasted sweet potato wedges seasoned with salt, pepper, and a little chili powder. When shopping for pork, look for all-natural tenderloins, which have the best flavor and texture. Avoid pork that has been injected with additives, which can give the meat an unpleasant, rubbery texture.**

Trim the pork of any silverskin and excess fat and cut each tenderloin on the diagonal into four pieces about 2 inches thick. Turn the pieces so they're lying on a cut side and, using a meat mallet or a small heavy skillet, lightly pound the steaks until they're about ½ inch thick.

In a small bowl, mix together the chili powder, cumin, brown sugar, garlic powder, 2 teaspoons salt, and 1 teaspoon pepper. Rub this spice mixture all over the pork and let it sit for at least 15 minutes at room temperature or refrigerate for up to 2 hours.

Heat a gas grill to medium-high or prepare a medium charcoal fire. When the grill is ready, cook the pork, covered, until nice grill marks form, about 3 minutes. Flip and continue cooking until just firm to the touch but still a little pink in the center (an instant-read thermometer inserted into the center of each steak should register 140°F), 3 to 4 more minutes.

Transfer the pork to a large serving platter and let rest, tented with foil. Meanwhile, stir together the honey, vinegar, tomato paste, chipotle and adobo sauce, and mustard, and season with salt and pepper to taste. Spoon the sauce over the pork and serve. *—Tony Rosenfeld*

## Cut pork tenderloin to suit the cooking method

**B**oneless, versatile pork tenderloin can be cut however you please—into thick steaks, thin medallions, or even as a butterflied roast. There's nothing tricky about cutting pork tenderloin; just use a sharp knife and cut the pork against the grain into even pieces.

### Steaks

Pounded flat, these are perfect for grilling, sort of like a tender version of a chop. The steaks are meaty enough that they won't cook through too quickly, which makes them great for the grill.

### Medallions

These thin rounds cook quickly, so they're best sautéed on the stovetop, which allows you to control the heat and avoid over-cooking the lean, tender meat.

### Butterflied

Butterflying means slicing the tenderloin almost all the way through lengthwise; you can then open the tenderloin like a book and stuff it with flavorful ingredients. Roasting is the way to go with stuffed tenderloin to ensure that it cooks evenly.

# Spicy Korean-Style Pork Medallions with Asian Slaw

See photo on page 179.

*Serves four to six.*

1 large or 2 small pork tenderloins (about 1¼ pounds)

⅓ cup soy sauce

¼ cup rice vinegar

3 tablespoons light brown sugar

2 medium cloves garlic, minced

1½ tablespoons peeled and minced fresh ginger

1 tablespoon Asian sesame oil

1 tablespoon Asian chile sauce (like Sriracha)

1 pound Napa cabbage, thinly sliced (about 6 cups)

1 cup grated carrots (about 2 medium carrots)

4 scallions (both white and green parts), trimmed and thinly sliced

5 tablespoons canola or peanut oil

Kosher salt

**Mild pork takes on the sweet-spicy flavors of a Korean-inspired marinade, which doubles as a sauce. The pork medallions sit right on a cabbage slaw, which lets all the wonderful juices mix and mingle.**

Trim the pork of any silverskin and excess fat, and cut on the diagonal into ½-inch-thick medallions.

In a small measuring cup, whisk together the soy sauce, 2 tablespoons of the vinegar, 2 tablespoons of the brown sugar, the garlic, ginger, ½ tablespoon of the sesame oil, and 2 teaspoons of the chile sauce. Toss ½ cup of this mixture with the pork medallions in a large bowl; reserve the remaining mixture to use as a sauce. Let the pork sit at room temperature for 25 minutes or refrigerate for up to 2 hours.

Meanwhile, in another large bowl, toss the cabbage and carrots with half of the scallions, 1 tablespoon of the canola oil, 1 teaspoon salt, and the remaining 2 tablespoons vinegar, 1 tablespoon brown sugar, ½ tablespoon sesame oil, and 1 teaspoon chile sauce. Let sit for 15 minutes, toss again, and transfer to a large serving platter.

Heat 2 tablespoons of the canola oil in a heavy, 12-inch skillet over medium-high heat until shimmering hot. Remove the pork from the marinade, shaking off the excess, and transfer the pork to a clean plate. Discard the marinade. Add half of the pork medallions to the skillet, spacing them evenly. Cook them without touching until well browned, about 2 minutes. Flip and cook until the pork is just cooked through (slice into a piece to check), about 2 more minutes. Set the pork on top of the slaw. Pour out the oil and wipe the pan with paper towels (if the drippings on the bottom of the pan look like they may burn, wash the pan). Return the pan to medium-high heat. Add the remaining 2 tablespoons canola oil and cook the remaining medallions in the same manner. Top the slaw with the remaining pork and pour the reserved soy-ginger sauce over the medallions. Serve immediately, sprinkled with the remaining scallions. *—Tony Rosenfeld*

# Sautéed Pork Chops with Grape, Rosemary & Red-Wine Pan Sauce

**Use pork chops that are ½ to 1 inch thick so they cook quickly without drying out. To add a tangy note to the sauce, finish with a few drops of balsamic vinegar when you swirl in the butter.**

Season both sides of the pork chops with salt and pepper. Heat 1 tablespoon of the butter in a heavy, 10-inch or larger skillet on medium-high heat. When the butter has stopped foaming, add four of the pork chops and sear until the edges are browned and the middles are just beginning to brown, 1½ to 2 minutes. Flip the chops and cook until just cooked through, 30 to 60 seconds. Transfer the pork to a plate and cover with foil. Repeat with the remaining chops and transfer to the plate.

Add the grapes, wine, and rosemary to the skillet and bring the mixture to a boil, scraping the skillet with a wooden spoon to incorporate any browned bits stuck to the bottom into the sauce. Boil until syrupy, 3 to 4 minutes. Add the broth and any accumulated juices from the pork chops and boil the sauce, stirring occasionally, until reduced by about half, another 3 to 4 minutes. Reduce the heat to low, add the remaining 2 tablespoons butter, and swirl around in the pan until melted. Serve the chops topped with the sauce. *−Eva Katz*

*Serves four.*

8 thin boneless pork chops (about 1¼ pounds total)

Kosher salt and freshly ground black pepper

3 tablespoons unsalted butter

1 cup seedless red grapes, halved

½ cup dry red wine

1 teaspoon chopped fresh rosemary

½ cup homemade or canned low-salt chicken broth

# Grilled Caribbean-Spice Pork Chops with Pineapple Salsa

*Serves six.*

**For the spice rub:**

1 tablespoon dark brown sugar

2 teaspoons ground coriander

2 teaspoons ground cumin

1½ teaspoons garlic powder

1 teaspoon kosher salt

¾ teaspoon ground ginger

½ teaspoon turmeric

**For the salsa:**

½ to ¾ medium fresh pineapple, peeled, quartered, cored, and cut into small dice (about 2 cups)

4 large radishes, trimmed and cut into small dice (about ¾ cup)

½ medium orange or yellow bell pepper, cored and cut into small dice (about ⅔ cup)

3 tablespoons chopped fresh cilantro

2 tablespoons fresh lime juice; more to taste

Kosher salt and freshly ground black pepper

**For the chops:**

6 boneless pork loin chops, about ¾ inch thick

1½ tablespoons canola or vegetable oil

**Make your spice rub and salsa before you grill the meat.**

**Make the spice rub:** In a small bowl, combine the brown sugar, coriander, cumin, garlic powder, salt, ginger, and turmeric.

**Make the salsa:** In a medium bowl, combine the pineapple, radishes, bell pepper, cilantro, lime juice, and ¼ teaspoon each salt and pepper. Let stand while you grill the meat. Before serving, taste and adjust the lime juice, salt, and pepper to taste.

**Grill the chops:** Build a hot charcoal fire or heat a gas grill with all burners on high for at least 10 minutes. While the grill heats, lightly coat both sides of the pork chops with the oil and rub with the spice rub. Clean the hot grate with a wire brush; oil the grate.

Grill the meat (uncovered for charcoal; covered for gas) over direct heat on the hottest part of the grill, taking care not to crowd the meat. Cook until the meat forms impressive grill marks on one side, 2 to 3 minutes. Turn and continue to grill (uncovered for charcoal; covered for gas) until the meat is just firm to touch and just cooked through, 3 to 4 minutes, depending on thickness.

Transfer the chops to a serving platter and let rest for 5 minutes. Serve with the salsa spooned alongside or over the chops. *—Pam Anderson*

# 7
# Fish &
# Shellfish

p230

p254

**Etta's New Crab Cakes**
**(recipe on page 264)**

# Spice-Rubbed Tilapia with Tomatillo, Black Bean & Mango Salad

*Serves four.*

One 15-ounce can black beans, drained and rinsed

½ pound tomatillos, papery covering discarded, fruit rinsed, and cut into small dice

1 ripe medium mango, peeled, pitted, and cut into small dice

½ cup small-diced red onion (from about a quarter of a large onion)

⅓ cup fresh lime juice

⅓ cup plus 2 tablespoons vegetable oil

¼ cup chopped fresh cilantro

Freshly ground black pepper

1½ teaspoons chili powder

1 teaspoon ground cumin

1 teaspoon dried oregano

Kosher salt

4 skinless tilapia fillets (about 4 ounces each)

**Tomatillos, which look like small green tomatoes surrounded by a papery husk, add their refreshing flavor to this colorful accompaniment. For other salad combinations, try chickpeas or red beans in place of the black beans, and red tomato or cucumber in place of the tomatillo.**

Put a heatproof serving platter on a rack in the center of the oven and heat the oven to 200°F.

In a medium bowl, combine the beans, tomatillos, mango, red onion, lime juice, ⅓ cup of the oil, the cilantro, and a few grinds of pepper; toss gently. Let the salad sit at room temperature while you cook the fish.

Mix ¼ teaspoon pepper with the chili powder, cumin, oregano, and 1 teaspoon salt. Rub both sides of the tilapia fillets with the mixture. In a 12-inch nonstick skillet, heat the remaining 2 tablespoons oil over medium-high heat until hot. Cook two of the tilapia fillets until lightly browned and the flesh is opaque and cooked through, about 2 minutes per side. Transfer the fish to the platter in the oven to keep warm while you cook the remaining fillets.

Spoon half of the salad on top of the cooked fillets and serve with the remaining salad on the side. *—Leslie Glover Pendleton*

It takes just three easy steps to boost the flavor of this mild, quick-cooking fish.

1 **Coat** Coat the fillets with breadcrumbs, herbs, spices, or nuts, which will form a flavorful crust.

2 **Sear or pan-fry** Use either method to set the coating and give the fish a browned exterior and rich flavor.

3 **Garnish** Give tilapia a final flavor boost with a tangy sauce or salad, a splash of vinegar, or just a squeeze of lemon.

# Herb-Coated Tilapia with Lemon

*Serves four.*

1 medium lemon

¾ cup chopped fresh herbs (any combination of parsley, thyme, mint, chives, or cilantro)

4 skinless tilapia fillets (about 4 ounces each)

Kosher salt and freshly ground black pepper

2 tablespoons extra-virgin olive oil

**Tilapia has firm white flesh and a mild, sweet flavor that goes with just about everything. If you're serving this dish to company, you might want to cut wedges from a lemon that hasn't been zested. To test for doneness, use the tip of a knife to peek into the middle of a fillet; the flesh should be opaque but still moist.**

Finely grate the zest from the lemon, then cut the lemon in quarters and set aside.

Mix the herbs and lemon zest on a plate. Sprinkle the fillets with ¾ teaspoon salt and ¼ teaspoon pepper and coat both sides of each fillet with herbs, pressing them on so they adhere.

In a 12-inch nonstick skillet, heat the oil over medium heat until hot. Cook the tilapia until the flesh is opaque and just cooked through, about 2 minutes per side. Serve the tilapia with the lemon quarters, for squeezing at the table.
*—Leslie Glover Pendleton*

**tip:** In the supermarket, tilapia is usually sold skinned and filleted. Sometimes the flesh is solid white, sometimes it has a pinkish tone, and often the fillets have a stripe of dark meat down the middle—all of these variations are fine. However, make sure that your fillets have a firm appearance, with no soft spots. Like all fish, tilapia should have a delicate, clean aroma of the sea.

# Crispy Breaded Tilapia
# with Classic Tartar Sauce

*Serves four.*

½ cup mayonnaise

2 tablespoons minced red onion

2 tablespoons sweet pickle
  relish or dill pickle relish

2 tablespoons minced fresh
  flat-leaf parsley

1 tablespoon capers, drained,
  rinsed, and chopped

2 teaspoons fresh lemon juice

⅓ cup all-purpose flour

2 large eggs

2 cups fresh white breadcrumbs

Kosher salt and freshly ground
  black pepper

4 skinless tilapia fillets (about
  4 ounces each)

Vegetable oil for the pan

1 large lemon, cut into wedges

**If you're in the mood for fried fish, this will hit the spot—without any deep frying. Tartar sauce is a cinch to make and tastes so much better than the stuff in jars. You can even make it a few days ahead.**

Position a rack in the center of the oven and heat the oven to 200°F. Line a baking sheet with paper towels and set aside.

In a small bowl, stir together the mayonnaise, onion, relish, parsley, capers, and lemon juice. Cover and refrigerate.

Line up three wide shallow dishes. Put the flour in the first; beat the eggs lightly in the second; put the breadcrumbs in the third. Season the tilapia with salt and pepper. Working with one fillet at a time, coat it with flour and shake off the excess. Then dip the fillet in the egg and dredge it in the breadcrumbs, patting them on to help them adhere. Set each breaded fillet on a plate or tray as you finish it.

Pour the oil ¼ inch deep into a 10- to 12-inch skillet. Heat over medium heat until it is hot but not smoking, or until a breadcrumb sizzles and browns quickly when dropped in the oil. Cook two of the fillets until they are crisp and browned, 2 to 3 minutes per side. Transfer to the baking sheet, sprinkle with salt, and keep warm in the oven while you cook the remaining two fillets.

Serve immediately with lemon wedges and the tartar sauce.

*—Leslie Glover Pendleton*

# Peanut-Crusted Tilapia with Frizzled Ginger & Scallions

*Serves two.*

⅓ cup vegetable oil

3 medium scallions, cut lengthwise into fine matchsticks (about ½ cup)

One 2x1 ¼-inch knob of fresh ginger, peeled and cut into fine matchsticks (about ¼ cup)

Kosher salt

2 tablespoons all-purpose flour

1 large egg

½ cup salted peanuts, finely chopped

2 skinless tilapia fillets (about 4 ounces each)

4 teaspoons seasoned rice vinegar, or to taste

Freshly ground black pepper

**Crispy ginger and scallions are simply irresistible; delicious with this fish, they're also a great garnish for scallops and even mashed potatoes. Instead of peanuts, try coating the tilapia with cashews or sesame seeds.**

In a 10- to 12-inch, heavy, nonstick skillet, heat the oil over medium-high heat until hot. Add the scallions and ginger and cook, stirring occasionally, until just golden, with some green still visible on the scallions, 2 to 4 minutes. Remove the skillet from the heat and, with a slotted spoon, transfer the vegetables to paper towels to drain (leave the oil in the skillet). Toss the ginger and scallions lightly with salt.

Line up three wide, shallow dishes. Put the flour in the first; beat the egg in the second; put the peanuts in the third. Season the tilapia fillets with salt. Dredge one fillet in the flour, shaking off the excess. Dip the fillet in the egg, then coat it with peanuts. Set the fillet on a plate and repeat with the second fillet.

Reheat the oil in the skillet over medium-high heat. Add the fillets and cook until golden on each side and the flesh is opaque and cooked through, 3 to 4 minutes per side (reduce the heat if they brown too fast).

Place the tilapia on dinner plates, sprinkle with the rice vinegar and pepper to taste, top with the frizzled vegetables, and serve immediately.

*—Leslie Glover Pendleton*

# Flounder Poached in Coconut, Ginger & Basil Broth

*Serves six.*

6 skinless flounder fillets (1 to
   1½ pounds total)

Kosher salt

Ground white pepper

1 tablespoon grated fresh
   ginger

1 cup roughly chopped fresh
   sweet basil or Thai basil

1 tablespoon vegetable or
   extra-virgin olive oil

1 large shallot, thinly sliced
   (about ¼ cup)

One 2-inch piece fresh
   ginger, peeled and cut into
   matchsticks

2 cloves garlic, minced

2 ribs celery, sliced ⅛ inch
   thick on the diagonal (about
   2 cups)

1 small fresh hot red chile (or
   jalapeño), sliced into thin
   rings (seeds intact)

1 cup homemade or canned low-
   salt chicken broth

One 5.5-ounce can unsweetened
   coconut milk

4 scallions, thinly sliced on the
   diagonal (about 1 cup)

2 tablespoons fish sauce

2 tablespoons fresh lime juice

1 tablespoon mirin (Japanese
   sweet rice wine)

1 teaspoon finely grated
   lime zest

1 cup jasmine rice, cooked
   according to package
   directions

**For a festive presentation, try tying the fillets with dark green scallion tops instead of using toothpicks. Dip the green tops in boiling water for 15 seconds so they're pliable and tie in a loose knot around the rolled fish fillets. If you can't find the smaller size can of coconut milk called for in this recipe, measure out ¾ cup from a larger can; the remainder will keep in the freezer for up to a month.**

Set the fillets on a work surface, skin side down. Season lightly with salt and white pepper. Divide the 1 tablespoon grated ginger among the fillets and spread it over them as evenly as you can. Sprinkle about 1 tablespoon of the chopped basil over the fillets. Roll each fillet, starting at the thicker end. Secure each roll with a toothpick and sprinkle lightly with a little more salt and white pepper. Set aside.

In a 4-quart Dutch oven with a tight-fitting lid (or other heavy-duty pot just large enough to hold the fish snugly), heat the oil over high heat until it shimmers. Add the shallot, ginger matchsticks, and garlic and cook for 1 minute, stirring constantly. Add the celery and cook for 30 seconds, stirring constantly. Add the chile and continue to cook, stirring, until the celery starts to soften, about 2 minutes. Add the broth and heat for 2 minutes. Turn off the heat and arrange the rolled fish in a single layer over the celery mixture. Pour the coconut milk over the fish and turn the heat to high. As soon as the coconut milk comes to a simmer, reduce the heat to medium low and cover. Simmer until the fish is opaque and cooked through, 8 to 10 minutes. If you're unsure, flake apart a section to see if it's done. Remove the pot from the heat. Carefully transfer the fish with a slotted spoon or fish spatula to a small, warm platter.

Return the pot to high heat. Add the remaining basil, along with the scallions, fish sauce, lime juice, mirin, and lime zest. Bring the broth just to a simmer, then taste and add more salt or mirin if needed.

For each serving, place a small mound of hot jasmine rice in a shallow bowl, top with a fish roll, and remove the toothpick. Ladle the hot broth over each fish roll and serve immediately. *—Jessica Bard*

# Broiled Flounder with a Parmesan "Caesar" Glaze

*Serves four to six.*

8 skinless flounder fillets (4 to 5 ounces each)

Kosher salt and freshly ground black pepper

⅓ cup good-quality mayonnaise

½ cup freshly grated Parmigiano-Reggiano, (preferably grated on the small holes of a box grater)

1½ tablespoons loosely packed finely grated lemon zest (from 1 large lemon)

1 tablespoon fresh lemon juice

½ teaspoon Worcestershire sauce

1 small clove garlic, minced

2 tablespoons coarsely chopped fresh flat-leaf parsley

**The flavors of Caesar salad dressing—Parmesan cheese, lemon juice, Worcestershire sauce, and garlic—perfectly accent mild flounder fillets.**

Position a rack 4 inches from the broiler element and heat the broiler on high. Spray a broiler pan with nonstick cooking spray.

Lightly season both sides of the fillets with salt and pepper. Set a fillet before you, skinned side up, and starting at the narrow end, roll it up. Repeat with the remaining fillets. Arrange the rolls, seam side down, in the prepared pan. Broil until the tops are lightly browned, 7 to 8 minutes.

Meanwhile, whisk together the mayonnaise, Parmigiano, lemon zest and juice, Worcestershire, and garlic in a small bowl. Season with pepper to taste.

When the tops of the fillets are lightly browned, remove the fish from the broiler. Spread equal amounts of the mayonnaise mixture over the top of each fillet. Return to the broiler until the topping is golden brown and bubbling, 1½ to 2 minutes.

Transfer the fillets to four dinner plates and sprinkle with the parsley. Serve immediately. —*Rick Rodgers*

# Sautéed Snapper with Broken Black-Olive Vinaigrette

**A "broken" vinaigrette is simply one that's not meant to be creamy and emulsified. The olives, oil, lemon zest and juice will drizzle themselves all over the fish, creating different flavor combinations in every bite. To turn this delicate fish during cooking, use a thin, angled spatula with a curved lip.**

Mix the olives, ⅓ cup of the oil, the lemon zest and juice, garlic, and red pepper together in a small bowl with a fork; the vinaigrette doesn't need to emulsify. Season with salt to taste.

Pull out any bones in the fish with needlenose pliers or tweezers. Season both sides of the fish with salt and dredge very lightly in the flour. Heat 2 tablespoons of the oil in a large nonstick skillet over medium heat. When hot, add two of the fillets, skin side up; cook until light golden brown, 4 to 5 minutes. With a thin, slotted metal spatula, turn the fish and cook until the second side is lightly browned and the fish is cooked through, about 3 minutes. Transfer the fillets, skin side down, to a plate and cover to keep warm. Repeat with the remaining fillets.

Stir the vinaigrette, toss enough of it with the arugula to coat lightly (1 to 2 tablespoons), and portion it among four plates. Lay the fish on top, spoon the remaining vinaigrette over the fillets, and serve with a wedge of lemon.

*—Rick Rodgers*

*Serves four.*

⅓ cup coarsely chopped pitted Kalamata olives

⅓ cup plus 2 tablespoons extra-virgin olive oil

1½ tablespoons loosely packed finely grated lemon zest (from 1 large lemon)

1 tablespoon fresh lemon juice

1 small clove garlic, minced

⅛ teaspoon crushed red pepper flakes

Kosher salt

4 skin-on snapper fillets (about 6 ounces each)

⅓ cup all-purpose flour for dredging

5 ounces (5 cups loosely packed) baby arugula, washed and spun dry

4 lemon wedges, for serving

# Sichuan Braised Cod

*Serves four.*

½ cup plus 2 teaspoons cornstarch

2 tablespoons rice vinegar; more to taste

¾ cup homemade or canned low-salt chicken broth

1½ tablespoons soy sauce

1 tablespoon ketchup

1½ pounds thick cod fillets ("cod loins"), cut into 4 uniform pieces

Kosher salt and freshly ground black pepper

2 large eggs

3 tablespoons canola or peanut oil

10 dried Thai or other small whole chiles

4 scallions, thinly sliced, white and green parts separated

1½ tablespoons peeled and minced fresh ginger

**Most of us aren't accustomed to cooking something as delicate as fish fillets at very high heat. To avoid overcooking, make sure all the components are prepped and ready before you begin. Serve the fish with plenty of steamed white rice to soak up the sauce.**

In a small bowl, mix together 2 teaspoons of the cornstarch and the vinegar. Add the broth, soy sauce, and ketchup.

Season the fish with ½ teaspoon salt and ½ teaspoon pepper. Spread the remaining ½ cup cornstarch on a plate and beat the eggs together in a wide bowl. Dredge the fish in the cornstarch. Heat 2 tablespoons of the oil in a 12-inch nonstick pan over medium-high heat until shimmering hot. Soak the fish in the eggs for a couple of seconds, then add to the pan. Cook, flipping after 3 minutes, until the fish is browned and a little firm to the touch, about 5 minutes total (it should not be cooked all the way through). Transfer the fish to a large plate.

Add the remaining 1 tablespoon oil to the pan, then the chiles, scallion whites, and ginger. Cook, stirring, until the scallions become translucent and browned in places, about 2 minutes. Give the ketchup-cornstarch mixture a quick stir, then pour it into the pan. It should come to a boil and thicken quickly. Reduce the heat to medium low, return the fish to the pan, and flip it a couple of times to coat it in the sauce. Cover the pan, leaving the lid slightly askew, and cook until the fish is just cooked through and starting to flake, 3 to 5 minutes. Taste the sauce for salt and vinegar and add more to taste.

Serve immediately with the sauce spooned over the fish and sprinkled with the scallion greens. *—Tony Rosenfeld*

# Roasted Trout with Lemon & Walnut Browned Butter

*Serves four to six.*

8 rainbow trout fillets (2 to
  2½ pounds total)

Kosher salt and freshly ground
  black pepper

½ cup (1 stick) unsalted butter

¼ cup finely chopped fresh flat-
  leaf parsley

2 tablespoons finely chopped
  fresh tarragon

Twenty-four ⅛-inch-thick lemon
  slices (from 2 to 3 lemons)

¼ cup chopped walnuts

**Quick to make yet delicious and beautiful, this brightly flavored fish dish is perfect for an impromptu dinner with friends. In the store, rainbow trout are sometimes sold as whole, cleaned fish. If this is how you find them, ask the fish seller to cut them into fillets and remove the fins. Serve with buttered baby red potatoes tossed with chopped fresh dill.**

Position a rack in the center of the oven and heat the oven to 450°F.

Arrange the trout skin side down on a foil-lined rimmed baking sheet. Sprinkle 2 teaspoons salt and 1 teaspoon pepper evenly over the trout. In a small saucepan, melt the butter and drizzle 4 tablespoons of it evenly over the fillets. Sprinkle the trout evenly with the parsley and tarragon. Arrange 3 lemon slices over each fillet. Roast until the fillets flake easily when pricked with a fork, 10 to 12 minutes.

Meanwhile, set the saucepan with the remaining melted butter over medium heat. Cook until lightly browned and fragrant, 3 to 5 minutes. Immediately remove from the heat and stir in the walnuts; keep warm.

When the trout is done, use a large spatula to transfer the fillets to dinner plates—if the skin sticks to the foil, lift up only the flesh. Swirl the walnut butter around, then spoon it over the trout and serve. —*Julianna Grimes Bottcher*

# Creole Salmon Cake Sandwiches

*Yields eight cakes; serves four.*

**For the salmon cakes:**

1 pound salmon fillets (preferably wild), skin and pin bones removed, then cut into 1-inch chunks

1 large egg

1 tablespoon country-style (grainy, but not whole-grain) Dijon mustard

2 teaspoons finely grated lemon zest

1 teaspoon hot sauce, preferably Crystal® brand

Kosher salt and freshly ground black pepper

1 tablespoon chopped fresh thyme

2 tablespoons extra-virgin olive oil

**For the sandwiches:**

Four 5- to 6-inch hoagie or sub rolls or lengths of soft French or Italian bread from a baguette-type loaf (the bread shouldn't be too dense nor the crust too crunchy)

½ cup mayonnaise, or to taste

Giardiniera Relish (see recipe below)

The relish that accompanies these slightly spicy cakes is a bit like the pickley olive salad you get in a New Orleans muffuletta sandwich. Perhaps that's why the relish and cakes taste so good tucked into a hoagie roll. Be careful not to process the salmon too finely; you don't want a completely smooth purée. If you don't have a food processor, you can use a chef's knife to very finely chop the raw fish.

**Make the salmon cakes:** Put the salmon in a food processor and pulse until chopped medium coarse, two or three 1-second pulses. Take care not to overprocess; there should still be some chunks. In a medium bowl, lightly beat the egg. Add the salmon and combine with a rubber spatula. Add the mustard, lemon zest, hot sauce, 1½ teaspoons salt, and ½ teaspoon pepper; mix until well combined. Cover the bowl with plastic and chill for at least 30 minutes or up to 4 hours.

Remove the salmon mixture from the refrigerator, turn it out onto a baking sheet, and portion it into eight equal mounds. With wet hands, gently shape each one into a 2½-inch-wide patty. Sprinkle a pinch of the thyme on both sides of each cake.

Heat the oil in a 12-inch nonstick skillet over medium-high heat. When the oil is hot, add the cakes and reduce the heat to medium. Cook the cakes, turning once, until nicely browned on both sides and the interior no longer looks raw, 5 to 6 minutes total. Be careful not to overcook. Transfer the cakes to a plate and cover to keep them warm.

**Make the sandwiches:** Slice each roll in half and pull out a little bit of the insides. Spread some mayonnaise on the bottom halves of each roll and place two salmon cakes over each bottom half. Scoop some of the giardiniera relish over the top halves of the rolls, including some of the juices, and gently press the two sides of each sandwich together. Cut each sandwich in half and serve. *—Tom Douglas*

## Giardiniera Relish

*Yields about 2 cups.*

Giardiniera is an Italian-style mixed pickle that typically contains pearl onions, cauliflower, hot peppers, cucumbers, carrots, and celery. You can find it in glass jars in the supermarket.

2 cups drained Italian giardiniera pickle

½ cup coarsely chopped pimento-stuffed green olives

¼ cup extra-virgin olive oil

3 tablespoons chopped fresh flat-leaf parsley

Freshly ground black pepper

Stem and seed any whole peppers from the giardiniera, then coarsely chop all the giardiniera. Put the chopped vegetables in a medium bowl and add the olives, oil, parsley, and ¼ teaspoon pepper. Mix well. Serve immediately or refrigerate, covered, for up to five days.

# Baked Salmon with Citrus Vinaigrette

*Serves four.*

1 medium shallot, finely diced

1½ tablespoons Champagne
vinegar or white-wine vinegar

2 teaspoons fresh lemon juice

2 teaspoons fresh orange juice

1½ teaspoons finely chopped
lemon zest

1½ teaspoons finely chopped
orange zest

Kosher salt

Four 5-ounce skinless, center-
cut salmon fillets

¼ cup extra-virgin olive oil;
more for the salmon

Fresh chervil leaves or 1 tablespoon roughly chopped fresh
cilantro, for garnish

**This salmon goes beautifully with a simple salad of shaved fennel and radishes tossed with fresh lemon juice. The citrus vinaigrette is also lovely on lighter fish, such as sole or flounder, or even drizzled over sliced grilled chicken breast.**

Position a rack in the center of the oven and heat the oven to 400°F.

In a small bowl, combine the shallot, vinegar, citrus juices and zests, and a pinch of salt. Let the mixture sit for 5 to 10 minutes.

Meanwhile, season the salmon with salt, put it on an oiled rimmed baking sheet, and drizzle a thin stream of oil on top. Bake until it's done to your liking, about 6 minutes for medium, and 8 minutes for medium well, (keep in mind that it will continue to cook after it comes out of the oven).

Whisk the ¼ cup oil into the shallot mixture, taste, and adjust the seasoning with a drop of vinegar if necessary. Transfer the salmon to four dinner plates, spoon about 2 tablespoons of the vinaigrette onto each portion, sprinkle the chervil leaves or cilantro on top, and serve. —*Tasha DeSerio*

# Broiled Salmon with a White Bean, Kale & Bacon Ragoût

*Serves four.*

¼ pound thick-cut bacon (about 4 thick slices), cut crosswise into thin strips

3 tablespoons extra-virgin olive oil

2 cloves garlic, minced

3 cups packed thinly sliced kale leaves (stems removed)

1½ cups homemade or canned low-salt chicken broth

One 15.5-ounce can cannellini beans, rinsed well and drained

Four 6-ounce skinless salmon fillets

Kosher salt and freshly ground black pepper

1 tablespoon chopped fresh thyme

**The bacon does double-duty here: It flavors the kale-bean mixture as well as the broiled salmon.**

Position a rack 6 inches from the broiler element and heat the broiler on high.

In a heavy skillet over medium heat, cook the bacon in the oil, stirring occasionally, until the bacon renders much of its fat and starts to brown, about 5 minutes. Use a spoon to remove 2 tablespoons of the bacon fat from the skillet and reserve in a small bowl.

Add the garlic to the bacon in the skillet. Cook, stirring, until the garlic starts to sizzle, about 30 seconds. Raise the heat to high, add the kale, and cook, stirring, until it starts to wilt, about 1 minute. Add the broth and beans and bring to a boil. Reduce the heat to medium, cover the skillet, and cook for 5 minutes. Remove from the heat and keep warm.

While the beans are cooking, line a heavy-duty rimmed baking sheet with foil and arrange the salmon on it, skin side down. Drizzle the reserved bacon fat over the salmon and season with ½ teaspoon salt and a few generous grinds of pepper. Broil until slightly firm to the touch, 7 to 10 minutes for medium (the salmon will be dark pink in the middle). Sprinkle half of the thyme over the salmon. Stir the remaining thyme into the beans and kale and season with salt and pepper to taste.

To serve, spoon equal portions of the beans and kale onto dinner plates and top each plate with a piece of salmon. Serve immediately. *—Tony Rosenfeld*

# Roasted Salmon & Asparagus with Lemon Oil

*Serves four.*

1 large lemon

3 tablespoons extra-virgin olive oil; more for the pan

20 thin stalks asparagus (10 to 12 ounces), trimmed

Kosher salt and freshly ground black pepper

Four 6- to 8-ounce skin-on salmon fillets (preferably about 1 inch thick)

**What could be better for a busy weeknight? The entrée and side dish cook at the same time, on the same pan, for just a few minutes. With so little prep time and clean up, this is a recipe you'll be turning to again and again.**

Position a rack in the center of the oven and heat the oven to 450°F.

Finely grate the zest from the lemon, preferably with a rasp-style grater. In a small bowl, combine the zest with 2 tablespoons of the oil. Cut the lemon in half and set aside.

On one side of a heavy, rimmed baking sheet, toss the asparagus with the remaining 1 tablespoon oil, ¾ teaspoon salt, and ½ teaspoon pepper. Spread out the asparagus in a single layer. Lightly coat the other side of the baking sheet with oil and place the salmon fillets, skin side down, on the oiled area. Sprinkle with 1 teaspoon salt and ½ teaspoon pepper. Roast until the asparagus are tender and the salmon is cooked to your liking (cut into a fillet with a paring knife to check), 10 to 13 minutes for medium. Keep in mind that the fish will continue to cook a bit more after it comes out of the oven. If the asparagus needs more time to cook, transfer the salmon to a platter, tent it loosely with foil, and return the asparagus to the oven until tender.

Arrange the salmon and asparagus on a platter and drizzle the lemon oil all over both. Squeeze a little juice from a lemon half over the salmon and serve immediately. *—Tony Rosenfeld*

# Spice-Crusted Salmon

**Full-flavored salmon stands up beautifully to the robust spices in this dish. Serve with sautéed sugar snap peas and a wedge of lemon.**

Position a rack in the center of the oven and heat the oven to 450°F.

Combine the ginger, sesame seeds, coriander seeds, cumin seeds, fennel seeds, red pepper, and garlic in a food processor and process until the mixture is finely chopped, about 30 seconds. With the motor running, drizzle the oil through the feed tube and process, stopping to scrape down the sides, until the mixture forms a paste, about 20 seconds.

Rub oil on the salmon skin and put the salmon, skin side down, on a rack set on a rimmed baking sheet. Sprinkle 2 teaspoons salt evenly over the salmon. Using your hands, spread the spice paste over the salmon. Roast until the salmon is cooked to your liking, 16 to 18 minutes for medium-rare.

—*Julianna Grimes Bottcher*

*Serves six.*

¼ cup peeled and coarsely chopped fresh ginger

2 tablespoons sesame seeds

2 tablespoons coriander seeds

1 tablespoon cumin seeds

1 tablespoon fennel seeds

½ teaspoon crushed red pepper flakes

1 clove garlic, peeled

3 tablespoons extra-virgin olive oil; more for oiling the salmon

One 2½-pound skin-on salmon fillet

Kosher salt

# Cajun Swordfish with Quick, Creamy Rémoulade Sauce

*Serves two.*

¼ cup mayonnaise

1 teaspoon whole-grain mustard

1 teaspoon prepared horseradish, squeezed dry with a paper towel

1 teaspoon capers, rinsed, drained, and chopped

¾ teaspoon hot paprika

¾ teaspoon dried thyme

¾ teaspoon dried oregano

½ teaspoon garlic powder

Kosher salt and freshly ground black pepper

2 swordfish steaks, ½ inch thick (6 to 8 ounces each), trimmed of any skin or dark flesh

1 tablespoon vegetable oil

**Each bite of this quick-to-make fish dish is a study in yummy contrast: earthiness and heat from the Cajun spices playing against creamy, tangy rémoulade sauce. Serve the fish with some white rice tossed with beans and chopped cilantro. If you want to double the recipe, use two pans for the fish.**

In a small bowl, combine the mayonnaise, mustard, horseradish, and capers; stir until well blended.

In another small bowl, combine the paprika, thyme, oregano, garlic powder, ½ teaspoon salt, and ⅛ teaspoon pepper.

Brush the swordfish with 1 teaspoon of the oil. Spread equal amounts of the paprika mixture over both sides of the swordfish and let sit for 10 minutes.

In a large cast-iron or heavy-duty skillet, heat the remaining 2 teaspoons oil over medium-high heat until very hot. Add the swordfish and cook until well browned, 4 to 5 minutes. Flip the swordfish and continue to cook until cooked through (cut into it to check) and the second side is well browned, another 3 to 5 minutes. Serve with the rémoulade sauce. *—David Bonom*

# Paella with Shrimp, Clams & Mussels

**Intensly flavored rice is the hallmark of a great paella like this one. If you can't get Spanish bomba rice, use another medium-grain rice, such as Goya brand, but add only 3½ cups of broth to the rice instead of 4¾ cups.**

Put the saffron in a large mortar and grind to a powder with a pestle (or crumble the saffron into a 1-cup liquid measuring cup and grind it with the back of a spoon). Heat the clam juice to simmering in a saucepan or in a microwave. Pour it into the mortar (or cup) with the saffron and set aside to infuse.

Grate the onion half on the largest holes of a box grater to get about ¼ cup grated onion; set aside. Grate both tomato halves on the box grater all the way down the skin. Discard the skin.

Put the oil in a 14-inch paella pan. Set over medium heat, add the grated onion, and cook until it softens and darkens slightly, 2 to 3 minutes. Add the grated tomato, chopped garlic, pimentón, and ¼ teaspoon of the salt; cook gently in the center of the pan, stirring frequently, until the mixture, called a sofrito, becomes dark red and is a very thick purée, 20 to 30 minutes. (As it thickens, lower the heat to keep it from burning, and if it starts sticking to the pan, stir in a little water.)

While the sofrito cooks, pick through the mussels to find the prettiest eight; reserve these in the refrigerator. Put the shrimp shells in a large saucepan set over medium-high heat and cook, stirring, until they're dry and pink, 2 to 3 minutes. Add the water or fish stock and all the remaining mussels, and bring to a boil over high heat. Reduce the heat and simmer for 10 minutes. Strain the broth into a bowl, discarding the shrimp shells and the mussels. Wipe out the saucepan and pour the broth back into it. Add the saffron-infused clam juice to the broth and bring to a gentle simmer. Add the remaining ½ teaspoon salt, taste, and add more if necessary; it should be quite well salted, but not salty. Cover and reduce the heat to very low.

When the sofrito is done, add the rice and cook over medium heat, stirring constantly to combine it with the sofrito, for 2 minutes. Increase the heat to high and pour 4¾ cups of the hot broth (if you don't have enough, supplement with water) into the paella pan. Use a spoon to spread the rice evenly, but don't stir for the remainder of the cooking. Adjust the heat to get a vigorous simmer, repositioning the pan to get bubbles all the way to the perimeter.

Arrange the clams in the pan, pushing them into the rice. When the rice just begins to appear at the level of the broth, after 8 to 10 minutes, arrange the reserved mussels in the pan. Lower the heat so the broth simmers very

*Serves four.*

Large pinch saffron (about 30 threads)

1 cup bottled clam juice

½ medium onion

1 large ripe tomato, halved horizontally

¼ cup extra-virgin olive oil

8 cloves garlic, coarsely chopped

¼ teaspoon pimentón (Spanish paprika, either sweet or hot; optional)

¾ teaspoon kosher salt; more to taste

½ pound mussels, cleaned (about 20)

⅓ pound large shrimp (about 12), peeled; shells reserved

5 cups water or fish stock

1½ cups Spanish bomba rice

8 medium clams, such as littlenecks (about 1 pound), cleaned

2 lemons, cut in half, for serving

gently throughout the pan. After another 5 minutes, arrange the shrimp in the pan, pressing them lightly into the rice. Continue cooking until the liquid is absorbed, the shrimp are pink, the shellfish are open, and the rice is tender but toothy (taste a few grains below the top layer), about another 5 minutes. (The rice needs to simmer for a total of about 20 minutes, so if it seems like the broth is evaporating too quickly, drizzle some more broth or water on top. If the rice isn't cooking evenly, lay a sheet of foil loosely over the pan to trap the heat.)

Check for socarrat (the delicious browned rice that has stuck to the bottom of the pan) by using a spoon to feel for resistance on the bottom of the pan. Check in various spots. If there is none, increase the heat to medium high and carefully cook, moving the pan around, until you hear crackling and feel resistance, 1 to 2 minutes; if you smell any burning, remove the pan from the heat.

Remove the pan from the heat and cover tightly with foil. Let the paella rest for 5 to 10 minutes. Put the pan on the table, remove the foil, and invite everyone to squeeze lemon over the section in front of them. Traditionally, paella is eaten directly from the pan, starting at the perimeter and working toward the center; boundaries become clear as you go. *—Sarah Jay*

## Buying saffron: the redder, the better

Let's clarify one thing right off the bat: Saffron is indeed "the most expensive spice in the world" by weight, but you need so little when cooking that it's actually cheaper to use than many everyday flavorings—a single lemon often costs twice as much as a pinch of saffron. And a pinch, which is 20 to 25 threads, is all you need in most cases.

When buying saffron, keep two rules in mind. First, buy saffron in threads only. Powdered saffron can contain other products, and it's difficult to know whether you're buying the pure spice. Second, look for saffron that contains only short, deep red threads (they're actually the stigmas from the saffron crocus). Lesser grades of saffron include threads with some yellow areas (which is the style part of the flower). This isn't a bad thing, but the yellow part doesn't have the same coloring and flavoring power as the red stigmas, so the saffron isn't as potent.

# Steamed Mussels in Garlicky White-Wine Broth

*Serves four.*

3 cups dry white wine (Pinot Grigio works well)

4 pounds mussels, scrubbed and debearded

1 cup (2 sticks) unsalted butter, cut into ½-inch chunks

½ cup pitted Kalamata olives, drained and chopped

½ cup lightly packed coarsely chopped fresh flat-leaf parsley (about 1 small bunch)

3 medium cloves garlic, chopped

¼ cup lightly drained capers, coarsely chopped

6 to 8 drops Tabasco

**Serve these mussels with a soupspoon and some crusty bread to sop up the juices.**

Bring the wine to a boil in a large pot and let continue to boil for 4 minutes to reduce it slightly. Add the mussels, cover, and cook, shaking the pot frequently, until the mussels open, 3 to 5 minutes. With a slotted spoon, transfer them to four large bowls, discarding any that didn't open.

Add the butter, olives, parsley, garlic, capers, and Tabasco to the wine and stir gently until the butter blends with the wine. Spoon the buttery broth over the mussels and serve immediately. *—Arlene Jacobs*

tip: To debeard mussels, use your thumb and index finger to feel around the outside of each shell for any fibrous strands and pull. The beard should detach easily from the mussel. Do this as close to cooking time as possible since debearding the mussel kills it.

# Shrimp & Cannellini Salad with Tarragon Vinaigrette

*Serves four as a main course, six as an appetizer or "small plate."*

**2 tablespoons sherry vinegar**

**1 tablespoon Dijon mustard**

**1 tablespoon minced fresh tarragon**

**1 teaspoon minced garlic**

**Kosher salt and freshly ground black pepper**

**5 tablespoons extra-virgin olive oil**

**One 15- or 16-ounce can cannellini beans, rinsed and drained**

**1 ripe medium tomato, cut into medium dice (about 1 cup)**

**1 large shallot, sliced thinly into rings (about ¼ cup)**

**12 jumbo (16 to 20 per pound) shrimp, peeled and deveined**

**1 medium head red-leaf lettuce (or a lettuce mix), washed, spun dry, and torn into bite-size pieces (about 8 cups)**

**Tarragon adds a welcome freshness to this versatile salad. Serve the shrimp as an appetizer, a light lunch, or part of a springtime buffet.**

In a medium bowl, mix the vinegar with the mustard, tarragon, garlic, and ¼ teaspoon each salt and pepper. Slowly whisk in 4 tablespoons of the oil.

In a large bowl, combine the beans, tomato, and shallot. Add 3 tablespoons of the vinaigrette and stir gently to combine.

Toss the shrimp with the remaining 1 tablespoon oil and season with salt and a few grinds pepper. Heat a grill pan over high heat, then cook the shrimp until opaque throughout, 3 to 4 minutes per side.

Toss the lettuce with half of the remaining vinaigrette (add more to taste). For individual servings, portion the lettuce among the serving plates. Spoon the beans on top of the greens and top each salad with two or three shrimp, depending on how many servings you're making. To serve buffet style, arrange a layer of lettuce, the beans, and then the shrimp. *—Jessica Bard*

## For consistency, buy shrimp by the count, not the size

The next time you buy shrimp, take a closer look at the label and you'll notice a set of numbers divided by a slash, like this: 21/25. This number, called the "count," tells you the size of the shrimp. The count refers to the number of individual shrimp in 1 pound. So, for instance, when you buy 1 pound of 21/25 count shrimp, you can expect to get 21 to 25 shrimp. The smaller the numbers, the bigger the shrimp. Sometimes on big shrimp you'll see a count that looks like this: U/15 or U/10. This means there are "under 15" or "under 10" shrimp per pound.

When buying shrimp, the main advantage to using the count is that it's a reliable, consistent measure. Adjectives that describe the size, like "jumbo" or "large," aren't used consistently. It's not uncommon to find a particular count—say 51/60—labeled as "medium" in one store while another store just down the road calls them "small."

21/25 count

31/40 count

51/60 count

# Paprika Shrimp with Orange & Avocado Salsa

*Serves six.*

2 medium navel oranges

5 tablespoons extra-virgin olive oil

Kosher salt

1 ripe Hass avocado, pitted, peeled, and cut into medium dice

⅓ cup thinly sliced scallions (from about 4 slender scallions; both white and green parts)

1 tablespoon fresh lime juice

2 teaspoons sweet paprika, preferably Hungarian

½ teaspoon ground cumin

1 teaspoon Tabasco

1½ pounds large (21 to 25 per pound) shrimp, peeled and deveined

**Cumin and Tabasco give shrimp a zesty kick that pairs perfectly with a citrusy salsa. Saffron rice makes a nice accompaniment.**

In the oven, position a rack 4 inches from the broiler and heat the broiler to high.

Segment the oranges: Slice the ends off one of the oranges with a small, sharp knife. Stand the orange on one of its cut ends and slice off the skin in strips, cutting below the bitter white pith. Working over a small bowl, cut the orange segments free from the membrane, letting each one fall into the bowl as you go. Squeeze any remaining juice from the membranes into the bowl. Repeat with the other orange. Cut all of the orange segments in half crosswise and return them to the bowl. Add 2 tablespoons of the oil, ¾ teaspoon salt, the avocado, scallions, and lime juice to the oranges and toss gently to combine.

Combine the remaining 3 tablespoons oil, 1 teaspoon salt, the paprika, cumin, and Tabasco in a medium bowl; stir well. Add the shrimp, tossing to coat. Arrange the shrimp on a foil-lined rimmed baking sheet. Broil until opaque and cooked through, about 4 minutes. Serve the shrimp with the salsa. *—Julianna Grimes Bottcher*

**tip:** It's usually easier to slice or dice a ripe avocado before removing its skin. Cut the avocado in half lengthwise and remove the pit (whack it with the blade of a chef's knife and pull the pit out). Using a paring knife, cut the avocado diagonally into slices, without piercing the skin. For dicing, make a second set of diagonal slices perpendicular to the first. To remove the sliced or diced avocado from its skin, hold the avocado in the palm of your hand and, using a large spoon, carefully scoop out the slices.

# Spanish Rice with Shrimp

*Serves two as a main course,
four as a first course.*

½ pound shrimp (about 2 cups;
  18 to 20 large shrimp), peeled;
  shells reserved

½ ripe tomato, coarsely
  chopped

2 cups water

1 cup clam juice

Pinch crushed red pepper flakes
  (or cayenne)

⅛ teaspoon sweet paprika

1 teaspoon kosher salt

3 tablespoons olive oil

½ medium onion, chopped

4 large cloves garlic, coarsely
  chopped

1 cup medium-grain rice

2 tablespoons chopped fresh
  flat-leaf parsley (optional)

Lemon wedges, for serving

**Frozen shrimp works fine here, as long as it's uncooked and unpeeled.
Thaw the shrimp under cold running water first.**

Put the shrimp shells in a small saucepan with the tomato, water, clam juice, red pepper, paprika, and salt. Bring to a boil, reduce the heat to a simmer, cover, and cook for 10 minutes.

Meanwhile, heat a 10-inch skillet with the oil over medium-low heat. Add the onion and cook, stirring frequently, until softened, about 6 minutes. Add the garlic and cook until softened, 2 to 3 minutes.

Remove the shrimp shell broth from the heat and strain through a sieve into a 4-cup measure. You should have 2¾ cups liquid; if there is less, add water to compensate.

Increase the heat under the skillet to medium high. Stir in the rice and cook, stirring frequently, until it becomes somewhat translucent, about 1 minute. Add the strained broth, spread the rice into an even layer, and bring to a boil. Reduce the heat to medium and simmer vigorously for 5 minutes. Arrange the shrimp on top of the rice and simmer until the rice and liquid are at the same level, about another 5 minutes. Reduce the heat to medium low and simmer gently until the rice is just tender and the liquid is absorbed, about another 10 minutes. (It's all right if the rice starts to stick to the bottom of the pan; it can be brown, but don't let it burn.)

Remove from the heat, cover, and let rest for 10 minutes. Sprinkle with the parsley, if using, and serve with the lemon wedges. *—Sarah Jay*

# Shrimp & Scallop Cakes

*Yields eight cakes; serves four.*

2 whole star anise

4 tablespoons peanut or canola oil; more as needed for frying

2 cups stemmed and sliced (¼-inch-thick) fresh shiitake mushrooms (from about two 3½-ounce packages)

½ pound shrimp, any size, peeled and deveined

¾ pound dry-packed sea scallops

2 tablespoons mirin (sweetened rice wine)

2 tablespoons roughly chopped fresh cilantro, plus 8 cilantro leaves

2 tablespoons thinly sliced scallions (from about 2 scallions; both white and green parts)

½ teaspoon Asian sesame oil

Kosher salt

Gingered Soy Sauce (see page 263)

**An Asian take on fish cakes, these are fun to serve as little bites at a cocktail party. To make them mini, portion them into 24 small mounds, shape into small cakes, press a small cilantro leaf on each, and cook as directed. When buying scallops, choose those labeled "dry," "dry-packed," or "chemical free"; they taste better and brown better than treated scallops.**

Grind the star anise in a clean electric coffee grinder dedicated to spices.

Heat 2 tablespoons of the oil in a large nonstick skillet over medium-high heat. Add the shiitakes and sauté, stirring as needed, until cooked through, golden, and slightly crisp around the edges, 5 to 7 minutes. Transfer to a cutting board, let cool, then coarsely chop.

Coarsely chop the shrimp and transfer to a large bowl. Put the scallops in a food processor and process until smooth. Add the scallops to the bowl of shrimp. Add 1 teaspoon of the star anise, along with the shiitakes, mirin, cilantro, scallions, sesame oil, and ½ teaspoon salt. Combine well using a rubber spatula—don't worry about overmixing. Cover the bowl and chill for 30 minutes or more. Discard any remaining ground star anise or save for another use.

Turn the mixture out onto a baking sheet and portion it into eight equal mounds. With wet hands, shape each mound into a flattened cake about 2½ inches wide and ½ inch thick. Press a cilantro leaf, nice side up, onto the top of each cake.

Heat the oven to 200°F. Heat 1 tablespoon of the oil in a large nonstick skillet over medium heat. Using a rubber spatula, transfer four of the cakes to the pan with the cilantro-leaf side down. Cook until lightly browned on both sides and cooked through, turning once or twice with a spatula, 5 to 6 minutes total cooking time. Transfer to a plate, cover, and keep warm in the oven. Wipe the skillet clean, then cook the remaining cakes as above, using the remaining 1 tablespoon oil. Serve hot, with ramekins of the gingered soy sauce for dipping. —*Tom Douglas*

# Gingered Soy Sauce

*Yields about ²/₃ cup.*

**Sambal badjak and sambal oelek are Indonesian hot chile pastes. You can find them in well-stocked supermarkets and Asian specialty markets. You could also use Chinese chile paste.**

1 piece fresh ginger, about 1½x2 inches, peeled

⅓ cup soy sauce

3 tablespoons mirin (sweetened rice wine)

1 tablespoon plus 1 teaspoon granulated sugar

¾ teaspoon sambal badjak or sambal oelek, or to taste

2 teaspoons fresh lime juice

Grate the ginger on a box grater using the large holes. Put the ginger in your palm and squeeze the ginger juice into a small bowl; discard the grated ginger.

In a small saucepan, combine 1½ teaspoons of the ginger juice with the soy sauce, mirin, and sugar. Warm the mixture over medium heat, stirring, just until the sugar dissolves. Transfer to a small bowl and stir in the sambal and lime juice. Serve or store covered and refrigerated for up to three days.

# Etta's New Crab Cakes

See photo on page 225.

*Yields eight crab cakes; serves four.*

- 8 slices white sandwich bread
- 3 tablespoons plus 2 teaspoons coarsely chopped fresh flat-leaf parsley
- 1 large egg yolk
- 1 tablespoon cider vinegar
- 1 tablespoon Dijon mustard
- 1 tablespoon coarsely chopped red bell pepper
- 1 tablespoon coarsely chopped onion
- 1 teaspoon Tabasco
- ½ teaspoon sweet paprika
- ½ teaspoon chopped fresh thyme
- Kosher salt and freshly ground black pepper
- ¼ cup extra-virgin olive oil
- ¼ cup sour cream
- 1 pound fresh or pasteurized blue lump crabmeat, drained and picked clean of shell, or 1 pound fresh Dungeness crabmeat (if you use Dungeness, squeeze the crabmeat lightly to remove excess liquid)
- 6 tablespoons (¾ stick) unsalted butter
- Red-Eye Cocktail Sauce (see below)
- 4 lemon wedges, for serving

**Light and creamy inside with a nice golden crust, these are the most popular item at Etta's Seafood in Seattle.**

Tear up the bread and pulse it in a food processor to make fine, soft crumbs (you should have about 3½ cups). Pour the crumbs into a 9x13-inch (or similar-size) dish and mix in 3 tablespoons of the parsley.

In a food processor, combine the egg yolk, vinegar, mustard, bell pepper, onion, Tabasco, paprika, thyme, ½ teaspoon salt, ¼ teaspoon pepper, and the remaining 2 teaspoons parsley. Pulse to finely mince and combine all the ingredients. With the motor running, slowly add the oil through the feed tube until the mixture emulsifies and forms a thin mayonnaise. Transfer the mayonnaise to a large bowl and stir in the sour cream. Use a rubber spatula to gently fold in the crabmeat, taking care not to break up the lumps. Pour the crab mixture onto a large rimmed baking sheet and portion it into eight equal mounds. Gently shape each one into a patty about 3 inches wide and ½ inch thick. (The mixture will be quite wet.)

Using a spatula to move the patties, lightly dredge each patty on both sides in the breadcrumb mixture. Cover the crab cakes with plastic and chill for at least 1 hour. (You can leave the cakes right in the pan of breadcrumbs and chill them as long as overnight.)

Heat the oven to 200°F. Heat 3 tablespoons of the butter in a large nonstick skillet over medium heat. When the butter melts, add four crab cakes and gently fry until golden brown on both sides and heated through, turning just once with a spatula, about 4 minutes per side. Transfer the cakes to a plate (don't cover) and keep them warm in the oven. Wipe the skillet clean and cook the remaining cakes as above, using the remaining 3 tablespoons butter.

Serve hot, accompanied by ramekins of cocktail sauce and lemon wedges.
—*Tom Douglas*

## Red-Eye Cocktail Sauce

*Yields about 1¼ cups.*

**This makes enough sauce for a double batch of crab cakes, or you can save the sauce and use it with poached shrimp, pan-fried oysters, or other seafood.**

- 1½ teaspoons finely ground coffee, preferably dark or espresso roast
- 1 cup tomato ketchup
- 3 tablespoons prepared horseradish
- 1½ tablespoons fresh lemon juice
- 2¼ teaspoons Worcestershire sauce

Put the coffee in a paper coffee filter cone set in a strainer over a Pyrex measuring cup or small heatproof bowl. Bring a small amount of water to a boil. Pour about 2 tablespoons (the exact amount isn't important) boiling water into the filter cone and allow the liquid coffee to drain off. Discard the liquid and transfer the moistened coffee grounds from the paper cone to a bowl—you may need to scrape the coffee off the paper with a small spoon. Add the ketchup, horseradish, lemon juice, and Worcestershire and stir. Serve immediately, or cover and refrigerate for up to a week.

Picking and eating whole crabs is a party in itself—all you need is melted butter and few a friends to join you. Or try some of the sauces that accompany the seafood-cake recipes at left and on pages 242 and 262.

Here are some tips for cooking and picking live crabs, either for crab cakes or for a pick-and-eat crab feast.

## How to cook:

Get out your biggest pot, fill the pot with a couple of gallons of water, add some sliced lemons, crushed bay leaves, and a few tablespoons of salt and bring to a boil. Add the crabs, cover, and boil until the shells are bright red and the crabs are cooked through, 12 to 20 minutes for Dungeness crabs, 5 to 10 minutes for blues (blues may also be steamed). Put them in the sink and quickly rinse with cold water. Let them cool, but don't cover them with cold water because that will wash away their flavor.

Dungeness crab

Blue crab

## How to get to the crabmeat:

Though a Dungeness crab is shown here, blue crabs can be picked the same way. Dungeness crabs have the largest crabmeat-to-shell ratio, but expect, at best, only about ½ pound of crabmeat from a 2- to 3-pound crab.

**1** Pick up a cooked crab and pry the top shell from the body. Gently rinse the yellow substance, called the "mustard," from the crab, if you like.

**2** Remove and discard the triangular gills from both sides of the crab.

**3** Break the crab body in half and remove the tab-like apron from the bottom shell.

**4** Using your hands or a knife, break the body halves into sections between each leg.

**5** With your fingers, pick the white meat from each section. Try to pick out the crabmeat in the largest pieces possible. To break open the claws and leg knuckles, use kitchen shears or whack them with a mallet or the back of a chef's knife.

8 Sides

p270

p302

Roasted Ratatouille
(recipe on page 290)

# Boiled Asparagus with Salsa Verde

*Serves four as a side dish;*
*yields ¹/₂ cup sauce.*

¹/₃ cup extra-virgin olive oil

3 tablespoons minced fresh flat-
leaf parsley

1 tablespoon minced shallot

4 anchovy fillets, rinsed and
minced into a paste

2 teaspoons fresh lemon juice

2 teaspoons capers, rinsed and
finely minced

1 teaspoon grated lemon zest

Sea salt or kosher salt

1¹/₂ pounds asparagus, trimmed

This zippy salsa verde is also delicious on poached chicken, salmon, halibut, or steamed cauliflower. Be sure to grate the lemon zest before you juice the lemon. You can make the salsa verde up to 8 hours ahead.

**Make the salsa verde:** In a small bowl, combine the oil, parsley, shallot, anchovies, lemon juice, capers, and lemon zest. Stir to blend, then season with ¹/₈ teaspoon salt, or more to taste.

**Cook the asparagus:** Bring a large pot of salted water to a boil. Add the asparagus and cook until just tender, about 4 minutes for medium spears. Lift the asparagus out of the boiling water with tongs and pat dry on a clean dishtowel. Transfer to a platter, arranging the spears with the tips pointing in the same direction. Spoon the sauce over the warm spears and serve immediately. —*Janet Fletcher*

**tip:** Asparagus is commonly sold in bundles of about a pound, standing upright in a tray of water. Choose fresh-looking, firm spears with tight tips. Smell them first to make sure they don't give off an unpleasant odor (if they do, they're old). Check the cut ends of the stalks; they should be moist, not dried out. If dried ends are all that's available, cut about half an inch off the bottom. To make sure they keep their freshness, stand asparagus bundles in about an inch of water in a jar or a shallow tray and keep them in the refrigerator. Cook the spears within two or three days.

# Sautéed Asparagus with Butter & Parmigiano

*Serves four as a side dish.*

1½ pounds asparagus, trimmed

3 tablespoons unsalted butter

Kosher salt and freshly ground
black pepper

1 tablespoon minced fresh flat-
leaf parsley

¼ cup freshly grated
Parmigiano-Reggiano

You can embellish this simple dish by adding peas or fava beans to make a spring vegetable mix. Serve the asparagus or the mixed vegetables as a side dish for roast chicken, lamb, or pork. Or you can toss the sautéed asparagus with hot pasta for a simple but stunning seasonal main dish.

Slice the asparagus on a sharp diagonal about ½ inch thick, leaving the tips whole. Melt the butter in a 12-inch skillet over medium heat. Add the asparagus and season with ½ teaspoon salt and ¼ teaspoon pepper. Cook, stirring often, until the asparagus is just tender, 5 to 6 minutes, lowering the heat if needed to keep it from browning. Don't overcook; the asparagus will soften a little more as it cools.

Remove the pan from the heat. Stir in the parsley and 3 tablespoons of the cheese. Transfer to a serving bowl, top with the remaining cheese, and serve immediately. *—Janet Fletcher*

## Simple side dishes and more starring juicy, tender asparagus

- **For a bright appetizer or side dish,** sprinkle roasted or grilled asparagus with finely grated lemon zest and crushed toasted nuts (walnuts, pine nuts, or almonds would work well).

- **For an extra dash of flavor,** drizzle roasted or grilled spears with Asian sesame oil, then sprinkle on a little salt and some lightly toasted sesame seeds (white, black, or a mixture of the two).

- **Dress up steamed asparagus** simply and deliciously with a sesame-lemon mayonnaise. Add 3 tablespoons Asian sesame oil and 3 tablespoons fresh lemon juice to homemade or good-quality bottled mayonnaise. Drizzle over the asparagus or use as a dipping sauce.

- **Make a bright, flavorful asparagus and shrimp pasta.** Cut the spears into 1-inch pieces and blanch them briefly, then sauté the shrimp and asparagus with minced garlic and strips of sun-dried tomato. Finish with a little grated lemon zest and a squeeze of lemon juice and toss with bow ties or any small pasta shape.

- **Make a colorful and appetizing Niçoise-style composed salad** with steamed, boiled, or roasted asparagus, strips of roasted red pepper, canned cannellini beans or chickpeas, hard-boiled eggs, black olives, and grilled or oil-packed tuna on a bed of butter or romaine lettuce. Scatter with some toasted pine nuts and drizzle with a lemon or red-wine-vinegar vinaigrette.

# Grilled Asparagus with Fresh Tarragon Mayonnaise

*Serves four; yields about ²/₃ cup mayonnaise.*

1 large egg yolk, at room temperature

½ cup plus 1 tablespoon extra-virgin olive oil

2 teaspoons minced shallot

2 teaspoons minced fresh flat-leaf parsley

1 teaspoon minced fresh tarragon

1½ teaspoons fresh lemon juice; more to taste

Kosher salt

1½ pounds asparagus, trimmed

Here's the best way to eat these asparagus spears: with your fingers, dragging the spears through the mayonnaise. The tarragon mayonnaise is delicious with boiled asparagus, too. If you're worried about serving raw egg, replace the egg yolk with a pasteurized egg product.

**Make the mayonnaise:** Put the egg yolk in a small bowl. Add a few drops of lukewarm water and whisk well. Begin adding the ½ cup oil in a very thin stream, whisking constantly. When the sauce thickens and forms a creamy emulsion, you can add the oil a little faster. Whisk in the shallot, parsley, tarragon, and lemon juice. Season with ½ teaspoon salt or more to taste. If needed, whisk in a few drops of water to loosen the mayonnaise until it's spoonable, not stiff.

**Cook the asparagus:** Bring a large pot of salted water to a boil. Add the asparagus and blanch for 1 minute for small spears or 1½ minutes for medium spears. Transfer them with tongs to a bowl of ice water. When cool, lift the spears out of the ice water and thoroughly pat dry.

Prepare a hot charcoal fire or gas grill. Put the spears on a rimmed baking sheet or platter. Drizzle with the remaining 1 tablespoon oil, season with a generous pinch of salt, and toss with your hands to coat the spears evenly.

Position the grill grate as close to the coals or heat source as possible. Heat the grate, then arrange the asparagus on it directly over the heat with all the tips pointing in the same direction. (Be sure to arrange the asparagus perpendicular to the bars so they don't fall through.) Grill, turning the spears once with tongs, until they're blistered and lightly charred in spots, about 3 minutes total. Transfer to a platter and serve immediately, passing the mayonnaise separately. *—Janet Fletcher*

# Carrots with Curry-Yogurt Sauce

This sauce can be used with a variety of other vegetables, including cauliflower, potatoes, or green beans. It also could be drizzled over lamb or a side of chickpeas and couscous. Pay attention to the curry powder you use—some can be quite hot.

In a small bowl, stir the yogurt and cornstarch until well blended.

In a 1-quart saucepan, melt the butter over medium heat. Add the onion, sprinkle with a pinch of salt, and cook, stirring, frequently, until softened, 4 to 5 minutes. Add the garlic and ginger and cook, stirring frequently, until just golden brown, 4 to 5 minutes more (reduce the heat if the onion seems to be burning rather than browning). Add the curry powder and cumin and cook, stirring, 15 to 20 seconds. Reduce the heat to medium low, add the yogurt mixture, and stir until slightly thickened, about 1 minute. Season with ¼ teaspoon each salt and pepper, or to taste.

Meanwhile, bring an inch or so of water to a boil in a pot fitted with a steamer insert. Put the carrots in the steamer, sprinkle with salt, cover tightly, and steam until just tender, 6 to 8 minutes. To test for doneness, bite into a piece that you've quickly run under cold water (so that you don't burn your tongue).

Drizzle the sauce over the steamed carrots, sprinkle with the cilantro, if using, and serve. *–Jennifer Armentrout*

*Serves four to six.*

½ cup plain yogurt, preferably whole milk

1 teaspoon cornstarch

2 tablespoons unsalted butter

⅓ cup minced yellow onion (about half a small onion)

Kosher salt

1 teaspoon minced garlic

1 teaspoon peeled and minced fresh ginger

½ teaspoon curry powder

¼ teaspoon ground cumin

Freshly ground black pepper

2 tablespoons coarsely chopped fresh cilantro for garnish (optional)

1½ pounds carrots (about 8), peeled and sliced into ½-inch-thick rounds

# Roasted Carrots & Shallots with Oil-Cured Olives & Gremolata

*Serves six.*

½ cup finely chopped fresh
flat-leaf parsley

Finely chopped zest of
1 medium lemon (1½ to
2 tablespoons)

1 teaspoon minced garlic

2 pounds medium carrots

1 cup ¼-inch-thick-sliced
shallot rounds (3 or 4 medium
shallots)

1 tablespoon fresh thyme leaves

⅓ cup extra-virgin olive oil

1 teaspoon kosher salt

Freshly ground black pepper

¼ cup thinly sliced pitted
oil-cured olives

The sweet earthiness of the carrots pairs perfectly with the briny flavor of the olives in this side dish. To work ahead, you can clean and prep the carrots and slice the shallots the day before roasting. The gremolata—a brightly flavored mixture of parsley, lemon zest, and garlic—can be made up to 8 hours ahead. To prep the lemon zest for the gremolata, peel it off in long strips with a vegetable peeler, cut away any of the white pith, and chop the zest finely.

Position a rack in the center of the oven and heat the oven to 425°F.

Toss the parsley, lemon zest, and garlic together in a small bowl, cover with plastic wrap, and set aside.

Peel the carrots and slice in half lengthwise. If they're big, slice each half lengthwise again into long quarters. Put the carrots on a large rimmed baking sheet and toss with the shallots, thyme, oil, salt, and several grinds of pepper. Arrange the carrots in a single layer and roast, tossing occasionally, until they are tender and ever so slightly browned, 20 to 30 minutes.

Remove from the oven and toss in the olives and the gremolata. Adjust the seasoning with salt and pepper to taste and serve. —*Suzanne Goin*

# Baby Artichokes with Lemony Brown Butter Sauce & Chives

*Serves four.*

1¾ pounds baby artichokes (to yield 1 to 1¼ pounds trimmed artichokes; see below)

Kosher salt

¼ cup (½ stick) unsalted butter

2 tablespoons fresh lemon juice

Freshly ground black pepper

2 tablespoons thinly snipped fresh chives

Cute and tender, baby artichokes need a bit of prep work to get them ready for cooking, but when you get the hang of it, the work goes quickly. Once the artichokes are trimmed, everything is edible, including the choke—the fuzzy center, which is inedible when the choke matures. You can make the sauce an hour or so ahead. Gently reheat before drizzling on the steamed artichokes.

Bring an inch or so of water to a boil in a pot fit with a steamer insert. Put the artichokes in the steamer, sprinkle with salt, cover tightly, and steam until just tender. Pierce with a fork to check.

Meanwhile, in a 1-quart saucepan, melt the butter over medium heat. Cook the butter, whisking constantly, just until the milk solids turn a nutty brown color, 3 to 5 minutes. As soon as the butter is brown, take the pan off the heat and carefully pour in the lemon juice. Swirl to combine. Season with ¼ teaspoon salt and ⅛ teaspoon pepper, or to taste.

To serve, drizzle the sauce over the steamed artichokes and sprinkle with the chives. *—Jennifer Armentrout*

## How to trim a baby artichoke

The process for baby artichokes is the same as for the grown-up versions except that the little ones have no choke to worry about, so you save yourself that step.

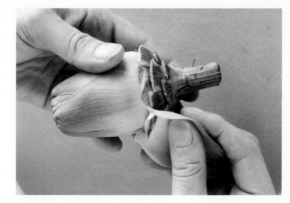

**1** Snap off and discard the outer leaves until you reach the tender, pale green interior cone of leaves.

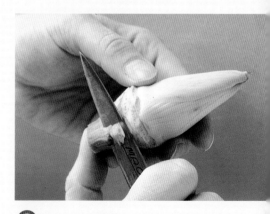

**2** With a paring knife, trim the stem to within 1 to 1½ inches of the base. Trim around the base to smooth off the nubbins left by the outer leaves, then trim off the fibrous outer layer of the stem.

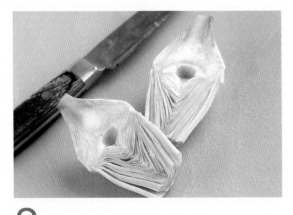

3 Cut ½ to 1 inch off the tip of the leaf cone, then cut the artichoke in half lengthwise.

4 To keep the artichokes from browning, float them in a bowl of lemon water until you're ready to cook them.

# Spanish Braised Spinach with Chickpeas

*Serves six.*

3 tablespoons olive oil

3 strips bacon

6 cloves garlic, 3 whole and 3 chopped medium fine

6 slices (¼ inch thick) baguette or crusty country bread

½ teaspoon ground cumin

¼ teaspoon paprika

1¼ pounds (two 10-ounce bags) fresh spinach, stemmed, washed well, drained, and coarsely chopped

One 15.5-ounce can chickpeas, rinsed and drained

1 cup plus 1 to 2 tablespoons water

Kosher salt and freshly ground black pepper

1 tablespoon sherry vinegar or other wine vinegar

**This side dish is quite hearty, and so would balance nicely with a light piece of flaky white fish, such as pan-fried cod, halibut, or sea bass. And don't be fooled by spinach: what may look like too much to start with will reduce tremendously when cooked.**

In a large, straight-sided skillet, heat the oil over medium heat and add the bacon. Cook, flipping occasionally, until it is golden and crisp, 6 to 8 minutes. Transfer to a plate lined with paper towels. Add the 3 whole cloves of garlic and the bread to the pan and sauté until the garlic is tender and golden and the bread is deep golden brown on both sides, 4 to 5 minutes. Using tongs or a slotted spoon, transfer the garlic cloves and four of the toasts to a mortar (or a small food processor). Set aside the remaining two slices of toast on a paper towel.

To the same skillet, add the chopped garlic, cumin, and paprika. Cook, stirring, until fragrant and the garlic begins to brown, 15 to 30 seconds. Increase the heat to medium high and immediately begin adding the spinach in batches, stirring to wilt. When it's all in the pan, add the chickpeas, 1 cup of the water, 1 teaspoon salt, and several grinds of pepper. Bring to a simmer.

Meanwhile, mash the bread slices and garlic in the mortar or process in the processor (don't mash the two reserved bread slices) with the vinegar and the 1 to 2 tablespoons water until puréed.

Stir the mashed bread mixture into the spinach, lower the heat to medium, and simmer until the liquid has reduced almost completely but the spinach is still moist, about 10 minutes. Crumble the bacon and stir it in. Taste and add more salt or vinegar if needed. Crumble the reserved toast over the spinach. Serve hot or warm. —*Sarah Jay*

# Sautéed Spinach with Shallots

*Serves six.*

5 tablespoons unsalted butter

¼ cup finely chopped shallots

¾ teaspoon ground coriander (preferably from toasted and freshly ground seeds)

Pinch crushed red pepper flakes

1¼ pounds (two 10-ounce bags) fresh spinach, stemmed and thoroughly washed but not dried

Kosher salt and freshly ground pepper (preferably white pepper)

Pinch freshly grated nutmeg, or to taste

**This side dish is simple enough to make during the week, yet elegant enough to serve when entertaining. Swiss chard leaves (stemmed) would make a fine substitution for the spinach in this recipe.**

Melt the butter in a 12-inch skillet over medium heat. Add the shallots, coriander, and red pepper and cook, stirring occasionally, until the shallots begin to soften but do not brown, 2 to 3 minutes. Increase the heat to medium high and begin adding the spinach, a large handful at a time, tossing with tongs, until it's all in the skillet. Cook, tossing frequently, until the spinach is wilted and bright green, about 2 minutes. If a lot of water remains, cook on high heat until the leaves are coated with butter but not soupy, another 1 to 2 minutes. Season to taste with salt, pepper, and nutmeg and serve.

*—Molly Stevens*

# Spiced Green Beans Braised with Tomato & Onions

**This classic Lebanese dish is flavored with hints of cinnamon and allspice. It's wonderful with any roasted meat but especially good with lamb.**

In a 12-inch skillet with a lid, heat the oil over medium heat. Add the onion and cook, stirring occasionally, until soft and lightly golden, 4 to 5 minutes. Add the green beans, salt, and pepper and stir well. Reduce the heat to medium low and cook, stirring occasionally, until the onion is caramelized and the beans start to soften and brown lightly, about 10 minutes.

Add the tomatoes, garlic, sugar, allspice, and cinnamon. Stir well, reduce the heat to low, cover, and cook, stirring occasionally, until the beans are very tender throughout, 15 to 20 minutes, or longer if a softer texture is desired. Season to taste with salt and pepper. Serve warm or at room temperature.

*—Ris Lacoste*

*Serves four to six.*

¼ cup extra-virgin olive oil

1 medium onion (about 8 ounces), halved lengthwise and thinly sliced lengthwise (about 2 cups)

1 pound fresh green beans, trimmed

½ teaspoon kosher salt; more as needed

¼ teaspoon freshly cracked black peppercorns; more as needed

2 cups canned diced tomatoes (from a 28-ounce can), drained

4 large cloves garlic, thinly sliced

1 teaspoon granulated sugar

¾ teaspoon ground allspice

½ teaspoon ground cinnamon

# Green Beans with Mustard-Tarragon Vinaigrette

*Serves four to six.*

4 quarts water

¼ cup plus ¼ teaspoon
  kosher salt

1 medium-small shallot, halved
  lengthwise and thinly sliced

2 tablespoons tarragon vinegar

1 tablespoon Dijon mustard

1 tablespoon roughly chopped
  fresh tarragon

¼ teaspoon freshly ground
  black pepper

¼ cup good-quality extra-virgin
  olive oil

1¼ pounds fresh green beans,
  trimmed

**This is a great way to serve green beans that are at their freshest. They should be consistently tender throughout—toothsome but not crunchy or fibrous.**

Combine the water and the ¼ cup salt in a large saucepan and bring to a boil. Meanwhile, in a medium bowl, whisk together the shallot, vinegar, mustard, tarragon, the remaining ¼ teaspoon salt, and the pepper. Slowly whisk in the oil. Set aside.

Add the beans to the boiling water, stir once or twice to distribute them, and cook until tender throughout but not soft, 4 to 5 minutes, depending on their size and freshness. Drain the beans in a colander.

Put the beans in a serving bowl and toss with all of the vinaigrette. Serve immediately. —*Ris Lacoste*

## Flavors that love green beans

You can add pizzazz to green beans with an ingredient (or a few) from this list.

- **Aromatic, pungent, and tangy:** anchovies, capers, fish sauce, garlic, hot chiles, shallots, scallions, soy sauce, vinegar

- **Cured, salty and cheesy:** bacon, prosciutto, Pecorino, Parmigiano- Reggiano, Asiago

- **Herbal:** basil, bay, chives, marjoram, parsley, sage, savory, tarragon, thyme

- **Spicy:** black pepper, cumin, coriander, curry powders or pastes, dried chiles, smoked paprika

- **Nutty:** almonds, hazelnuts, pine nuts, sesame seeds, walnuts

- **Rich and creamy:** butter, extra-virgin olive oil, sesame oil, aïoli or mayonnaise, crème fraîche, coconut milk

- **Fruity:** lemon and orange juice and zest, tomatoes (fresh, stewed, sun-dried, or roasted)

# Broccoli with Feta, Olive Oil-Fried Almonds & Currants

*Serves four to six.*

1 pound broccoli

1½ tablespoons dried currants

1 medium clove garlic, peeled

Kosher salt

2 tablespoons red-wine vinegar

Pinch cayenne

5 tablespoons extra-virgin olive oil

½ cup slivered blanched almonds

3 ounces feta (preferably French), crumbled (about ¾ cup)

⅓ cup roughly chopped fresh cilantro (optional)

**tip:** Boiling is the fastest method for cooking broccoli, but you need to take care not to overcook it. The boiled broccoli will continue to cook after it comes out of the pot, so stop cooking while it's still a few degrees underdone. For dishes in which you'll use the broccoli at room temperature, cool it quickly. While plunging it in ice water preserves the bright green color, it softens the flavor and texture. Instead, spread it on a baking sheet and let it cool at room temperature. If you're worried you might have overcooked the broccoli, put the baking sheet in the refrigerator to cool.

**The combination of sweet and salty makes this an ideal antipasto course, or try it as a side dish for grilled chicken or swordfish. Don't make the mistake, however, of boiling broccoli until it's limp and lifeless. Cook it until it has lost its crunch but still has a bit of toothiness left.**

Bring a large pot of generously salted water to a boil.

Meanwhile, tear off any broccoli leaves and trim the bottoms of the stems. Cut the florets just above where they join the large stem, then cut each floret lengthwise in half or in quarters through its stem (but not the buds). The top of each floret should be about the size of a quarter. Using a vegetable peeler or paring knife, peel the tough outer skin from the large stem, removing as little flesh as possible. Cut the stem into sticks about ¼ inch wide and 2 inches long.

Boil the florets and stem pieces until they're tender (pierce with a paring knife or taste a piece) but still offer a bit of resistance, about 3 minutes. Drain the broccoli, spread it on a baking sheet in an even layer, and set aside to cool—it will continue to cook as it cools.

Put the currants in a small bowl, add enough hot water to cover, and let sit until softened, about 10 minutes. Meanwhile, using a mortar and pestle or the flat side of a chef's knife, mash the garlic to a paste with a pinch of salt. Transfer the garlic to a small bowl and add the vinegar and cayenne. Let sit for about 10 minutes.

Warm 1 tablespoon of the oil in a small sauté pan over medium heat. Add the slivered almonds and fry, stirring frequently, until golden brown, 2 to 3 minutes. Transfer to a plate lined with paper towels and season with salt.

Drain the currants. Whisk the remaining 4 tablespoons oil into the vinegar mixture. Just before serving, combine the broccoli, currants, feta, and half of the almonds in a large bowl. Drizzle with the vinaigrette and toss gently to combine. Taste and season with a pinch more salt if necessary. Transfer to a serving platter, sprinkle with the remaining almonds and the cilantro, if using, and serve. *—Tasha DeSerio*

# Spicy Asian-Roasted Broccoli & Snap Peas

*Serves four.*

5 cups broccoli florets (from about 2 broccoli crowns)

3 cups (about 12 ounces) fresh sugar snap peas, trimmed

6 to 8 red or orange fresh Thai chiles, stemmed

3 tablespoons extra-virgin olive oil

2 tablespoons plus 1 teaspoon Asian sesame oil

1 teaspoon kosher salt

2 tablespoons chopped fresh cilantro

1½ tablespoons light-colored (white or yellow) miso

1 tablespoons honey

2 teaspoons sambal oelek (Asian chile paste)

1 teaspoon finely grated orange zest

1 teaspoon peeled and grated fresh ginger

1 clove garlic, minced

**If you have trouble finding fresh Thai chiles (also called bird chiles), try using the same amount of the dried version.**

Position a rack in the center of the oven and heat the oven to 450°F.

Put the broccoli, peas, and chiles in a large bowl; toss with 2 tablespoons of the olive oil and 2 tablespoons of the sesame oil. Sprinkle with salt and toss again. Transfer the vegetables to a 10x15-inch Pyrex dish and roast, stirring once, until the peas are lightly browned and the broccoli tops are quite dark in spots, about 22 minutes.

Meanwhile, in a small bowl, whisk together the remaining 1 tablespoon olive oil and 1 teaspoon sesame oil, the cilantro, miso, honey, sambal oelek, orange zest, ginger, and garlic. Pour the mixture over the roasted vegetables and toss to coat. Remove the chiles (or leave them in for color but warn diners not to eat them). Serve immediately. *—Julianna Grimes Bottcher*

# Broccoli with Balsamic-Bacon Vinaigrette Sauce

*Serves four to six.*

2 strips bacon, cut into ¼-inch dice

1 small shallot, minced

1½ tablespoons balsamic vinegar

1 tablespoon fresh lemon juice

¼ teaspoon Dijon mustard

3 tablespoons extra-virgin olive oil

Kosher salt and freshly ground black pepper

1¼ pounds broccoli, tops cut into 1-inch florets, stems sliced ¼ inch thick

**Steamed broccoli, simply sauced—the results are anything but bland. And if you can't get enough of this tangy-savory sauce, try it with Brussels sprouts, broccolini, potatoes, or green beans.**

**Make the sauce:** In a 1-quart saucepan over medium heat, cook the bacon, stirring occasionally, until crisp and golden, about 5 minutes. With a slotted spoon, transfer the bacon to a dish lined with paper towels, leaving the fat in the pan. Add the shallot to the bacon fat and cook, stirring occasionally, until softened, 1 to 2 minutes. Add 1 tablespoon of the vinegar and scrape with a spoon to dissolve the browned bits stuck to the pan bottom. Off the heat, stir in the remaining ½ tablespoon vinegar, the lemon juice, and mustard. Gradually whisk in the oil (don't worry if the sauce doesn't emulsify). Season with ¼ teaspoon salt and ⅛ teaspoon pepper, or to taste.

**Cook the broccoli:** Bring an inch or so of water to a boil in a pot fitted with a steamer insert. Put the broccoli in the steamer, sprinkle with salt, cover tightly, and steam until just tender, 3 to 4 minutes. The broccoli should be neither crisp nor soft but exactly in between. To check, bite into a piece that you've quickly run under cold water (so you don't burn your tongue). Transfer to a serving bowl.

Briefly reheat the sauce, if necessary. Drizzle over the steamed broccoli, sprinkle with the bacon bits, and serve. *—Jennifer Armentrout*

tip : The firm but juicy stems of broccoli are delicious, and they're often the sweetest part of the vegetable. But they cook at a different rate than the frilly, tender florets, so it's important to cut your broccoli so that all the pieces are perfectly steamed at the same time. Trim off any scraggly leaves and the dried stem end, then cut the stem into ¼-inch-thick slices and the top into florets about 1 inch long.

# Roasted Ratatouille

See photo on page 267.

*Yields 4 to 5 cups; serves four.*

- 2 small onions (about 5 ounces each), halved and cut into ¼-inch-thick half-moons
- 2 red bell peppers (6 to 7 ounces each), peeled (as much as possible with a vegetable peeler; serrated works best), cored, and cut into ¼-inch-wide strips
- 1 medium eggplant (about 1 pound), peeled if desired and sliced crosswise ½ inch thick, slices then cut in halves or quarters, depending on size
- 2 medium zucchini (7 to 8 ounces each), trimmed and cut into ¼-inch-thick rounds
- 15 cloves garlic, peeled
- ½ cup plus 2 tablespoons extra-virgin olive oil; more as needed
- 1 teaspoon chopped fresh rosemary
- Kosher salt
- 4 ripe medium tomatoes (about 1½ pounds total), peeled (with a serrated vegetable peeler; otherwise, skip the peeling), cored, and cut into ½-inch chunks
- ¼ cup thinly sliced fresh basil (a chiffonade)

**Roasting might seem like an untraditional way to make ratatouille, but it avoids two problems this French classic is prone to—bland flavor and a porridge-like texture. The high oven heat evaporates moisture from the vegetables and concentrates their flavors.**

Position racks in the top and bottom thirds of the oven and heat the oven to 400°F. Line two large rimmed baking sheets (12x16-inch sheet pans are a good size) with foil and top with a sheet of parchment.

In a large bowl, toss together the onions, peppers, eggplant, zucchini, garlic, oil, rosemary, and 1½ teaspoons salt. Spread the vegetables evenly over both sheets. Don't spread them too thin or they may burn (they shrink a lot as they cook).

Roast, stirring the vegetables a few times and swapping the positions of the pans once, until they are slightly collapsed or shriveled, starting to brown, and very tender, about 45 minutes. If the vegetables look like they may burn, turn down the heat or pile them closer together. If they look dry, drizzle on a little more oil.

Divide the tomatoes between the two pans and continue to roast until the tomatoes soften and shrink and the other vegetables are well browned, another 30 to 50 minutes.

Scrape all the vegetables and any juices into a serving bowl. Toss with the basil, taste for seasoning, and serve warm. *—Martha Holmberg*

# Ratatouille Vegetable Tart

*Serves four as a main dish, or eight as an appetizer.*

**Store-bought puff pastry makes a flaky base for savory ratatouille and cheese. Serve big squares for dinner, or smaller ones for appetizers.**

One 9½-inch square sheet puff pastry, fully thawed if frozen (thaw overnight in fridge if possible)

Flour, for rolling

8 oil-packed anchovy fillets, drained and chopped

1 to 1¼ cups Roasted Ratatouille (see page 290)

⅓ cup crumbled feta

2 tablespoons roughly chopped fresh flat-leaf parsley (optional)

Heat the oven to 425°F.

Lightly flour a work surface, lay the sheet of pastry out, and gently roll until it measures about 11x15 inches. Slide the pastry onto a baking sheet and prick all over with a fork, at about 1-inch intervals.

Gently stir the anchovies into the ratatouille, then spread it evenly over the pastry, to within an inch of the borders. Distribute the feta over the tart. Bake until the pastry is puffed and browned (including on the bottom), 18 to 25 minutes.

Slide onto a cutting board, sprinkle with the parsley, and cut into squares or strips. Serve warm or at room temperature.

# Great ideas for extra ratatouille

- **Fill an omelet** with a spoonful of ratatouille and some crumbled goat cheese.

- **Toss with hot penne pasta,** grated Parmigiano-Reggiano, and a few spoonfuls of pasta cooking water to loosen.

- **Layer lasagne noodles** with ratatouille, a little tomato sauce, fresh mozzarella, and grated Parmigiano-Reggiano; bake until warm and bubbly.

- **Mix with some chopped brine-cured black olives,** capers, and grated orange zest and pile onto toasted baguette slices as an appetizer.

- **Butterfly a boneless, skinless chicken breast,** pound to an even thickness, layer with a slice of prosciutto, a spoonful of ratatouille, and a sprinkling of Fontina. Roll up, secure with toothpicks, season with salt, dredge in flour, and sauté gently.

- **Arrange some in individual gratin dishes** or cazuelas with three jumbo peeled and deveined shrimp, Greek black olives, crumbled feta, and a drizzle of olive oil. Bake until the shrimp are pink and everything's hot and bubbly, and serve as a first course.

- **Grill some meaty fish steaks,** such as halibut, tuna, or swordfish, and top with a spoonful of ratatouille and a squeeze of lemon. Or use ratatouille as a bed for slices of grilled lamb.

- **Use a scoop of cold ratatouille** as part of a Niçoise salad, along with steamed new potatoes, green beans, tuna in oil, black olives, and hard-cooked egg. Drizzle with a lemon-garlic vinaigrette.

- **Make a Ratatouille Vegetable Tart,** above.

# Honeyed Cauliflower with Toasted Almonds

*Serves four as a substantial side dish.*

1 large (2-pound) head cauliflower

2 tablespoons honey (preferably a darker honey)

2 tablespoons sherry vinegar

3 to 4 tablespoons extra-virgin olive oil

Kosher salt

1 tablespoon coarsely chopped fresh thyme

¼ lemon

⅓ cup sliced almonds, toasted on a baking sheet in a 375°F oven until golden, 4 to 8 minutes

**If you need to convert anyone in your family to cauliflower, this is the recipe that will do the trick. The slow-sautéing method brings out a deep nuttiness in the cauliflower, which the sweet-sour honey glaze plays off of beautifully.**

Trim the cauliflower and carefully cut it into 2-inch-long, 1½-inch-wide florets; discard any small, crumbly pieces. Measure 6 cups of the florets and save any extra for another use. In a small bowl, whisk the honey and vinegar.

Heat 3 tablespoons of the oil in a 12-inch skillet over medium heat. Add the 6 cups of cauliflower, sprinkle with 1 teaspoon salt, and toss gently with tongs to coat with the oil. Arrange the cauliflower in one layer and let cook, undisturbed, until the bottoms are lightly browned, about 3 minutes. Using tongs, flip each floret to an unbrowned side and add another tablespoon of oil if the pan seems dry. Let cook, undisturbed again, for about 3 minutes to lightly brown that side. Repeat twice more for a total of about 6 more minutes, until all sides of the cauliflower have golden-brown spots. The stems of the florets will still be fairly firm, but the tops will be getting tender.

Raise the heat to medium high and add the honey-vinegar mixture and thyme. Toss to coat the cauliflower and continue to toss gently until the liquid reduces to a glaze on the florets, about 3 minutes. Remove the pan from the heat, taste a floret, and add more salt, if needed. Squeeze the lemon quarter over the cauliflower, add the toasted almonds, and toss to combine. Serve right away or let sit for up to 30 minutes and serve barely warm.

*—Susie Middleton*

# Grilled Baby Eggplant & Plum Tomatoes with Fresh Basil

**This dish is brilliant for entertaining because it tastes wonderful at room temperature, so you can make it ahead. Scoring the flesh of the eggplant before grilling it helps it cook to tender, smoky perfection. To make cheese shavings, run a vegetable peeler across the surface of a block of cheese—lightly for wispy shavings and with more force for substantial ones.**

With the cover down, heat a gas grill to high. Mince the garlic, sprinkle the salt over it, and scrape repeatedly with the flat side of a chef's knife until the garlic is mashed to a paste. Combine the garlic paste with the oil in a small bowl and add the thyme and a generous amount of pepper.

Trim the tops off each eggplant, then score the skin lengthwise with the tines of a fork. Cut each eggplant in half lengthwise and, using the sharp tip of a knife, score the cut sides in a crosshatch pattern, going halfway through the flesh, about ½ inch deep. Gently knock out any loose seeds from the tomatoes. Put the eggplant and tomatoes in a bowl large enough to hold them. Toss with the garlic oil and sprinkle with pepper.

With the lid down, grill the eggplant on both sides until tender and deeply colored but not burnt, about 10 minutes total. Grill the tomatoes, cut sides down, just until they're nicely warmed and slightly charred, 2 to 5 minutes total. Baste the vegetables while grilling with the remaining seasoned oil.

Mix the grilled eggplant and tomatoes on a serving platter and scatter the basil and cheese over them. Drizzle more oil on top or pass a bottle of extra-virgin olive oil at the table. —*Lauren Groveman*

*Serves six to eight.*

- 3 cloves garlic, peeled
- 2 teaspoons kosher salt
- ½ cup extra-virgin olive oil; more for drizzling
- 2 generous teaspoons minced fresh thyme
- Freshly ground black pepper
- 6 to 8 baby eggplant (about 2 pounds total)
- 1¼ pounds ripe but firm plum tomatoes (about 6), halved through the stem end
- 8 large basil leaves, stacked and sliced into ¼-inch-thick ribbons
- ½ cup shaved Parmigiano-Reggiano

# Grilled Tomatoes

*Serves six.*

6 firm medium tomatoes (about 2¼ pounds total)

Kosher salt

1½ tablespoons red-wine vinegar

3½ tablespoons extra-virgin olive oil

1 clove garlic, minced

1 small shallot, minced

Freshly ground black pepper

1 tablespoon chopped fresh flat-leaf parsley; whole leaves, for garnish

**Tomato halves are much easier to handle on the grill than tomato slices. These tomatoes would be delicious with your favorite vinaigrette or even drizzled with a pesto.**

Remove the green stem from the tomatoes but don't core them. Cut each tomato in half horizontally. Gently loosen the seeds with your fingertips. Turn the tomato over and shake to discard any loose seeds. Sprinkle the cut sides of the tomatoes well with salt. Set them cut side down on a wire rack and let drain for 30 minutes.

Prepare a charcoal grill so it's medium hot or heat a gas grill to high.

In a bowl, whisk the vinegar with 3 tablespoons of the oil, the garlic, and shallot. Season to taste with salt and pepper.

Lightly oil the drained tomatoes with the remaining ½ tablespoon oil. Arrange them cut side down on the hot grate and grill (turning halfway through) until the skins begin to blister and soften, 6 to 10 minutes.

Just before serving, add the chopped parsley to the vinaigrette. Transfer the tomatoes from the grill to a platter and drizzle with the vinaigrette. Garnish with the parsley leaves and serve hot, warm, or at room temperature.

*—Joanne Weir*

# Creamy Winter Greens Gratin

*Serves four.*

2 tablespoons unsalted butter

½ cup fresh breadcrumbs

Kosher salt and freshly ground black pepper

1 cup heavy cream

2 cloves garlic, smashed and peeled

2½ ounces bacon (about 3 strips) or 1½ ounces thinly sliced pancetta

2 cups cooked winter greens (spinach, Swiss chard, kale, or broccoli raab; see cooking directions at far right)

⅓ cup freshly grated Parmigiano-Reggiano, or a combination of Parmigiano and another hard cheese like Gruyère, Emmental, or aged Gouda

**This creamy, crumb-topped gratin will please even the pickiest. First you'll need to boil the greens—your choice of spinach, Swiss chard, kale, or broccoli raab, following the directions at right. You can also substitute any hard cheese for the Parmigiano.**

Heat the oven to 400°F. Have ready a shallow 4-cup ceramic gratin dish or casserole dish (any shape is fine as long as it's shallow), or four individual gratin dishes.

Melt 1 tablespoon of the butter and toss it in a small bowl with the breadcrumbs and a pinch of salt and a little pepper; set aside.

In a medium saucepan, bring the cream and garlic to a boil over medium-high heat (watch that it doesn't boil over), immediately lower the heat, and simmer vigorously until the cream reduces to about ¾ cup, 4 to 8 minutes. (Don't over-reduce.) Take the pan off the heat and remove and discard the garlic cloves. Let the cream cool slightly, stirring occasionally to keep a skin from forming. Season with ¼ teaspoon salt and a few grinds of pepper.

Meanwhile, in a large nonstick skillet, cook the bacon or pancetta over medium heat until crisped and browned, about 7 minutes. Transfer to paper towels and carefully pour off most of the excess fat in the skillet (but don't wipe it clean). Return the skillet to medium heat. Add the remaining 1 tablespoon butter and let it melt. Add the cooked greens, season with ¼ teaspoon salt if using bacon (omit the salt if using pancetta), and cook, stirring constantly, for 1 minute.

Transfer the greens to the gratin dish or dishes and spread them evenly. Crumble the bacon or pancetta over the greens, then sprinkle with the cheese. Pour the seasoned cream over all, and top with the buttered breadcrumbs. Bake until the gratin is brown and bubbly, about 25 minutes. Let rest for 10 to 15 minutes before serving. *–Susie Middleton*

To get the 2 cups of cooked greens you need for the gratin at left, be sure to start out with the amount of raw greens specified for each variety as described below.

To cook the greens, cut off and discard the tough stems (use a small, sharp paring knife and trim around the stem). Bring a large pot of lightly salted water to a boil, submerge all the greens, and cook just until tender. Drain well, then spread on a towel to absorb excess moisture. If the greens still seem very wet, squeeze them gently to remove excess liquid.

## Spinach

**Start with:**
1 pound mature spinach, stems removed and leaves roughly chopped to yield about 7 cups tightly packed (or 12 ounces)

**Cook for:**
30 seconds

## Swiss chard

**Start with:**
1¾ pounds chard, stems cut away and reserved for another use (slice, freeze, and add to your next vegetable soup) and leaves roughly chopped to yield about 9½ cups (or 12 ounces)

**Cook for:**
1 minute

## Kale

**Start with:**
1¼ pounds kale, tough stems trimmed away, leaves roughly chopped to yield 6 cups tightly packed

**Cook for:**
8 minutes

## Broccoli raab

**Start with:**
a 1-pound bunch broccoli raab, tough lower stems removed (almost half the bunch), as well as any discolored leaves, and the rest very roughly chopped to yield about 6 heaping cups

**Cook for:**
2 minutes

# Garlicky Cherry Tomato Gratin

*Serves four to six.*

3 tablespoons extra-virgin olive oil; more for the dish

1 teaspoon minced garlic

2 tablespoons fresh orange juice

1 teaspoon balsamic vinegar

1¾ pounds small red and yellow cherry tomatoes, halved (about 4½ cups)

1 teaspoon lightly chopped fresh thyme; plus ¼ teaspoon whole leaves

Kosher salt

1½ cups fresh breadcrumbs

**Use a combination of cherry tomato varieties to create great flavor and color. This is a perfect destination for those cute baskets of Sweet 100s on display at the farmers' market. Don't be tempted to use grape tomatoes, as their texture isn't as pleasing as that of true cherry tomatoes.**

Heat the oven to 350°F. Lightly oil a shallow 1½-quart baking dish (a ceramic gratin dish is nice; the shallower the better).

In a small (preferably nonstick) skillet, heat 2 tablespoons of the oil over medium-low heat. Add the garlic and cook until it softens and becomes fragrant (but does not brown), about 1 minute. Remove from the heat and let cool. Add the orange juice and vinegar and stir.

In a medium bowl, combine the tomatoes with the garlic-oil mixture, the chopped thyme, and ½ teaspoon salt; stir well. Spread evenly in the gratin dish.

In small bowl, mix the breadcrumbs with the remaining 1 tablespoon oil, whole thyme leaves, and ¼ teaspoon salt until well combined. Cover the tomatoes evenly with the crumb mixture.

Bake until the crumbs are nicely golden, 50 to 60 minutes. By this time, the juices will have been bubbling around the edges for some time. The tomatoes will be tender but not completely broken down. The longer you bake the gratin, the more flavorful it will be as the juices will reduce, but don't allow the crumbs to burn. —*Susie Middleton*

# Kale with Pancetta & Marjoram

**Pancetta is an Italian bacon that's cured with salt and spices but not smoked, so it's slightly sweeter and milder than American bacon. If you want that smokiness, however, you can use about 3 slices of thick-cut regular bacon instead. Or leave out the bacon altogether, add a bit more olive oil, and enjoy a delicious vegetarian version of this dish.**

Heat 2 tablespoons of the oil in a wide 8-quart pot with a lid over medium heat until shimmering. Add the pancetta and cook, stirring occasionally, until golden, 4 to 5 minutes. Add the onion and a few generous grinds of black pepper and cook, stirring occasionally, until the onion is softened and beginning to brown around the edges, 5 to 7 minutes. Add the garlic and cook until the onion is lightly caramelized, 4 to 6 minutes.

Pack the kale into the pot and sprinkle with the marjoram, red pepper, and ½ teaspoon salt. Cover and let wilt for 1 minute, then toss the kale and onion together with tongs, cover, and cook, removing the lid to toss occasionally, until just tender, about 10 minutes (taste a piece to check).

Toss the kale with the vinegar, the remaining tablespoon oil and, if necessary, additional salt and pepper to taste and serve. *—Allison Ehri*

*Yields about 4 cups;*
*serves four.*

**3 tablespoons extra-virgin olive oil**

**3 ounces pancetta, cut into ¼-inch dice**

**1 large yellow onion (12 ounces), halved lengthwise and thinly sliced lengthwise (about 3 cups)**

**Freshly ground black pepper**

**2 large cloves garlic, chopped**

**2½ pounds kale (about 2 bunches), stemmed, leaves torn into large pieces, rinsed well, and drained but not dried**

**2 teaspoons chopped fresh marjoram**

**⅛ to ¼ teaspoon crushed red pepper flakes**

**Kosher salt**

**1 teaspoon red-wine vinegar**

# Twice-Baked Potatoes with Cheese & Bacon

*Serves eight.*

4 medium russet potatoes (about 8 ounces each), scrubbed

3½ tablespoons unsalted butter, at room temperature

½ cup crème fraîche or sour cream, at room temperature

¼ cup half-and-half, warmed

¾ cup shredded sharp Cheddar or Gruyère

¼ cup lightly packed finely grated Parmigiano-Reggiano

5 strips bacon, cooked until crisp and crumbled

½ teaspoon kosher salt

Freshly ground black pepper

2 tablespoons snipped fresh chives or finely chopped scallions (both white and green parts; optional)

**tip:** To get a head start on entertaining, fill the potatoes, transfer them to a baking dish, cover tightly with plastic, and refrigerate for several hours or overnight. They can go directly from the refrigerator to the oven (obviously, remove the plastic wrap first).

**It's hard not to love the fluffy texture of mashed potatoes combined with the satisfyingly chewy texture of baked potato skins. Easy to make, these potatoes can be assembled ahead of time, too (see tip below).**

Position a rack in the center of the oven and heat the oven to 350°F. Set the potatoes directly on the oven rack and bake until tender all the way through, 1 to 1¼ hours. Transfer the potatoes to a work surface and let them cool for 10 to 15 minutes. Increase the oven temperature to 400°F.

Examine each potato to see if there's a way to halve it to give you two shallow, wide halves rather than taller, narrower ones. With a large chef's knife, slice each potato in half lengthwise, cutting cleanly—not sawing—so as not to tear the skin. Using a dishtowel or oven mitt to protect your hand from the heat, hold a potato half in one hand and gently scoop out the flesh with a spoon, leaving the shell ¼ to ⅛ inch thick. Repeat with the remaining halves. Force all the flesh through a potato ricer or mash it with a potato masher; transfer it to a mixing bowl.

With a wooden spoon, stir in 3 tablespoons of the butter, the crème fraîche, half-and-half, cheeses, bacon, salt, pepper to taste, and chives or scallions, if using, into the mashed potato flesh. Scoop the filling into the potato skins, compacting it lightly (just enough so that it holds together). For a rough-textured surface, mark it with the tines of a fork. Top each with bits of the remaining ½ tablespoon butter.

Arrange the potatoes on a baking sheet or in a large baking dish. Bake until heated through and beginning to brown in spots on top, 25 to 30 minutes (or 30 to 35 minutes if made ahead and refrigerated). Let sit for about 10 minutes before serving. *—Molly Stevens*

# Three-Cheese Potato Gratin

*Serves six to eight.*

2 teaspoons unsalted butter, at room temperature

1½ cups whole milk

1 cup heavy cream

2 large cloves garlic, smashed and peeled

2 to 3 sprigs fresh rosemary, 3 inches long

Pinch freshly grated nutmeg

4 ounces Swiss cheese, grated (about 1 cup)

2 ounces Parmigiano-Reggiano, grated (about ½ cup)

2 pounds russet potatoes (3 to 4 medium)

Kosher salt and freshly ground white pepper

4 ounces fresh goat cheese, crumbled (about ⅔ cup)

**Creamy and cheesy, tender and toothsome, this gratin is the essence of comfort food. If you'd like to make this less rich, use less cream and more milk.**

Position a rack in the center of the oven and heat the oven to 350°F. Line a rimmed baking sheet with foil. Grease a 9x13-inch baking dish with the butter.

Pour the milk and cream into a small saucepan. Add the garlic, rosemary, and nutmeg. Bring just to a simmer, cover, and remove from the heat. Set aside to infuse for at least 20 minutes. Combine the Swiss cheese and Parmigiano in a bowl.

Peel the potatoes and, using a mandoline or your sharpest knife, slice them into ⅛-inch-thick rounds. Arrange about one-third of the potatoes in a single overlapping layer in the baking dish, season with salt and white pepper, and top with one-third of the Swiss-Parmigiano mix. Scatter over half of the goat cheese. Add a second overlapping layer of potatoes, more salt and white pepper, another third of the Swiss-Parmigiano mix, and the remaining goat cheese. Make a third layer with the remaining potatoes and season with salt and white pepper. Press down lightly to compact the layers.

Remove the garlic and rosemary from the infused cream, and discard them. Set the cream over medium-high heat and watch carefully until it just begins to simmer; don't let it boil. Pour the cream over the potatoes and sprinkle the remaining Swiss-Parmigiano mix on top. Set the baking dish on the foil-lined baking sheet and bake until the top is deeply brown and the potatoes are completely tender when poked with a skewer, 1¼ to 1½ hours. Let sit for 10 to 15 minutes before serving. *—Molly Stevens*

## Why russets are dry and fluffy

Not only do russet potatoes have more starch than other varieties, they also have more of a particular type of starch known as amylose. These starch granules are relatively large, and when they're heated they absorb water from surrounding cells, which makes the potato dry. The amylose starch also swells up and separates, and this makes the potato seem light and fluffy. The result is a potato that's perfect for baking and mashing, not to mention absorbing butter and other enrichments.

# Smashed Potatoes with Horseradish Crème Fraîche

*Serves six.*

¾ cup crème fraîche

3 tablespoons prepared horseradish, more to taste

Kosher salt and freshly ground black pepper

1½ pounds small fingerling potatoes or baby potatoes, such as baby Yukon Golds or Red Bliss

¼ cup (½ stick) unsalted butter

2 tablespoons chopped fresh flat-leaf parsley

**For a twist on classic mashed potatoes, fingerlings or baby potatoes are boiled, crushed slightly, and enriched with butter. A little bit of horseradish added to the crème fraîche topping makes this dish a winner with roast beef.**

Combine the crème fraîche and horseradish in a small bowl. Season to taste with salt, pepper, and more horseradish, if you like.

Put the potatoes in a medium pot, cover with cold water (by about 2 inches), and add 1 tablespoon salt. Bring to a boil, turn down the heat to medium low, and simmer gently until the potatoes are tender when pierced with a skewer, 15 to 20 minutes. Reserve about ¼ cup of the water and drain the potatoes. At this point, you can hold the potatoes for a few hours (To reheat, immerse them in boiling water until they're heated through, about 5 minutes.)

Let the potatoes cool for a moment, then slightly smash them with a wooden spoon just until they crack open. Return the potatoes to the pot over medium heat. Add the butter and ¾ teaspoon salt. Stir to coat the potatoes with the butter. Add a few tablespoons of the reserved potato water to help coat and glaze the potatoes. Stir in the parsley, taste, and adjust the seasoning with salt and pepper. Top each serving with crème fraîche and a sprinkle of pepper. *—Suzanne Goin*

Ruby Crescent, Purple Peruvian, Russian Banana—these may sound like designer paint colors, but they're actually varieties of fingerling potatoes. These petite spuds, which somewhat resemble misshapen fingers (hence the name), come in many varieties. They all tend to have thinner skin and denser flesh than round potatoes like Yukon Golds or red-skins. Ruby Crescents and Purple Peruvians have a delicate, slightly sweet flavor, whereas the Russian Bananas are more robust and earthy.

Fingerlings are fairly all-purpose, lending themselves to roasting, sautéing, boiling, and steaming. Feel free to substitute fingerlings for baby potatoes in your favorite recipes. The Purples make for a delicious and dramatic potato salad on their own or as part of a mix; just cook the different varieties separately, as the cooking times may vary slightly.

For a real treat, try slicing fingerlings into ¼-inch-thick coins and poaching them at a simmer in olive oil until tender, about 15 minutes. If you're a garlic lover, throw in a handful of peeled, halved garlic cloves before poaching. Remove the potatoes from the oil with a slotted spoon and serve them sprinkled with coarse salt and freshly ground black pepper.

# Baked Sweet Potatoes with Maple-Pecan-Shallot Butter

*Serves four.*

7 tablespoons unsalted butter, at room temperature

2 medium shallots, halved and thinly sliced crosswise

¼ cup chopped pecans, toasted on a baking sheet in a 375°F oven until golden, 5 to 10 minutes

1 tablespoon real maple syrup

1 teaspoon chopped fresh thyme

Kosher salt

4 medium sweet potatoes of similar size (10 to 12 ounces each), scrubbed and patted dry

**A generous knob of this mildly sweet butter turns a simple baked potato into a special side. The butter can be refrigerated for up to 1 week or frozen for up to 2 months.**

Melt 1 tablespoon of the butter in a medium nonstick skillet over medium-low heat. Add the shallots and cook until well browned and slightly crisp, about 6 minutes. Set aside to cool.

In a small bowl, combine the remaining 6 tablespoons butter with the shallots, pecans, maple syrup, thyme, and ⅛ teaspoon salt. Blend together with a spoon or fork until evenly incorporated. Set aside for at least 1 hour at room temperature. (If not using within a few hours, cover and refrigerate. Bring the butter to room temperature before using.)

Position a rack in the center of the oven and heat the oven to 425°F. Lay the potatoes on a foil-lined rimmed baking sheet and bake until the flesh is very tender when pierced with a fork, 50 minutes to 1 hour.

To serve, make a cut along the top of each potato, push on the ends to pry it partially open, and fluff the flesh with a fork. Place a dollop of the maple-pecan-shallot butter inside each potato and pass extra butter at the table, if desired. *—Ruth Lively*

**tip:** As with any potato, peeled sweet potatoes will darken when exposed to air. To prevent this, keep cut potatoes fully submerged in a bowl of cold water until ready to cook, then pat dry and proceed with your recipe. Baked sweet potatoes keep well in the fridge for a week or longer, so you can have them on hand to mash or use as twice-baked, in a soup, or just warmed up whole and brightened with a knob of herb butter or a spoonful of pesto.

# Pan-Fried Yukon Gold Potatoes with Paprika

*Serves four to six.*

**1½ pounds Yukon Gold potatoes (3 or 4 medium potatoes), scrubbed but not peeled**

**5 tablespoons extra-virgin olive oil**

**¾ teaspoon kosher salt; more to taste**

**1 teaspoon paprika, preferably Hungarian sweet or Spanish smoked paprika**

**Freshly ground black pepper**

If you have smoked Spanish paprika (called pimentón), this is a great place to use it. Use a pan large enough to hold the potatoes in one layer so they don't steam in their own moisture. If stored properly in a cool, dark place, preferably with high humidity, Yukon Golds don't turn brown as quickly as other potatoes once they're cut. Still, if you're prepping the potatoes ahead, it's a good idea to keep them covered in water or coat them lightly with oil.

Cut the potatoes in half, then cut them in thick slices lengthwise, ½ to ¾ inch wide. Stack the slices and cut them in half lengthwise, then cut crosswise to get ¾-inch-wide pieces.

Heat 4 tablespoons of the oil in an 11- to 12-inch skillet, preferably cast iron, over medium-high heat. When the oil is shimmering hot, add the potatoes and stir immediately to coat them with the oil. Sprinkle with the ¾ teaspoon salt and stir again. Fry the potatoes, stirring frequently, until they're tender in the center and nicely browned on the outside, 25 to 30 minutes. (If the potatoes seem to be browning too fast, reduce the heat to medium or medium-low.)

Turn off the heat. Push the potatoes to one side of the pan and pour the remaining 1 tablespoon oil into the empty space in the pan. Stir the paprika into the oil and let sizzle for about 5 seconds. Stir the potatoes into the paprika oil until well coated. Stir in several grinds of pepper. Taste for salt and add more if necessary. Serve hot.

*—Ruth Lively*

## Herb-roasted:

For herb-roasted potatoes, roast whole small Yukon Golds tossed with olive oil and seasoned with coarse sea salt and pepper in a hot oven until tender. During the last 20 minutes of cooking, add a handful of chopped fresh sage, rosemary, winter savory, or several sprigs of thyme or a combination. Toss together and finish cooking.

## Braised with artichokes:

To turn out a flavorful Mediterranean braise, brown quartered trimmed artichokes and quartered Yukon Golds in olive oil, then add olives, a few thin slices of lemon, slivered garlic, fresh or dried oregano, salt and pepper, and some chicken or vegetable stock. Cover and simmer until the vegetables are tender and the liquid has reduced to a few tablespoons, 30 to 35 minutes.

## Garlicky mashed:

For garlic mashed potatoes, cover 1½ pounds of quartered Yukon Golds and a head of peeled garlic with water, boil until tender, and drain. Immediately mash with a hand masher to your desired smoothness. Add salt, pepper, half a stick of butter, and, if desired, a little half-and-half or cream.

## Boiled and smashed:

After boiling Yukon Golds in their jackets, smash them roughly with a fork right on the dinner plate, then drizzle with good extra-virgin olive oil and sprinkle on sea salt, a grind of black pepper, and a scattering of chopped fresh chives.

## In a gratin:

For a simple but rich gratin, layer very thin slices of Yukon Golds in a generously buttered dish or skillet, arranging them so the slices just overlap. Sprinkle each layer lightly with salt and pepper, a little crushed pink peppercorn, rosemary leaves, and a bit of grated hard cheese, like Asiago or Parmigiano-Reggiano. Make three to four layers in all. Pour a little heavy cream over all and bake at 375°F for 35 to 40 minutes, until golden.

## As a soup:

For a delicious and simple soup, sweat chopped leeks and celery in a little olive oil or butter, then simmer the leeks and celery with diced potatoes in chicken or vegetable stock or water. Season with salt and pepper. When the vegetables are tender, purée and serve hot or cold, with a dollop of sour cream topped with chopped fresh chives.

# Grilled Corn on the Cob with Lime-Cayenne Butter

*Serves eight to ten.*

½ cup (1 stick) unsalted butter
Juice of 1 lime
1 teaspoon kosher salt
½ teaspoon cayenne
8 to 10 ears corn

**The tart and spicy butter offers a nice contrast to the sweet, smoky flavors of the grilled corn. While a charcoal fire creates the best flavors, the butter will enhance corn cooked on a gas grill, too.**

Melt the butter in a small saucepan and stir in the lime juice, salt, and cayenne. Keep warm.

Peel off all but one or two layers of the corn husks. Pull the remaining husks down, but not off, and remove the bulk of the silks (the rest will come off easily after they char). Pull up the husks; it's okay if some kernels peek through.

Prepare a hot charcoal fire or heat a gas grill to high. Put the corn on the grate while the coals are still red hot. (Cover if using a gas grill.) Grill the corn, turning often, until the outer layer of husk is completely charred. Depending on your fire, this could take from 5 to 10 minutes. You can push the corn to a cooler spot if you're grilling other things for your meal, or transfer the grilled corn to a platter and keep it warm in the charred husks.

Just before serving, peel off the husk and brush away any remaining silks. Brown the kernels on the grill briefly, turning the corn frequently to develop a roasty color and a little additional smoke flavor, about 1 minute. (If the corn spends too long on the grill without the protection of the husk, the kernels will become dry and a bit chewy.)

Brush the warm cayenne butter on the hot grilled corn and serve immediately. *—Lisa Hanauer*

# Roasted Rosemary Butternut Squash & Shallots

**The key to perfectly roasted vegetables is to spread them out in one layer on a heavy-duty baking sheet—any closer and they'll steam rather than roast.**

Position a rack in the center of the oven and heat the oven to 450°F.

Put the squash on a heavy-duty rimmed baking sheet. Peel and quarter each shallot and add them to the squash. Drizzle the oil over the vegetables; toss to coat. Sprinkle with the rosemary, salt, sugar, and pepper; toss to coat. Distribute the vegetables evenly on the baking sheet. Roast for 20 minutes. Stir, then continue roasting until the vegetables are tender and lightly browned, another 10 to 15 minutes. Before serving, taste and season with more salt if needed. *—Julianna Grimes Bottcher*

*Serves four.*

3 cups peeled butternut squash cut into ¾-inch dice (from about a 2-pound squash)

4 medium shallots

2 tablespoons extra-virgin olive oil

1 teaspoon chopped fresh rosemary

1 teaspoon kosher salt

½ teaspoon granulated sugar

½ teaspoon freshly ground black pepper

# Sautéed Butternut Squash with Lemon, Walnuts & Parsley

*Serves two to three.*

2 tablespoons extra-virgin olive oil

2 tablespoons unsalted butter

3 cups peeled butternut squash cut into ½-inch dice (from about a 2-pound squash)

Kosher salt and freshly ground black pepper

¼ cup loosely packed fresh flat-leaf parsley leaves, chopped

⅓ cup chopped walnuts, toasted on a baking sheet in a 375°F oven until golden, 5 to 10 minutes

1½ teaspoons freshly grated lemon zest

**The high heat of the sauté pan gives butternut squash a golden, crisp exterior and deep rich flavor. For best results, avoid using a nonstick pan, which will prevent the squash from browning properly. A straight-sided sauté pan with a stainless-steel interior works best.**

Heat the oil and butter together in a 10-inch straight-sided sauté pan over medium-high heat. When the oil is hot and the butter has melted, add the squash, 1 teaspoon salt, and ½ teaspoon pepper. Cook, stirring occasionally, until the squash is lightly browned and tender, 8 to 10 minutes. Transfer to a serving bowl.

Add the parsley, walnuts, and lemon zest to the squash and toss to combine. Serve immediately. *—Julianna Grimes Bottcher*

## Peeling and cubing butternut squash

**1** Square off the ends and cut the squash in two just above the bulbous end. Stand the sections on the flat ends and use a sharp knife (or vegetable peeler) to remove the tough outer peel, slicing from top to bottom.

**2** Cut the rounded end in half lengthwise and scoop out the seeds.

**3** Cut the squash into uniform ½- or ¾-inch cubes, so they'll cook evenly.

# 9 Desserts

p328

p358

**Chocolate-Raspberry Cookies & Cream**
(recipe on page 317)

# Pomegranate Sangria Gelatin

*Serves six.*

2 cups pure pomegranate juice, such as Pom® brand

4 teaspoons unflavored gelatin powder

⅓ cup granulated sugar

1 cup dry white wine

¼ cup strained fresh orange juice

2 tablespoons strained fresh lime juice

1½ cups mixed small-diced or sliced fresh fruit, such as berries, peaches, plums, mangos, oranges, honeydew melon, grapes, or bananas

Small sprigs fresh mint, for garnish (optional)

**If you think of gelatin desserts as strictly for kids, you might be surprised at how pleasing a homemade version can be. With unflavored gelatin powder, you can make gelatin desserts out of just about any liquid, including your favorite juice-based cocktails. Check your supermarket's fresh produce or bottled juice section for pomegranate juice.**

Pour 1 cup of the pomegranate juice into a small saucepan. Sprinkle the gelatin and then the sugar over the juice. Let sit for 5 minutes. Set the saucepan over medium heat and stir until the gelatin and sugar completely dissolve. Off the heat, stir in the remaining 1 cup pomegranate juice, along with the wine, orange juice, and lime juice. Pour the mixture into six wineglasses or footed dessert glasses. Refrigerate until firm, 3 to 4 hours.

To serve, mound the mixed fruit on top of the gelatin and garnish with the mint sprigs, if using. *–Jennifer Armentrout*

# Chocolate-Raspberry Cookies & Cream

**This is best made the night before serving. If you can't find crème fraîche, you can use all heavy cream instead.**

Put 1 cup of the raspberries in a small bowl, sprinkle with 2 tablespoons of the sugar, mash with a fork, and let sit a few minutes.

Meanwhile, put the remaining berries and 2 more tablespoons of sugar in a food processor (or blender) and process until the berries form a purée. Strain through a fine mesh strainer into a small bowl, pressing with a rubber spatula to get the seeds out. Squeeze in a few drops of lemon juice and add a tiny pinch of salt. Taste and add more sugar or lemon if needed. The sauce should be thin enough to drizzle. If it seems too thick, add a few drops of water. Cover and refrigerate.

In a medium bowl, combine the cream, crème fraîche, and the remaining 1 tablespoon sugar and whip with a hand-held electric mixer until the mixture forms firm, thick peaks. Add the mashed berry mixture and lightly fold into the cream mixture with a rubber spatula, leaving streaks.

Reserve 6 of the cookies for decoration and crunch up the rest into uneven pieces—not too small. Fold the cookies into the cream. Cover with plastic wrap, pressing the wrap onto the surface of the cream, and chill until the cookie pieces are thoroughly softened, at least 2 hours and preferably overnight.

To serve, use an ice cream scoop or large spoon to scoop out a mound of cookies and cream into a small bowl or onto a plate. Drizzle a ribbon of raspberry sauce around the plate, tuck a whole cookie into the cream, decorate with a mint sprig, and serve. —*Martha Holmberg*

See photo on page 315.

*Yields 2½ cups cream and ¾ cup sauce; serves six.*

3 cups frozen raspberries (about 12 ounces), thawed

5 tablespoons granulated sugar; more if needed

Few drops fresh lemon juice

Kosher salt

⅔ cup heavy cream

⅓ cup crème fraîche

21 Famous Chocolate Wafers® (thin chocolate cookies)

6 sprigs fresh mint

# Clementine Granita

*Yields about 1 quart; serves four.*

¾ cup granulated sugar

2 tablespoons finely chopped clementine zest (from 2 to 3 medium clementines)

Kosher salt

¾ cup water

3 cups fresh clementine juice, with pulp (from 18 to 20 medium clementines or about 4 pounds)

**Although a frozen dessert might not be your first thought in deep winter when citrus fruits are in season, this granita is a refreshingly light and delightful finish to a rich winter meal, and it's a snap to make. If you have an ice cream freezer, this recipe works equally well as a sorbet.**

In a small saucepan, stir the sugar, zest, a pinch of salt, and the water. Bring to a boil over medium heat and cook, stirring, until the sugar dissolves and the syrup is clear, about 2 minutes. Set aside to cool slightly as you juice the clementines.

Stir the juice and sugar syrup together, pour into a small metal pan (such as a loaf pan), cover with plastic wrap, and freeze for 2 hours. Stir the mixture with a spoon, breaking up the portions that have become solid, and return to the freezer. Stir every 30 minutes until the mixture is evenly icy and granular, about 2 hours more.

Cover and return the granita to the freezer until ready to serve, up to one week. To serve, scrape with a spoon to loosen the mixture and spoon into small bowls or glasses. *–Ruth Lively*

## More clementine dessert inspirations

Clementines, which you'll find in the market from October through February, are often sold by the case. Though they'll keep for up to a week at room temperature, and longer in the crisper drawer, you may find yourself looking for ways to use them up. Below are some delicious options.

- **For a sweet garnish,** poach clementine sections and zest in a heavy syrup of 2 parts sugar to 1 part water until soft and tender, then cool and store in the syrup. Use as a garnish for cheesecake or a dense chocolate cake.

- **Try a warm gratin** of clementines with zabaglione. Pour a Grand Marnier®-flavored zabaglione (custard sauce) over clementine sections in a shallow ovenproof dish and run under the broiler for a few minutes to brown the top.

- **For a zesty compote,** simmer clementine sections with pear and apple slices in a light syrup of 1 part sugar to 2 parts water (perhaps using white or sweet wine for part of the liquid), a vanilla bean, star anise or cardamom, and a strip of clementine zest, until the fruit is tender. Let cool in the syrup. Serve with pound cake or over vanilla ice cream.

- **Make a citrusy upside-down cake** using clementine sections. Add a little zest to the batter, too, if you wish.

# Vanilla & Ginger Roasted Plums

*Serves six.*

Unsalted butter for the baking dish

6 ripe but firm black or red plums

3 to 4 tablespoons granulated sugar

1 teaspoon grated lemon zest

1 tablespoon fresh lemon juice

1 tablespoon rum, preferably dark

1½ teaspoons pure vanilla extract

½ teaspoon peeled and grated fresh ginger

Pinch kosher salt

Vanilla ice cream, for serving

**As the plums roast, they release juices that you'll want to spoon over the finished dessert. Make sure you don't overcook the plums or they'll fall apart.**

Heat the oven to 425°F. Generously butter an 8x11-inch baking dish (or one just large enough to hold the plums in one layer).

Cut the plums in half, discard the pits, and slice each halved plum into four wedges.

In a large bowl, toss the plums with 3 tablespoons of the sugar, the lemon zest and juice, rum, vanilla, ginger, and salt. Toss well. Taste one of the plum wedges; if it's still tart, sprinkle in the remaining 1 tablespoon sugar. Pour into the prepared baking dish and roast, gently stirring occasionally, until the plums are tender and juicy, 10 to 20 minutes. Don't overcook them.

Let the plums cool for at least 5 minutes or up to an hour before serving. Serve them hot or warm with vanilla ice cream and spoon the juices over the top.
—*Molly Stevens*

# Lemon Shortbread Bars

*Yields 2 dozen 2-inch-square bars.*

## For the crust:

Nonstick cooking spray, vegetable oil, or melted butter for the pan

14 tablespoons (1¾ sticks) unsalted butter, melted and cooled to just warm

½ cup granulated sugar

½ teaspoon table salt

2 cups plus 2 tablespoons (9½ ounces) unbleached all-purpose flour

## For the lemon topping:

4 large eggs

1¼ cups granulated sugar

3 tablespoons unbleached all-purpose flour

⅛ teaspoon table salt

¾ cup strained fresh lemon juice (from 3 to 4 lemons)

1 tablespoon packed finely grated fresh lemon zest (from 2 lemons, using a rasp-style grater)

1 tablespoon confectioners' sugar

---

**With its sweet-tart flavor and creamy, delicate texture, the lemon topping on these bars is similar to lemon curd but easier to make. The crust has the buttery tenderness of shortbread without the tendency to crumble.**

**Make the crust:** Line a straight-sided 13x9-inch metal baking pan with foil, letting the ends create an overhanging edge for easy removal. Lightly coat the sides of the foil (not the bottom) with nonstick cooking spray, oil, or melted butter to prevent the lemon topping from sticking.

In a medium bowl, stir together the butter, granulated sugar, and salt. Stir in the flour to make a stiff dough. Press the dough evenly into the bottom of the prepared pan. Prick the dough all over with a fork. Refrigerate for 30 minutes (or freeze for 5 to 7 minutes), until the dough is firm.

Meanwhile, position a rack near the center of the oven and heat the oven to 325°F. Bake the crust until golden and set, about 30 minutes.

**Make the topping:** In a medium bowl, whisk the eggs, granulated sugar, flour, and salt together until smooth, about 1 minute. Whisk in the lemon juice and zest. Pour the topping over the hot crust. Return the pan to the oven and increase the heat to 350°F. Bake until the topping is set in the center (it no longer wiggles when the pan is moved) and the edges are golden, 20 to 25 minutes.

Set the pan on a wire rack to cool until the crust is completely firm, at least 1 hour. (For faster cooling, put the bars in the fridge once the pan is no longer piping hot, or even outside in winter.)

When the bottom of the pan is cool, carefully lift the bars from the pan using the foil sides and transfer them to a cutting board. Separate the foil from the bars by sliding a metal spatula between them. Sift the confectioners' sugar over the lemon topping. Cut the bars into 2-inch squares. These will keep, refrigerated, for 3 to 4 days. Serve at room temperature. —*Nicole Rees*

## Tricks for making lemon bars with a perfect shortbread crust

**1** Melt the butter and stir it into the sugar and salt for a crust that's rich yet sturdy.

**2** Chill the dough in the pan so it bakes without puffing or shrinking and has a perfectly crisp texture.

**3** Fully bake the crust before you add the lemon topping—it's the key to keeping that crispness.

Lemon Shortbread Bars, Caramel Turtle Bars (page 329), and
Peanut Butter & Chocolate Shortbread Bars (page 325).

# Caramel Turtle Bars

*Yields about 4 dozen 1½-inch-square bars.*

## For the crust:

Nonstick cooking spray, vegetable oil, or melted butter for the pan

14 tablespoons (1¾ sticks) unsalted butter, melted and cooled to just warm

½ cup packed light brown sugar

½ teaspoon table salt

2 cups (9 ounces) unbleached all-purpose flour

## For the caramel topping:

2 cups pecan halves, toasted on a baking sheet in a 375°F oven until golden, 5 to 10 minutes, then coarsely chopped

1 cup packed light brown sugar

¾ cup heavy cream

½ cup (1 stick) unsalted butter, cut into chunks

½ cup light corn syrup

¼ teaspoon table salt

## For the ganache:

6 tablespoons heavy cream

2 ounces good-quality bittersweet chocolate, finely chopped (about ½ cup)

**A buttery shortbread crust provides the base for a layer of crunchy pecans topped with chewy caramel and a drizzling of chocolate. You'll need a zip-top baggie to make the decorative ganache crosshatching and a candy thermometer for the caramel topping.**

**Make the shortbread crust:** Line a straight-sided 13x9-inch metal baking pan with foil, letting the ends create an overhanging edge for easy removal. Lightly coat the sides of the foil (not the bottom) with nonstick cooking spray, oil, or melted butter to prevent the caramel from sticking.

In a medium bowl, stir together the butter, brown sugar, and salt. Stir in the flour to make a stiff dough. Press the mixture evenly into the bottom of the prepared pan. Prick the dough all over with a fork. Refrigerate for 30 minutes (or freeze for 5 to 7 minutes), until the dough is firm.

Meanwhile, position a rack near the center of the oven and heat the oven to 325°F. Bake the dough for 20 minutes, then decrease the oven temperature to 300°F and bake until the crust is golden all over and completely set, about 15 more minutes.

**Make the topping:** Sprinkle the pecans evenly over the crust.

In a heavy, medium saucepan, bring the brown sugar, cream, butter, corn syrup, and salt to a boil over medium-high heat, stirring until all the ingredients are melted and smooth. Let the mixture continue to boil, without stirring, until a candy thermometer registers 240°F, about 6 more minutes. Turn off the heat and immediately (but carefully) pour the caramel evenly over the prepared crust. Let the bars cool completely, about 2 hours, before garnishing with the ganache.

**Make the ganache:** Put the chocolate in a small heatproof bowl. In a small saucepan, bring the heavy cream to a boil. Remove from the heat and pour over the chocolate. Let sit for 3 minutes, then stir gently with a rubber spatula until combined and smooth.

Fill a plastic zip-top baggie with the ganache, snip the tip off a corner, and drizzle it decoratively over the caramel bars (you don't have to use all the ganache; any extra will keep in the fridge for five days). Let the ganache set for 30 minutes to an hour.

Carefully lift the bars from the pan using the foil sides and transfer them to a cutting board. Separate the foil from the bars by sliding a metal spatula between them. Cut the bars into 1½-inch squares. They will keep at room temperature for 1 week. *–Nicole Rees*

# Peanut Butter & Chocolate Shortbread Bars

The combination of a creamy peanut-butter spread and bittersweet chocolate ganache make these hard to resist. Cut into miniature squares, these bar cookies are great for serving at a dessert buffet or for snacking on any time.

**Make the peanut shortbread:** Line a straight-sided 13x9-inch metal baking pan with foil, letting the ends create an overhanging edge for easy removal.

In a medium bowl, stir the melted butter, granulated sugar, and salt. Stir in the flour and peanuts to make a stiff dough. Press the mixture evenly into the bottom of the prepared pan. Prick the dough all over with a fork. Refrigerate for 30 minutes (or freeze for 5 to 7 minutes), until the dough is firm.

Meanwhile, position a rack near the center of the oven. Heat the oven to 325°F, then bake the dough for 20 minutes. Reduce the oven temperature to 300°F and bake until the crust is golden brown all over and completely set, another 20 to 25 minutes. Let the crust cool completely before topping.

**Make the peanut butter filling:** In a stand mixer fitted with the paddle attachment (or in a large bowl with a hand mixer), beat together the peanut butter and butter on medium speed until smooth, about 1 minute. Add about half of the confectioners' sugar along with the vanilla and hot water. Beat on low speed until combined, then on medium speed until smooth and fluffy, about 1 more minute. Beat in the remaining confectioners' sugar until the mixture is smooth and thick, like frosting, about 1 more minute. If the filling seems too stiff, add another 1 tablespoon hot water and beat for another minute.

With a knife or metal offset spatula, spread the filling over the fully cooled crust. The filling may not spread smoothly and evenly, but don't worry; the ganache will cover it.

**Make the ganache:** Put the chocolate in a small heatproof bowl. In a small saucepan, bring the heavy cream to a boil. Remove from the heat and pour over the chocolate. Let sit for 3 minutes, then stir gently with a rubber spatula until combined and smooth. Spread the ganache over the peanut-butter filling with an offset spatula to coat evenly. Let the bars sit for at least 3 hours to allow the ganache to set before cutting (or refrigerate for 1 hour).

Carefully lift the bars from the pan using the foil sides and transfer them to a cutting board. Separate the foil from the bars by sliding a spatula between them. Cut the bars into 1½-inch squares. They will keep at room temperature for 1 week. —*Nicole Rees*

*Yields 4 dozen 1½-inch-square bars.*

### For the crust:

¾ cup (1¾ sticks) unsalted butter, melted and cooled to just warm

½ cup granulated sugar

½ teaspoon table salt

2 cups plus 2 tablespoons (9½ ounces) unbleached all-purpose flour

½ cup unsalted peanuts, finely chopped

### For the peanut-butter filling:

1 cup creamy peanut butter (not natural but an emulsified variety such as Jif®)

6 tablespoons (¾ stick) unsalted butter, at room temperature

1½ cups (6 ounces) confectioners' sugar

1 teaspoon pure vanilla extract

1 tablespoon hot water, more as needed

### For the ganache:

5 ounces good-quality bittersweet chocolate, such as Lindt Excellence®, chopped (about 1 heaping cup)

½ cup plus 2 tablespoons heavy cream

# Cranberry Streusel Shortbread Bars

*Yields about thirty-five 1¾-inch-square bars.*

## For the crust and streusel:

1 cup plus 5 tablespoons unsalted butter, melted and cooled to just warm

1 cup granulated sugar

¾ teaspoon table salt

2 large egg yolks

3 cups plus 3 tablespoons (14¼ ounces) unbleached all-purpose flour

## For the cranberry topping:

One 12-ounce bag fresh or frozen cranberries, picked over, rinsed, and drained

1 cup granulated sugar

¼ cup water

**A tangy cranberry filling keeps the rich shortbread crust and sweet streusel in check. Cut the bars larger and you have dessert.**

**Make the crust:** Line a straight-sided 13x9-inch metal baking pan with foil, letting the ends create an overhanging edge for easy removal. In a medium bowl, stir together the butter, ¾ cup of the sugar, and the salt. Whisk in the egg yolks. Stir in the flour to make a stiff dough. Transfer about 2 cups of the dough to the prepared pan and press the mixture evenly into the bottom. Prick the dough all over with a fork. Refrigerate for 30 minutes (or freeze for 5 to 7 minutes), until the dough is firm.

Meanwhile, position a rack near the center of the oven and another near the top. Heat the oven to 325°F, then bake the dough until the crust begins to set but does not brown at all on the edges (the center will not be firm yet), about 20 minutes.

**Make the streusel:** With your fingers, combine the remaining ¼ cup sugar with the reserved dough until crumbly. The mixture should hold together when pressed, but readily break into smaller pieces.

**Make the cranberry topping:** In a medium saucepan, bring the cranberries, sugar, and water to a boil. Reduce the heat to medium high and continue to boil until the liquid is reduced to a thick syrup, 5 to 8 minutes. Remove the pan from the heat and let cool 5 to 10 minutes—the syrup will continue to thicken as it cools.

Spread the cranberry mixture evenly over the hot crust. Scatter the streusel over the cranberries (don't crumble the streusel too much or the texture will be sandy). Increase the oven temperature to 350°F and bake the bars near the top of the oven until the streusel is golden and set, about 25 minutes. (Baking these bars at the top of the oven helps the streusel brown faster without overbrowning the crust.)

Place the pan on a wire rack to cool until the crust is completely firm, at least 1 hour. (For faster cooling, put the bars in the fridge once the pan is no longer piping hot, or even outside in winter.)

When the bottom of the pan is cool, carefully lift the bars from the pan using the foil sides and transfer them to a cutting board. Separate the foil from the bars by sliding a metal spatula between them. Cut the bars into 1¾-inch squares. They will keep at room temperature for 1 week. —*Nicole Rees*

# Nutty Chocolate Shortbread Wedges

**This is a nontraditional shortbread because it contains an egg yolk. It gives the shortbread a softer, less sandy texture.**

**Make the shortbread:** Position a rack in the middle of the oven and heat the oven to 350°F. Lightly butter the bottom and sides of a 9½-inch fluted tart pan with a removable bottom.

In a medium bowl, combine the butter, sugar, cocoa, and salt. Beat with an electric mixer on medium speed until well blended. Scrape the bowl. Add the egg yolk and vanilla and continue beating on medium speed until just combined. Add the flour and mix on low speed, scraping the bowl as needed, until the flour mixes in and the dough begins to clump together, about 1 minute.

Scrape the dough into the prepared pan, scattering the pieces of dough evenly. Using your fingertips (lightly floured, if necessary), pat the dough onto the bottom (not up the sides) of the pan to create an even layer. Bake until the top no longer looks wet and the dough just barely begins to pull away slightly from the sides of the pan, about 25 minutes.

**Make the glaze:** Do this shortly before the shortbread is done. Melt the chocolate and butter together in the top of a double boiler or in a microwave oven. Stir until smooth. When the shortbread is done, transfer the pan to a wire rack. Pour the warm glaze over the shortbread and, using an offset spatula, spread the glaze evenly to within ½ inch of the edge. Scatter the nuts evenly over the glaze and gently press them into the glaze. Let cool completely until the glaze is set. Remove the shortbread from the tart pan and cut it into 12 or 16 wedges. Serve at room temperature. *—Abigail Johnson Dodge*

*Serves twelve or sixteen.*

**For the shortbread:**

½ cup (1 stick) unsalted butter, at room temperature; more for the pan

½ cup granulated sugar

¼ cup unsweetened cocoa powder, preferably Dutch-processed

¼ teaspoon table salt

1 large egg yolk

½ teaspoon pure vanilla extract

1 cup (4½ ounces) unbleached all-purpose flour

**For the glaze:**

3 ounces bittersweet or semisweet chocolate, coarsely chopped (a generous ½ cup)

2 tablespoons unsalted butter, cut into two pieces

½ cup (2 ounces) coarsely chopped pecans or walnuts, toasted on a baking sheet in a 375°F oven until golden, 5 to 10 minutes, or chopped pistachios

# Kahlúa Truffle Triangles

*Yields about 6 dozen 1½- to 2-inch triangles.*

## For the crust:

1½ cups (6¾ ounces) unbleached all-purpose flour

¾ cup confectioners' sugar

¼ teaspoon table salt

¾ cup (1¼ sticks) cold, unsalted butter, cut into 10 pieces; more for the pan

½ teaspoon pure vanilla extract

## For the filling:

1 pound semisweet or bittersweet chocolate, broken into squares or very coarsely chopped

¾ cup whole or 2% milk

½ cup (1 stick) unsalted butter, cut into 6 pieces

4 large eggs

⅔ cup granulated sugar

2 tablespoons Kahlúa® (or other coffee-flavored liquor)

**You can bake these decadent treats up to a month ahead: Wrap the cooled baking pan in heavy-duty plastic wrap and freeze (no need to cut them into triangles first). Avoid piling anything on top of the pan until completely frozen. The baked truffles can also be refrigerated, wrapped in plastic, for up to two days.**

**Make the crust:** Position a rack in the center of the oven and heat the oven to 350°F. Line the bottom and sides of a 9x13-inch baking pan with foil, allowing foil to overhang the long sides of the pan to act as handles for removing the cookie later. Lightly butter the foil.

In a food processor, combine the flour, confectioners' sugar, and salt and process briefly to combine, about 15 seconds. Scatter the cold butter pieces and vanilla over the flour mixture and process, using short pulses, until the dough begins to form small clumps, 1 to 1½ minutes. Turn the dough into the prepared pan. Using lightly floured fingertips, press it into the pan in a smooth, even layer. Bake until pale golden, especially around the edges, 22 to 25 minutes. Do not overbake or the crust will be hard and crispy. Transfer the pan to a wire rack and lower the oven temperature to 325°F.

**Make the filling:** In a medium bowl, melt the chocolate, milk, and butter together over a pot of barely simmering water or in the microwave. Whisk until smooth and set aside to cool slightly.

In a stand mixer fitted with a paddle attachment (or in a large bowl with a hand mixer), beat the eggs, granulated sugar, and Kahlúa together on medium-high speed until foamy and lighter in color, 2 minutes. Reduce the speed to low and gradually add the chocolate mixture. Stop the mixer and scrape down the bowl and beater. Beat on medium speed until well blended, about 30 seconds.

Pour the chocolate batter over the baked crust and spread evenly. Bake until the sides are slightly puffed and a toothpick inserted near the center comes out wet and gooey but not liquid, 30 to 35 minutes. Transfer the pan to a rack. As it cools, the center may sink a bit, leaving the edges slightly (about ½ inch) elevated. While the filling is still warm, use your fingertips to gently press the edges down to the level of the center, if necessary.

When completely cool, cover with plastic wrap and refrigerate until very cold, at least 12 hours or up to 2 days. To serve, using the foil as handles, lift the rectangle from the pan and set it on a cutting board. Tipping the rectangle, carefully peel away the foil. Using a hot knife, cut the rectangle lengthwise into 1½-inch strips, wiping the blade clean before each cut. Cut each strip on alternating diagonals to make small triangles. Let sit at room temperature for about 5 minutes before serving. —*Abigail Johnson Dodge*

# Rich, Fudgy Brownies

*Yields one 9-inch-square pan of brownies; serves sixteen.*

1 cup (2 sticks) unsalted butter; more softened butter for the pan

²⁄₃ cup (3 ounces) unbleached all-purpose flour; more for the pan

2 cups granulated sugar

4 large eggs, at room temperature

½ teaspoon pure vanilla extract

¾ cup (2½ ounces) unsweetened natural cocoa powder

½ teaspoon baking powder

½ teaspoon table salt

**Port-Soaked Dried Cherries** (optional; see page 331)

**Port-Ganache Topping** (optional; see page 331)

**This brownie recipe gives you two options: for a picnic or a snack, make the brownies with the first eight ingredients. For an elegant dessert, add the port-soaked dried cherries to the batter and frost the cooled brownies with the port-ganache topping.**

Position a rack in the center of the oven and heat the oven to 350°F. Butter and flour a 9-inch-square metal baking pan, tapping out the excess flour.

Melt the butter in a medium saucepan over medium heat. Remove the pan from the heat. Whisk or stir in the sugar, followed by all four of the eggs and the vanilla. Stir in the flour, cocoa, baking powder, and salt, starting slowly to keep the ingredients from flying out of the pan and stirring more vigorously as you go. Stir until the batter is smooth and uniform, about 1 minute. If you're using the port-soaked cherries, stir them in at this time, along with any remaining liquid from the saucepan.

Spread the batter in the prepared pan, smoothing it so it fills the pan evenly. Bake until a toothpick or a skewer inserted ¾ inch into the center of the brownies comes out with just a few moist clumps clinging to it, about 40 minutes. Let the brownies cool completely in the pan on a wire rack. If you're topping the brownies with the ganache, spread it evenly over the cooled brownies and give it about an hour to set (it will still be quite soft and gooey).

Cut into 16 squares. Keep the brownies at room temperature, well wrapped. You can freeze them, too.

—Nicole Rees

## Port-Ganache Topping

*Yields 1 generous cup.*

½ cup tawny port

½ cup heavy cream

6 ounces semisweet chocolate, finely chopped (about 1 cup)

In a small saucepan over medium heat, bring the port to a boil and boil until reduced to 2 tablespoons, 3 to 6 minutes. Pour it into a small cup or bowl. Thoroughly rinse the pan.

Bring the heavy cream to a boil in the pan over medium-high heat, stirring occasionally. Take the pan off the heat. Stir in the chopped chocolate and reduced port until the mixture is smooth and the chocolate is melted.

Pour the ganache into a bowl and cover the surface with plastic wrap to prevent a skin from forming. Put the bowl in a cool part of the kitchen and let cool to room temperature, stirring occasionally. When it's cool, spread it over the brownies as directed in the brownie recipe.

## Port-Soaked Dried Cherries

*Yields ½ cup.*

½ cup dried cherries, very coarsely chopped (or whole dried cranberries)

⅓ cup tawny port

In a small saucepan, bring the cherries and port to a boil over medium heat. Reduce the heat to low and cook for 2 minutes. Take the pan off the heat and let cool to room temperature.

# Nutty Caramel Thumbprints

*Yields about 2 dozen cookies.*

## For the cookies:

1 cup (2 sticks) unsalted butter, at room temperature

⅔ cup (2½ ounces) confectioners' sugar

1½ teaspoons pure vanilla extract

½ teaspoon table salt

2¼ cups (10 ounces) unbleached all-purpose flour

## For the caramel filling:

22 small caramels (6 ounces), such as Kraft® brand

3 tablespoons heavy cream

⅓ cup finely chopped pecans, lightly toasted on a baking sheet in a 375°F oven, 5 to 10 minutes

This fun variation on the classic thumbprint cookie is perfect for holiday entertaining because you can make the cookies in stages, fitting preparation into your busy schedule: Bake the cookies and freeze, unfilled, for up to one month or store them at room temperature for five days. (Layer them between parchment or waxed paper in an airtight container.) You can fill the cookies up to three days ahead. Arrange them on a sheet pan in a single layer and cover tightly with plastic wrap (don't let it touch the caramel tops). Store at room temperature.

**Make the cookies:** Position a rack in the center of the oven and heat the oven to 350°F. Line two cookie sheets with parchment or nonstick baking liners.

In a stand mixer fitted with a paddle attachment (or in a large bowl with a hand mixer), beat the butter, confectioners' sugar, vanilla, and salt together on medium speed until well blended and smooth, about 3 minutes. Scrape down the bowl and beater. Add the flour and mix on low speed until a soft dough forms, about 1 minute.

Using two teaspoon measures, scoop up about two teaspoons of dough at a time and, using your palms, roll into smooth balls that are 1 to 1¼ inches in diameter. Arrange them about 1½ inches apart on the prepared cookie sheets. Using the back of a ½ teaspoon measure, press down into the middle of each mound to make a well that is almost as deep as the dough ball. (If the edges crack or break open, it's best to reroll and try again—the finished cookie will look better and hold the caramel without leaking.)

Bake one sheet at a time until the tops of the cookies look dry and the edges are golden brown, 15 to 20 minutes. Let the cookies cool on the cookie sheet for 5 minutes, then transfer them to a wire rack to cool completely.

**Make the caramel filling:** In a small saucepan, combine the unwrapped caramels and heavy cream. Set the pan over very low heat and cook, stirring constantly, until the caramels have melted and the mixture is smooth, 4 to 6 minutes. Use the caramel while warm.

Arrange the cooled cookies on a cookie sheet or jellyroll pan. Using a small spoon or spatula, drizzle the warm caramel into each indentation, filling to the rim but not overflowing. Scatter the nuts over the caramel and press lightly into the caramel. Let cool completely before storing or serving.

*—Abigail Johnson Dodge*

tip: This thumbprint recipe offers a great time-saver: using melted store-bought caramels as filling for the cookies. Look for individually wrapped caramels in the candy aisle of the supermarket.

# Pistachio-Cranberry Biscotti Straws

*Yields about 2½ dozen biscotti.*

1¼ cups (5⅝ ounces) all-purpose flour

½ cup granulated sugar

1 teaspoon baking powder

¼ teaspoon table salt

¾ cup (3½ ounces) unsalted shelled pistachio nuts

½ cup (2½ ounces) sweetened dried cranberries

1 large egg

1 large egg white

1 tablespoon finely grated orange zest (from about 2 oranges)

1 tablespoon fresh orange juice

¾ teaspoon pure vanilla extract

**These slender cookies can be made ahead—well ahead. The cooled biscotti can be frozen for up to six weeks or stored at room temperature for up to three weeks, layered between sheets of parchment or waxed paper in an airtight container.**

Position a rack in the center of the oven and heat the oven to 325°F. Line a large cookie sheet with parchment or a nonstick baking liner.

In a stand mixer fitted with the paddle attachment (or in a large bowl if mixing by hand), mix the flour, sugar, baking powder, and salt on low speed (or with a wooden spoon if mixing by hand) until well blended. Briefly mix in the nuts and cranberries.

In a small bowl or a 1-cup glass measure, whisk together the whole egg, egg white, orange zest and juice, and vanilla. With the mixer on low speed (or with the spoon), slowly pour in the egg mixture. Continue mixing until the dough is well blended and forms a sticky, moist dough, 1 to 2 minutes.

Dump the dough onto the prepared cookie sheet. Using slightly damp hands, shape the dough into a 7x11½-inch rectangle, wetting your hands as needed. Press and shape the dough as evenly as possible.

Bake until the rectangle is golden brown on top and slightly darker brown around the edges, about 25 minutes. Transfer the cookie sheet to a wire rack to cool for about 10 minutes, until it can be easily handled.

Transfer the biscotti to a cutting board; use a metal spatula to loosen it from the parchment if necessary. Using a serrated knife, cut the biscotti crosswise into slices about ⅓ inch thick. (Use a gentle sawing motion to break through the crust. After that, a firm push down on the knife is all that's needed.) Discard the parchment, return the slices to the cookie sheet, and arrange them with a cut side down. (It's all right if they touch because they don't spread.)

Bake until the biscotti are light golden brown and feel dry, about 14 minutes. Transfer the cookie sheet to a rack and cool the biscotti completely; they'll crisp as they cool. *—Abigail Johnson Dodge*

# Coffee Thins

The brown sugar and espresso flavor in these crisp cookies is as sophisticated as it gets, so these are a treat for the grown-ups. You can keep a log of dough in the fridge for up to three days, baking just a few when friends drop by.

Combine the flour, cinnamon, and salt in a small bowl.

In a large bowl, beat the butter and brown sugar together with a wooden spoon or an electric mixer until well blended; stir in the dissolved coffee. Add the flour mixture; mix until the dough is blended and begins to clump together (if you're using an electric mixer, set it on low speed). Pile the dough onto a large piece of plastic wrap. Using the wrap to help shape the dough, form it into a squared-off log 7 inches long. Chill until quite firm, at least 6 hours and up to 3 days.

Heat the oven to 350°F. Cut the dough in ¼-inch-thick slices; set them 1 inch apart on parchment-lined baking sheets. Bake until the tops look dry and the edges are slightly browned, about 12 minutes. Transfer to a wire rack to cool completely. —*Abigail Johnson Dodge*

*Yields about 28 cookies.*

1¼ cups (5½ ounces) unbleached all-purpose flour

Pinch ground cinnamon

Pinch table salt

½ cup (1 stick) unsalted butter, at room temperature

⅓ cup firmly packed dark brown sugar

1 teaspoon instant coffee or espresso powder, dissolved in 2 teaspoons coffee-flavored liqueur or water

# Toasted Almond Butter Thins

*Yields about 12 dozen cookies.*

2 cups (9 ounces) slivered blanched almonds, toasted on a baking sheet in a 375°F oven until golden, 4 to 8 minutes

1 cup plus 2 tablespoons (4½ ounces) cake flour

1 cup (4½ ounces) unbleached all-purpose flour

1 cup (2 sticks) unsalted butter, at room temperature

¾ teaspoon table salt

2½ cups (10 ounces) confectioners' sugar

1 large egg, at room temperature

**Perfect with an espresso or fragrant herbal tea, these delicate, sophisticated cookies taste like they're straight from *la pâtisserie.***

Combine the almonds and both flours in a medium bowl; set aside.

In a stand mixer fitted with the paddle attachment (or in a large bowl with a hand mixer), cream the butter on medium speed until soft and creamy. Add the salt and confectioners' sugar; mix on medium-low speed until thoroughly combined, about 5 minutes, scraping the bowl down as needed. Reduce the speed to low, add the egg, and mix until blended. Add the flour mixture; as soon as the dough comes together, stop the mixer.

Scrape the dough onto a large sheet of plastic wrap. Using the wrap to help shape and protect the dough, gently press it into a rectangle that's about 4½x8 inches and about 1½ inches thick. Wrap in plastic and refrigerate until the dough is firm enough to slice, at least 3 hours.

Heat the oven to 400°F. Line a baking sheet with parchment. Unwrap the dough, trim the edges, and slice it into three 1½-inch-square logs. Slice each log into square cookies between ⅛ and ¼ inch thick. Lay the squares ½ inch apart on the baking sheet. Bake until lightly browned around the edges, about 8 minutes, rotating the sheet halfway through. Leave the cookies on the sheet until they're cool enough to handle (about 10 minutes), then transfer them to a wire rack to cool completely. *–Joanne Chang*

# Blueberry-Lemon Cornmeal Cake

The combination of cornmeal and buttermilk offers both texture and tang. To top it off, there are blueberries in every bite. You can make this cake ahead—the flavor actually improves with a little age. Just cover the cooled cake in plastic wrap and store for up to five days at room temperature.

Position a rack in the center of the oven and heat the oven to 350°F. Lightly butter a 9x2-inch round cake pan. Line the bottom with a parchment round cut to fit the pan, lightly flour the sides, and tap out the excess.

**Make the cake:** In a medium bowl, whisk together the flour, cornmeal, baking powder, baking soda, and salt until well blended. In a stand mixer fitted with the paddle attachment (or a large bowl with a hand mixer), beat the butter, sugar, and lemon zest together on medium-high speed until well blended and fluffy, about 3 minutes. Add the eggs, one at a time, beating on medium speed until just blended and adding the lemon juice with the second egg (the batter will appear curdled; don't worry). Using a wide rubber spatula, fold in half the dry ingredients, then the buttermilk, then the remaining dry ingredients. Scrape the batter into the prepared pan and spread evenly. Bake for 15 minutes.

**Make the topping:** Combine the blueberries, sugar, and flour in a small bowl. Using a table fork, mix the ingredients, lightly crushing the blueberries and evenly coating them with the flour and sugar. After the cake has baked for 15 minutes, slide the oven rack out and quickly scatter the blueberries evenly over the top of the cake (discard any flour and sugar that doesn't adhere to the berries). Continue baking until a toothpick inserted in the center of the cake comes out clean, another 23 to 25 minutes.

Let the cake cool on a wire rack for 15 minutes. Run a knife around the inside edge of the pan. Using a dry dishtowel to protect your hands, lay the rack on top of the cake pan and, holding onto both rack and pan, and invert the cake. Lift the pan from the cake. Peel away the parchment. Lay a flat serving plate on the bottom of the cake and flip the cake one more time so the blueberries are on top. Serve warm or at room temperature. —*Abigail Johnson Dodge*

*Serves eight to ten.*

**For the cake:**

1⅓ cups (6 ounces) unbleached all-purpose flour; more for the pan

¼ cup (1½ ounces) finely ground yellow cornmeal

1 teaspoon baking powder

¼ teaspoon baking soda

¼ teaspoon table salt

6 tablespoons (¾ stick) unsalted butter, at room temperature; more for the pan

1 cup granulated sugar

1 teaspoon finely grated lemon zest

2 large eggs

1 tablespoon fresh lemon juice

½ cup buttermilk

**For the topping:**

1 cup fresh blueberries, picked over for stems

1 tablespoon granulated sugar

1 tablespoon unbleached all-purpose flour

# Lemon-Caramel Icebox Cake

*Serves twelve.*

## For the lemon curd:

4 large eggs

4 large egg yolks

3 tablespoons finely grated lemon zest (from about 3 lemons)

½ cup granulated sugar

⅔ cup fresh lemon juice

10 tablespoons (1¼ sticks) unsalted butter, cut into pieces

## For the caramel:

¾ cup granulated sugar

2 tablespoons light corn syrup

¼ cup water

¼ cup plus 2 tablespoons heavy cream

¼ teaspoon pure vanilla extract

## For assembly:

1½ cups graham cracker crumbs (from about 10 crackers), lightly toasted in a 350°F oven until they just take on some color, about 7 minutes

¼ cup (½ stick) unsalted butter, melted

1½ cups heavy cream

2 large egg whites

5 tablespoons granulated sugar; more for the pan

In this gorgeous cake, tart lemon curd gets tempered by a surprise layer of caramel sauce made pleasantly chewy by the cold. Although the cake looks complex, it's easy to make in stages; the caramel and the lemon curd can be made days ahead and refrigerated. Warm the caramel to a pourable consistency before using.

**Make the lemon curd:** Bring a medium saucepan filled halfway with water to a simmer. In a medium stainless-steel bowl that fits over the pan without touching the water, whisk together the whole eggs, yolks, lemon zest, sugar, and lemon juice. Put the bowl over (not touching) the simmering water and whisk until the mixture thickens and becomes smooth and custard-like, about 10 minutes; remove from the heat. Whisk in the butter a piece at a time. Strain the curd through a fine mesh strainer into a bowl. Put plastic wrap directly on its surface to keep a skin from forming and refrigerate.

**Make the caramel:** In a heavy, medium saucepan, combine the sugar, corn syrup, and water; stir until the sugar dissolves. Cook over high heat until the mixture turns dark amber. Don't stir the caramel while it cooks; instead, swirl the pan gently to get an even color. Remove from the heat and whisk in the cream (be careful, it will splatter). Return the mixture to the heat, whisk until smooth, then whisk in the vanilla. Let cool to room temperature.

**Assemble the cake:** Spray a 9-inch springform pan with nonstick cooking spray or grease it lightly. Dust the pan with sugar and knock out any excess. Combine the toasted graham cracker crumbs and melted butter, rubbing them together with your fingertips to combine thoroughly. Sprinkle half of the crumbs over the bottom of the prepared pan and pat down; reserve the rest.

In a large bowl, beat the cream to firm peaks with an electric mixer. Fold in the cooled lemon curd. Spoon half of the lemon cream over the cracker crust and spread it evenly to the edges of the pan. Sprinkle the remaining crumbs over the lemon cream. Spread the remaining lemon cream over the crumbs. Pour a little more than half of the caramel over the lemon cream, reserving the rest in the refrigerator. Put the cake in the freezer while you make the meringue topping.

Whisk the egg whites and sugar together in a double boiler over medium-high heat (as you did with the lemon curd) and cook until the mixture is warm and the sugar is dissolved, about 2 minutes. With an electric mixer, beat the whites to stiff peaks. Spread the meringue on the top of the cake. Freeze the cake, unwrapped, overnight. (For longer storage, wrap it in plastic once the meringue has firmed up; unwrap before defrosting.)

About an hour before serving, transfer the cake to the refrigerator. Just before serving, reheat the remaining caramel sauce if you want to drizzle some on the plate. Brown the meringue by running it under a hot broiler, rotating the cake if necessary, until evenly browned (or brown it with a propane torch). Run a thin knife around the sides of the cake and remove the springform. Cut the cake into slices with a warm knife. If the cake seems very frozen, let the slices soften somewhat before serving. Serve with a drizzle of the warm caramel sauce. —*Heather Ho*

# Pumpkin Swirl Cheesecakes

*Yields 12 mini cheesecakes.*

Cooking spray

Two 8-ounce packages cream cheese, at room temperature

²⁄₃ cup granulated sugar

1½ teaspoons pure vanilla extract

Pinch table salt

2 large eggs

⅓ cup canned pure solid-pack pumpkin

2¼ teaspoons all-purpose flour

½ teaspoon ground cinnamon

¼ teaspoon ground ginger

⅛ teaspoon ground nutmeg

**The mini cheesecakes can be refrigerated, covered, for three days or frozen for one month. Freeze the cooled cheesecakes in their tin in heavy-duty zip-top plastic bags, or remove them from the tin and arrange in airtight containers.**

Position a rack in the center of the oven and heat the oven to 300°F. Line a standard 12-cup muffin tin (each cup approximately 2¾ inches in diameter) with foil liners (or line two 6-cup tins) and coat lightly with cooking spray.

In a stand mixer fitted with the paddle attachment (or in a large bowl with a hand mixer), beat the cream cheese on medium-high speed until very smooth and fluffy, stopping to scrape down the bowl as necessary, about 4 minutes. Add the sugar, vanilla, and salt and continue beating until well blended and smooth, scraping down the bowl frequently, about 1 minute; there should be no lumps. Add the eggs, one at a time, beating on medium speed until just blended. (Don't overbeat once the eggs are added or the cheesecakes will puff and crack during baking.)

Transfer ²⁄₃ cup of the batter to a small bowl. Add the pumpkin, flour, cinnamon, ginger, and nutmeg to the small bowl and stir with a wooden spoon until well blended.

Divide the plain batter among the muffin cups (about 2 generous tablespoons in each). Then divide the pumpkin batter evenly among the cups (about 1 generous tablespoon in each). Drag the tip of a wooden skewer, toothpick, or paring knife through the two batters in a random, swirly pattern to create a marbled look.

Bake until the centers of the cheesecakes barely jiggle when nudged, 15 to 18 minutes. Set the muffin tin on a wire rack and let cool completely. Cover and refrigerate until very cold, at least 6 hours or up to 3 days.
—*Abigail Johnson Dodge*

# Gingery Plum Cake

*Serves eight to ten.*

**For the cake:**

1⅓ cups (6 ounces) unbleached all-purpose flour; more for the pan

1 teaspoon ground ginger

¾ teaspoon baking powder

¼ teaspoon baking soda

¼ teaspoon table salt

6 tablespoons (¾ stick) unsalted butter, at room temperature; more for the pan

1 cup packed light brown sugar

2 large eggs

1 teaspoon pure vanilla extract

⅔ cup sour cream

**For the topping:**

1 plum (or pluot or ripe apricot), halved, pitted, and cut into ⅛- to ¼-inch-thick slices

2 teaspoons peeled and finely grated fresh ginger

3 tablespoons packed light brown sugar

1 tablespoon unbleached all-purpose flour

Whipped cream, for garnish (optional)

This moist cake gets a double dose of ginger, from the ground spice in the cake batter and the fresh ginger in the topping. Plums are a natural partner for warm, citrusy ginger, but apricots or pluots can also work in this recipe.

Position a rack in the center of the oven and heat the oven to 350°F. Lightly butter a 9x2-inch round cake pan. Line the bottom with a parchment circle cut to fit the pan and lightly flour the sides, tapping out the excess.

**Make the cake:** In a medium bowl, whisk together the flour, ground ginger, baking powder, baking soda, and salt. In a stand mixer fitted with the paddle attachment (or with a hand-held mixer), beat the butter and sugar on medium-high speed until well blended and fluffy, about 3 minutes. Add the eggs, one at a time, beating on medium speed until just blended and adding the vanilla with the second egg. Using a wide rubber spatula, fold in half the dry ingredients, then the sour cream, then the remaining dry ingredients. Scrape the batter into the prepared pan and spread evenly. Bake for 15 minutes.

**Make the topping:** Combine the sliced fruit and grated ginger in a small bowl and toss until the ginger is well distributed. Add the sugar and flour. Using a table fork, mix to coat the fruit evenly. After the cake has baked for 15 minutes, scatter the topping evenly over the cake, working quickly. Don't worry about the fruit looking perfect—this is a rustic cake. Continue baking until a toothpick inserted in the center of the cake comes out clean, another 35 to 40 minutes.

Let the cake cool on a wire rack for 15 minutes. Run a knife around the inside edge of the pan. Using a dry dishtowel to protect your hands, lay the rack on top of the cake pan and, holding onto both pan and rack, invert the cake. Lift the pan from the cake. Peel away the parchment. Lay a flat serving plate on the bottom of the cake and flip the cake one more time so the fruit is on top. Serve warm or at room temperature, with whipped cream if you like. —*Abigail Johnson Dodge*

**tip:** In this recipe, Blueberry-Lemon Cornmeal Cake (page 337), and Raspberry-Peach Cake (page 344), adding the fruit after the cake batter has been baking for 15 minutes keeps it from sinking to the bottom.

# Raspberry-Peach Cake

*Serves eight to ten.*

## For the cake:

1⅓ cups (6 ounces) unbleached all-purpose flour; more for the pan

1 teaspoon baking powder

¼ teaspoon baking soda

¼ teaspoon table salt

6 tablespoons (¾ stick) unsalted butter, at room temperature; more for the pan

1 cup granulated sugar

2 large eggs

1½ teaspoons finely grated orange zest

½ teaspoon pure vanilla extract

⅔ cup plain yogurt

## For the topping:

½ large, ripe peach or nectarine, halved, pitted, and cut into very thin slices (aim for ¹⁄₁₆ inch)

¾ cup fresh raspberries

1 tablespoon granulated sugar

1 tablespoon unbleached all-purpose flour

**This cake is perfect for a summer picnic and terrific for breakfast, too. Add a drizzle of raspberry sauce or a dollop of lightly sweetened whipped cream and the cake turns into a great finale for any summer dinner.**

Position a rack in the center of the oven and heat the oven to 350°F. Lightly butter a 9x2-inch round cake pan. Line the bottom with a parchment circle cut to fit the pan, lightly flour the sides, and tap out the excess.

**Make the cake:** In a medium bowl, whisk the flour, baking powder, baking soda, and salt together until well blended. In a stand mixer fitted with the paddle attachment (or a large bowl with a hand mixer), beat the butter and sugar together on medium-high speed until well blended and fluffy, about 3 minutes. Add the eggs, one at a time, beating on medium speed until just blended and adding the orange zest and vanilla with the second egg. Using a wide rubber spatula, fold in half the dry ingredients, then the yogurt, then the remaining dry ingredients. Scrape the batter into the prepared pan and spread evenly. Bake for 15 minutes.

**Make the topping:** Combine the peach slices, raspberries, sugar, and flour in a small bowl. Using a table fork, mix the ingredients to evenly coat the fruit and lightly crush the raspberries. After the cake has baked for 15 minutes, slide the oven rack out and scatter the fruit evenly over the top of the cake, working quickly. Continue baking until a toothpick inserted in the center of the cake comes out clean, another 25 to 30 minutes.

Let the cake cool on a wire rack for 15 minutes. Run a knife around the inside edge of the pan to loosen the cake. Using a dry dishtowel to protect your hands, lay the rack on top of the cake pan and, holding onto both rack and pan, invert the cake. Lift the pan from the cake. Peel away the parchment. Set a flat plate on the bottom of the cake and flip the cake one more time so that the fruit is on top. Serve warm or at room temperature. —*Abigail Johnson Dodge*

## How to pit a peach

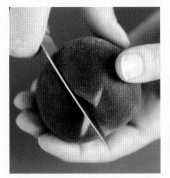

**1** Using a paring knife, start at the stem end of the fruit and cut through to the pit. Run the knife all the way around the fruit, keeping the blade up against the pit, finishing where you started.

**2** Hold the fruit in your hand and gently twist each half in opposite directions until one half comes free from the pit. Set that half aside.

**3** Remove the pit from the remaining half by loosening one end with your finger or the tip of a knife.

**4** If the pit doesn't come free, don't force it. You'll only damage the flesh if you force out the pit. Instead, cut off a few sections. You will then be able to wiggle the pit free.

# Cranberry & Almond Bundt Cake

*Yields 1 large Bundt® cake or 12 miniature Bundt cakes.*

**1½ cups (6¾ ounces) unbleached all-purpose flour; more for the pan**

**1½ teaspoons baking powder**

**¼ teaspoon table salt**

**1 cup (2 sticks) unsalted butter, softened at room temperature; more for the pan**

**7 ounces (about ⅔ cup) almond paste (not marzipan)**

**1 cup granulated sugar**

**4 large eggs, at room temperature**

**1 teaspoon pure vanilla extract**

**¼ cup milk, at room temperature**

**1½ cups fresh cranberries, picked through, rinsed, and coarsely chopped, or frozen cranberries, thawed and coarsely chopped**

**Confectioners' sugar for dusting (optional)**

**When baked in a specially shaped pan, Bundt cakes look extremely elegant, yet they're actually super-easy to make. A high amount of butter, sugar, and eggs gives this cake excellent staying power. Wrapped well, it can last a week at room temperature (but rarely is left to) and up to a month in the freezer.**

Position a rack in the center of the oven and heat the oven to 350°F. Butter and flour a 10- or 12-cup Bundt or kugelhopf pan (or twelve 1-cup mini Bundt pans). Tap out any excess flour.

Sift together the flour, baking powder, and salt. In a stand mixer fitted with the paddle attachment (or in a large bowl with a hand mixer), beat the butter and almond paste together on medium speed until smooth, 1 to 2 minutes. Add the granulated sugar and beat until light and fluffy, about 2 minutes. Beat in the eggs one at a time, stopping to scrape the sides of the bowl down after each addition. Beat in the vanilla. With the mixer on low speed, alternate adding the flour mixture and the milk, beginning and ending with the flour. Stop the mixer at least one more time to scrape down the bowl, then beat at medium speed until the batter is smooth, about 20 seconds. Fold in the cranberries with a rubber spatula.

Spoon the batter into the prepared pan (or pans), spreading it evenly with a rubber spatula. Run a knife through the batter to eliminate any air pockets. Bake until a wooden skewer inserted in the center comes out clean, 40 to 45 minutes (about 20 minutes for mini cakes). Set the pan on a wire rack to cool for 20 minutes. Invert the cake onto the rack, remove the pan, and let the cake cool completely. If you're making the cake ahead, wrap it while still barely warm. Serve at room temperature, dusting the top with confectioners' sugar, if you like.
—*Nicole Rees*

# Fastest Fudge Cake

If time is of the essence, know that this cake, which is made with cocoa powder and therefore requires no chocolate melting, is delicious on its own; but it's even better topped with the ganache.

Position a rack in the lower third of the oven and heat the oven to 350°F. Grease the bottom of an 8x2- or 9x2-inch round cake pan or line it with parchment.

In a small bowl, whisk together the flour, cocoa, baking soda, and salt. Sift only if the cocoa remains lumpy after whisking. In a large bowl, combine the melted butter and brown sugar with a wooden spoon or rubber spatula. Add the eggs and vanilla; stir until well blended. Add the flour mixture all at once and stir just until all the flour is moistened. Pour the hot water over the batter; stir just until it's incorporated and the batter is smooth. Scrape the batter into the prepared pan. Bake until a toothpick inserted in the center comes out clean, about 30 minutes for a 9-inch pan; 35 to 40 minutes for an 8-inch pan.

Let cool in the pan on a wire rack for 10 minutes. Run a thin knife around the edge and invert the cake (peel off the parchment if necessary). Invert it again onto the rack and let cool completely.

Once cool, set the rack over a baking sheet or foil. Pour the warm ganache over the cake and use an offset spatula to spread it over the top of the cake and down the sides. Let set for about an hour before serving. —Alice Medrich

*Serves eight to ten.*

1 cup (4½ ounces) unbleached all-purpose flour

¼ cup plus 2 tablespoons unsweetened natural cocoa powder (not Dutch-processed)

½ teaspoon baking soda

¼ teaspoon table salt

½ cup (1 stick) unsalted butter, melted and kept warm

1¼ cups packed light brown sugar

2 large eggs

1 teaspoon pure vanilla extract

½ cup hot water

1 cup warm Ganache (optional; see recipe below)

## Ganache

*Yields 1½ cups.*

You'll have a bit of this ganache left over after icing the cake; use it as a sauce for ice cream or another dessert. It keeps for a week in the refrigerator. Rewarm gently.

8 ounces bittersweet or semisweet chocolate, finely chopped
1 cup heavy cream; more as needed
Granulated sugar (optional)

Put the chocolate in a medium heatproof bowl. In a small saucepan, bring the cream to a boil. Pour the hot cream over the chocolate and whisk gently until the chocolate is completely melted and smooth. (If using a 70% bittersweet chocolate, the ganache might be a bit thick; add more cream, 1 tablespoon at a time, to thin it. You might also want to add a couple of teaspoons of sugar when you add the hot cream.)

# Four-Layer Cake with Raspberry Whipped Cream & Jumble Berries

*Yields one four-layer cake; serves twelve.*

## For the cake:

Nonstick cooking spray

2¾ cups (10½ ounces) cake flour

1½ cups granulated sugar

3¾ teaspoons baking powder

¾ teaspoon table salt

¾ cup (1½ sticks) unsalted butter, cut into tablespoon-size pieces, at room temperature

¾ cup whole or low-fat milk, at room temperature

1½ teaspoons pure vanilla extract

4 large eggs, at room temperature

## For the filling:

3 cups heavy or whipping cream

7 tablespoons granulated sugar

2¼ cups raspberry purée (purée the fruit in a blender and strain)

6¼ cups berries (strawberries, blueberries, raspberries, blackberries, or a combination, large berries sliced)

Whipped cream is an easy filling for a gorgeous berry-stacked cake. You can bake the cakes a day ahead, but assemble with the whipped cream and berries shortly before serving. You can substitute strawberry purée for the raspberry purée. You may not need all of the whipped cream; save the extra for topping other desserts.

**Make the cake:** Position a rack in the center of the oven and heat the oven to 350°F. Lightly coat two 9x2-inch round cake pans with nonstick cooking spray and line the bottoms with parchment.

Sift the flour, sugar, baking powder, and salt into the bowl of a stand mixer fitted with the paddle attachment (or a large bowl, if using a hand mixer). Mix on low speed (#2 on a KitchenAid® mixer) until well combined. Add the softened butter pieces and mix on low speed for 20 to 30 seconds to incorporate the butter into the dry ingredients—the mixture should look a little lumpy, with the largest lumps being about the size of a hazelnut. Add the milk and vanilla. Mix on medium speed (#5 on a KitchenAid) for 1 minute to thoroughly blend the ingredients and aerate the batter. Scrape down the sides of the bowl with a rubber spatula. Add the eggs one at a time, mixing on medium speed for about 15 seconds after each addition. Scrape down the bowl after the second egg.

Divide the batter equally between the two prepared pans. Use a small offset spatula or spoon to spread the batter evenly in each pan. Bake until the

cakes are golden brown and the tops feel firm but spring back a little when tapped lightly with a finger, and a pick inserted in the center comes out clean, 30 to 35 minutes. Set the pans on a wire rack, run a table knife around the edge of each cake, and let cool in the pans for 30 minutes. Invert the cakes onto the rack, lift the pans, peel off the parchment, and let the cakes cool completely. If baking ahead, wrap the cakes tightly in plastic after cooling.

**Make the whipped cream:** Chill the bowl and beaters of the mixer for 20 minutes in the refrigerator or 5 minutes in the freezer. Pour the heavy cream into the bowl and whisk on medium-high speed until it just starts to thicken. Slow the speed down to medium and gradually pour in the sugar and berry purée. Continue to whisk until soft peaks form. Continue to whisk by hand until the cream is smooth, and stiff peaks form (the cream will stand up straight when the whisk is raised).

**Assemble the cake:** Level the cakes, if necessary, and slice each cake into two layers (see "Cutting layers," below), making a total of four layers of cake.

Place the bottom layer on a flat serving platter or a cake stand lined with strips of waxed paper to keep it clean while assembling the cake. Top the layer with a scant 1½ cups whipped cream, spreading the cream to the edges of the cake with a metal offset spatula so that it's almost dripping over the sides. Top with 1½ cups berries, making sure some of the berries are around the edges of the cake so you can see them between the layers. Repeat with the next two layers. For the final layer, spread about 1½ cups whipped cream on top of the cake with the spatula. You may not need all of the whipped cream. Arrange the berries artfully on top of the cream. *—Katherine Eastman Seeley*

**tip:** To have more control over the final thickness of the whipped cream, finish whisking it by hand. Check the texture by lifting the whisk.

## Cutting layers for even cakes

If the tops of the cakes have mounded unevenly, level them by removing the top crust with a long serrated knife.

To slice one cake into two layers, start by tracing a line around the middle of the cake with a long serrated knife. Then slowly rotate the cake while following that line with the knife and cut through the cake toward the center. After a few rotations you will have sliced the cake in two.

If you don't get a straight cut, match the unevenly cut slices when assembling the cake, to prevent your finished cake from tilting.

# Four-Layer Cake with Chocolate Buttercream & Raspberry Jam

*Yields one four-layer cake; serves twelve.*

## For the cake:

Nonstick cooking spray

2¾ cups (10½ ounces) cake flour

1½ cups granulated sugar

3¾ teaspoons baking powder

¾ teaspoon table salt

¾ cup (1½ sticks) unsalted butter, cut into tablespoon-size pieces, at room temperature

¾ cup whole or low-fat milk, at room temperature

1½ teaspoons pure vanilla extract

4 large eggs, at room temperature

## For the buttercream and jam filling:

¾ cup seedless raspberry jam

3 tablespoons brandy or Grand Marnier

5 large egg whites

1¼ cups granulated sugar

½ cup plus 2 tablespoons light corn syrup

2½ cups (5 sticks) unsalted butter, at room temperature

12 ounces bittersweet chocolate, melted

This impressive layer cake is easier to make than it looks. The frosting is incredibly airy and smooth and less complicated than traditional buttercream. The hardest part to making the cake is remembering to bring the butter, milk, and eggs to room temperature before you start.

**Make the cake:** Position a rack in the center of the oven and heat the oven to 350°F. Lightly coat two 9x2-inch round cake pans with nonstick cooking spray and line the bottoms with parchment.

Sift the flour, sugar, baking powder, and salt into the bowl of a stand mixer fitted with the paddle attachment (or a large bowl if using a hand mixer). Mix on low speed (#2 on a KitchenAid mixer) until well combined. Add the softened butter pieces and mix on low speed for 20 to 30 seconds to incorporate the butter into the dry ingredients—the mixture should look a little lumpy, with the largest lumps being about the size of a hazelnut. Add the milk and vanilla. Mix on medium speed (#5 on a KitchenAid) for 1 minute to thoroughly blend the ingredients and aerate the batter. Scrape the sides of the bowl down with a rubber spatula. Add the eggs one at a time, mixing on medium speed for about 15 seconds after each addition. Scrape down the bowl after the second egg.

Divide the batter equally between the two prepared pans. Use a small offset spatula or spoon to spread the batter evenly in each pan. Bake until the cakes are golden brown and the tops feel firm but spring back a little when tapped lightly with a finger, and a pick inserted in the center of the cake comes out clean, 30 to 35 minutes. Set the pans on a wire rack, run a table knife around the edge of each cake, and let cool in the pans for 30 minutes. Invert the cakes onto the rack, lift the pans, peel off the parchment, and let the cakes cool completely. If baking ahead, wrap the cakes tightly in plastic after cooling.

**Make the filling and frosting:** In a small bowl, mix the jam with the brandy or Grand Marnier. Set aside.

Place the egg whites in the (clean, dry) bowl of the stand mixer fitted with the whisk attachment (or a large bowl, if using a hand mixer—wash and dry the beaters), and whisk on medium-high speed until foamy. Sprinkle in 6 tablespoons of the sugar and beat on high speed to medium peaks (the whites should be smooth, full, and shiny, and the peaks should curl a little). Turn off the mixer.

Combine the remaining ¾ cup plus 2 tablespoons sugar and the corn syrup in a 3-quart saucepan over medium-high heat, stirring briefly to dissolve the sugar. Continue to cook just until the mixture comes to a rolling boil. Immediately remove the syrup from the heat, turn the mixer onto medium-high speed, and slowly pour the syrup down the side of the bowl in a steady stream, being very careful not to let the syrup hit the whisk.

Reduce the speed to medium and continue whisking until the whites are barely warm, 5 to 7 minutes. Add the butter 1 tablespoon at a time. Reduce the speed to low and add the melted chocolate. Increase the speed to medium to blend and continue beating until the frosting is smooth and creamy.

**Assemble the cake:** Level the cakes, if necessary, and slice each cake into two layers (see "Cutting layers," page 349), making a total of four layers of cake.

Place the bottom layer on a flat serving platter or a cake stand lined with strips of waxed paper to keep it clean while assembling the cake. Top the layer with a scant 1½ cups of the buttercream, spreading it evenly with a metal offset spatula almost to the cake's edge. Spread a third of the jam on the next cake layer, flip it, and lay it over the buttercream filling, jam side down. Repeat with the next two layers. Set the top layer over the third layer of filling.

**Apply a crumb coating:** Before frosting the cake, it helps to apply a light coat of frosting (called the crumb coating) to seal the cake crumbs in. To do this, spoon about ½ cup of the buttercream into a small bowl. Spread it in a very thin layer over the entire cake with a small metal offset spatula. You should be able to see the cake layers through the icing. Chill the cake for about 20 minutes, until the icing is firm. Proceed to frost the cake.

**Frost the cake:** Spread the icing thickly and evenly over the entire cake with a large metal offset spatula. Don't worry about getting a smooth, perfect finish; just make sure the cake is completely covered and the frosting is spread uniformly. You shouldn't be able to see the layers underneath the buttercream. With the back of a teaspoon, smear the icing and pull it upward to form curls and swirls over the entire cake. *—Katherine Eastman Seeley*

**tip:** Pour the hot syrup slowly down the side of the bowl in a thin stream. If the syrup hits the whisk, it will splatter and harden inside the bowl.

# Double-Ginger Pound Cake with Brown Sugar Mascarpone Whipped Cream

*Serves twelve.*

## For the cake:

1 cup (2 sticks) unsalted butter, at room temperature; plus ½ to 1 tablespoon, melted, for the pan

2⅔ cups (12 ounces) unbleached all-purpose flour, more for the pan

2½ teaspoons baking powder

2½ teaspoons ground ginger

¾ teaspoon table salt

¼ teaspoon baking soda

¾ cup granulated sugar

¾ cup firmly packed light brown sugar

1 teaspoon pure vanilla extract

4 large eggs

¾ cup buttermilk

½ cup finely chopped crystallized ginger

1 to 2 teaspoons confectioners' sugar (optional)

## For the brown sugar whipped cream:

8 ounces mascarpone

1 cup heavy cream

¼ cup firmly packed light brown sugar

1 teaspoon pure vanilla extract

**Dress up the cake with a simple dusting of confectioners' sugar. A sugar shaker is a handy tool for this, but a sieve works too. You can bake the cake up to five days ahead but don't dust with sugar. Wrap the cooled cake in plastic wrap and store at room temperature.**

**Make the cake:** Position a rack in the center of the oven and heat the oven to 325°F. Grease a 10-cup fluted tube pan with the melted butter, using a brush to get into all the nooks and crannies. Lightly flour the pan, tapping out any excess flour.

In a medium bowl, combine the flour, baking powder, ground ginger, salt, and baking soda. Whisk until well blended and set aside.

In a stand mixer fitted with a paddle attachment (or in a large bowl with a hand mixer), beat the butter on medium-high speed until smooth, 1 to 2 minutes. Scrape down the sides of the bowl, then add the granulated sugar, brown sugar, and vanilla. Continue beating until very well combined and fluffy, about 4 more minutes. Add the eggs, one at a time, beating well after each addition and scraping down the bowl as necessary. Add slightly more than half the flour mixture and stir with a rubber spatula until just blended. Add the buttermilk and stir until just blended. Add the crystallized ginger to the remaining flour mixture and use your fingers to break up the clumps of ginger. Add the flour mixture to the batter and stir gently until just blended.

Scrape the batter into the prepared pan and spread evenly. Bake until a cake tester or toothpick inserted in the center comes out with just a few small, moist crumbs attached, 50 to 55 minutes. Set the pan on a wire rack and let cool for about 15 minutes. If necessary, run a knife between the cake and the top edge of the pan to loosen the cake. Invert the cake onto the rack, lift off the pan, and allow the cake to cool completely. If using confectioners' sugar, sift it over the cake just before serving.

**Make the whipped cream:** In a medium bowl, combine the mascarpone, heavy cream, brown sugar, and vanilla. Using an electric mixer, beat on low speed until combined, about 1 minute. Increase the speed to medium high and continue beating until the cream is thick and holds firm peaks, 30 to 90 seconds. Be careful not to overwhip or the cream will become grainy. Serve with the cake. *—Abigail Johnson Dodge*

# Tiramisù

*Serves ten to twelve.*

5 cups hot brewed espresso (or double-strength drip coffee made with espresso roast)

1 cup plus 2 tablespoons granulated sugar

2 tablespoons rum, or more to taste (optional)

4 large eggs, separated

2 cups (16 ounces) mascarpone

About 46 ladyfingers or savoiardi cookies (see the directions at right for recommendations)

2 tablespoons unsweetened cocoa powder or 1 to 2 ounces bittersweet chocolate

Coffee-dipped ladyfingers and fluffy mascarpone cream are the hallmarks of this luscious Italian dessert. For the best texture, the ladyfingers have to be just barely soaked through with coffee, moist but not soggy and falling apart. You'll find two main types of ladyfingers in grocery stores: packaged, cookie-style ladyfingers (usually imported from Italy) and soft, spongy ladyfingers commonly sold in clear packages in the bakery section. The latter won't do the trick. They get too soggy too fast, resulting in a sopping mess. Use the cookie-style ladyfingers instead. Ballocco, Bonomi, and Elledi brands work well. They take only 1 to 3 seconds to soak through. Real Torino® brand also works, but it has a slightly denser texture and needs significantly more soaking time (10 to 12 seconds).

Pour the coffee in a large bowl and add 2 tablespoons of the sugar while it's still hot. Stir well and let cool to room temperature. Add the rum, if using.

Combine the egg yolks and the remaining 1 cup sugar in a large bowl and beat with an electric mixer on medium-high speed until the yolks are pale yellow and fluffy, about 5 minutes. (The mixture will be fairly thick at first.) Add the mascarpone and beat until it's fully incorporated into a smooth cream, 2 to 3 minutes more.

Thoroughly wash and dry the beaters, then beat the egg whites in a medium bowl on medium-high speed until they form medium-stiff peaks when you lift the beaters (the tips should curl over onto themselves just a little). With a rubber spatula, fold about one-quarter of the beaten whites into the mascarpone cream to lighten it. Then gently fold in the remaining whites, taking care not to deflate them. Cover with plastic wrap and refrigerate.

Submerge one ladyfinger in the cooled coffee until the coffee penetrates about halfway through, leaving the core dry (break it to check). This can take from 1 to 12 seconds, depending on the type of ladyfinger. You don't want the ladyfinger to get completely soaked or it'll become soggy and fall apart. You should be able to feel that the outside is soft, but the inside is still firm.

Once you've determined the correct soaking time, submerge each lady-finger individually, gently shake out excess coffee, and immediately set it in a 9x13-inch baking dish; continue until you have one tight layer that covers the bottom of the dish. (You may need to break a few ladyfingers to fit in snugly.) Spread one-half of the mascarpone cream evenly on top of the ladyfingers.

Repeat the soaking procedure with the remaining ladyfingers to create a second snug layer, arranging them on top of the mascarpone cream as you did for the first layer. Spread the rest of the mascarpone cream evenly on top. Cover the dish with plastic wrap and refrigerate for at least 2 hours.

Before serving, sift the cocoa powder or finely grate the chocolate over the top to evenly cover. —*Laura Giannatempo*

## Assembling the tiramisù is easy

**1** Break one ladyfinger after you've dipped it in the cooled coffee to check that the coffee has penetrated only half-way through, leaving the core dry. The outside will be quite soft, but the inside should be firm.

**2** Evenly spread half the mascarpone cream with a spatula over a tight layer of ladyfingers arranged in a 9x13-inch baking dish.

**3** Use a fine mesh sieve to finish off the tiramisù with a generous dusting of cocoa powder just before serving.

# Chocolate Caramel Tart with Macadamia Nuts & Crème Fraîche Whipped Cream

*Serves twelve to sixteen.*

### For the crust:

1⅓ cups (6 ounces) unbleached all-purpose flour; plus a little more for rolling

3 tablespoons granulated sugar

¼ teaspoon kosher salt

½ cup (1 stick) cold unsalted butter, cut into small cubes

2 tablespoons heavy cream

1 large egg yolk

### For the filling:

1¼ cups macadamia nuts

2 cups heavy cream

3 tablespoons unsalted butter, cut into chunks

1 cup plus 1½ tablespoons granulated sugar

¼ cup light corn syrup

½ vanilla bean, split and scraped, seeds and pods reserved

¼ cup water

6 ounces 70% bittersweet chocolate, chopped (about 1¼ cups)

½ cup whole milk

¼ cup crème fraîche

**Not only is this tart gorgeous, but it also feeds a crowd, making it perfect for entertaining.**

**Make the crust:** In a stand mixer fitted with the paddle attachment, combine the flour, sugar, salt, and butter and mix on medium speed until the butter blends into the flour and the mixture resembles a coarse meal. Mix the cream and egg yolk together in a small bowl. With the mixer on low speed, gradually add the cream mixture and mix until just combined. Do not overwork the dough.

Transfer the dough to a work surface and bring it together with your hands. Shape the dough into a 1-inch-thick disk. If the dough seems too soft to roll out, put it in the refrigerator for 5 to 10 minutes to firm it up a little. Set the dough on a lightly floured work surface, sprinkle a little flour over it, and roll it out into a ⅛-inch-thick circle 14 to 15 inches in diameter, reflouring the dough and work surface as necessary.  Starting at one side, roll and wrap the dough around the rolling pin to pick it up. Unroll the dough over an 11-inch fluted tart pan with a removable bottom and gently fit it loosely in the pan, lifting the edges and pressing the dough into the corners with your fingers. To remove the excess dough, roll the pin lightly over the top of the pan, cutting a nice, clean edge. Cover loosely with plastic wrap and chill for 1 hour.

Position a rack in the center of the oven and heat the oven to 375°F. Prick the bottom of the crust with a fork and line it with a piece of parchment or several opened-out basket-style coffee filters. Fill the lined tart shell with dried beans or pie weights and bake until set around the edges, about 15 minutes. Take the tart out of the oven and carefully lift out the paper and pie weights (if using coffee filters, spoon out most of the weights first). Return the tart to the oven and bake until the crust is fully baked and golden brown all over, another 10 to 15 minutes. (Do not underbake or the crust will be soggy.) Let cool completely on a wire rack.

**Make the filling:** While the crust is baking, spread the nuts on a baking sheet and toast (in the same oven) until they are golden brown and smell nutty, 10 to 12 minutes. Let them cool, then chop coarsely.

In a small pot, bring ¾ cup of the cream and the butter to a simmer. Set aside. Combine 1 cup of the sugar with the corn syrup, vanilla bean seeds and pod, and water in a 3- or 4-quart heavy saucepan. Bring to a boil over high heat, stirring frequently with a wooden spoon, until the mixture becomes caramel-colored. Remove from the heat and immediately (but slowly and carefully; you don't want the hot sugar to overflow or splatter) whisk in the

hot cream mixture. Pour the caramel into the baked tart shell and pick out the vanilla bean halves with a fork or tongs. Sprinkle about two-thirds of the macadamia nuts on top of the caramel. Let cool completely in the refrigerator.

When the tart is cool, put the chocolate in a large bowl. In a small saucepan, bring ½ cup of the cream, the milk, and the remaining 1½ tablespoons sugar to a boil over medium-high heat. As soon as it boils, pour it over the chocolate. Let stand for 2 minutes, then stir very gently with a whisk until smooth and thoroughly combined. Let cool at room temperature for 5 minutes, then pour the chocolate filling over the completely chilled tart, covering the nuts and caramel.

Chill the tart in the refrigerator for at least 4 hours, until completely set. Unmold the tart, using a long, thin metal spatula to release it from the pan bottom. Place it on a cutting board or serving plate, depending on how you intend to serve it. Just before serving, whip the remaining ¾ cup cream and the crème fraîche to soft peaks using an electric mixer. Top each serving with a dollop of the whipped cream and scatter the remaining macadamia nuts over and around. —*Suzanne Goin*

**tip:** Be careful when making the caramel filling. Turn off the heat and whisk in the hot cream cautiously, a little at a time, so it doesn't overflow all over the stove (and you). Also, let the caramel set completely before you pour the chocolate filling over it (let the chocolate cool slightly before pouring).

# Mixed Berry Tarts with Lemony Filling

*Yields eight 4³⁄₄-inch tarts.*

## For the lemon curd:

3 large eggs

²⁄₃ cup granulated sugar

½ cup strained fresh lemon juice (from about 2 large lemons)

6 tablespoons (¾ stick) unsalted butter

1 tablespoon finely grated lemon zest

## For the shortbread pastry:

2 cups (9 ounces) bleached all-purpose flour

14 tablespoons (1¾ sticks) chilled unsalted butter, cut into 1-inch pieces

1 large egg, lightly beaten

2 tablespoons granulated sugar

1 tablespoon chilled heavy cream

2 teaspoons fresh lemon juice

1 teaspoon table salt

Non-stick cooking spray

## For assembling the tarts:

½ cup heavy cream

1 cup each fresh raspberries, blueberries, and blackberries or boysenberries, rinsed, picked over, dried, and placed in separate bowls

**You can decorate these delicious tarts with berries before serving them, or set out dishes of berries and let guests garnish their own tarts with the berries of their choice.**

**Make the lemon curd:** In a medium bowl, whisk the eggs until well blended. Combine the sugar, lemon juice, butter, and lemon zest in a 1- to 2-quart saucepan. Gently heat over medium-low heat until the butter has melted. Don't let the mixture come to a boil. Remove the pan from the heat and whisk the lemon mixture into the beaten eggs. Pour the mixture back into the saucepan and cook gently over medium-low heat, stirring constantly with the whisk, until the mixture thickens and reaches at least 160°F, about 5 minutes. Again, don't let the mixture boil. Let the lemon curd cool briefly before transferring it to a heatproof container. Press a piece of plastic wrap directly onto the surface of the curd and poke a few holes in it with the tip of a knife—this will keep a skin from forming on the curd. Refrigerate until completely chilled. The curd will continue to thicken as it cools. It will keep, covered, in the refrigerator for up to a week.

**Make the shortbread pastry shells:** Have ready eight 4³⁄₄-inch fluted tart pans with removable bottoms.

In a food processor, combine the flour, butter, egg, sugar, cream, lemon juice, and salt and pulse until the dough starts gathering together in big clumps. Turn the dough out onto a work surface and gather it together. Working quickly, shape the dough into an 8-inch log and divide it into eight equal pieces. Lightly flour your surface and roll a piece of dough into a 5-inch round. Gently press the dough into a tart pan. Repeat with the remaining dough. Put the tarts on a baking sheet and chill in the refrigerator for 15 minutes. Meanwhile, heat the oven to 400°F.

Cut out eight roughly 6-inch-square pieces of foil and spray one side lightly with nonstick cooking spray. Line each tart with a square of foil, oiled side down, being sure to gently fold the foil over the top edge of the tart. Place a handful of pie weights, raw rice, or dried beans into each lined tart. Transfer the tarts (still on the baking sheet) to the oven and bake until the crust turns golden brown and starts to pull away from the sides of the pans, 25 to 30 minutes. (Check the color by carefully lifting up the foil on a few of the tarts.) Let the tarts cool on the baking sheet on a wire rack for 5 minutes, then carefully remove the lining and weights. Let cool completely on the baking sheet on the rack.

**Assemble the tarts:** In a medium bowl, whip the cream to soft peaks. Add 1 cup of the lemon curd (you will have leftovers) and gently fold together with a rubber spatula until combined. Divide the mixture among the pastry shells

and smooth the filling with the spatula or the back of a spoon. The filling should be no higher than the edge of the tart shell. Carefully remove the outer rings and bottoms of the tart shells (use a metal spatula for the bottoms) and arrange the tarts on a large platter or individual plates. Top each tart with a mixture of raspberries, blueberries, and blackberries and serve immediately.
—*Janie Hibler*

tip: The great thing about pastries is that you can make each component separately, when you have a few minutes in your schedule, then pull them all together at the last minute. The lemon curd can be made ahead and stored, covered, for up to a week in the refrigerator. You can combine the lemon curd and whipped cream and hold the filling for about 2 hours in the fridge. The shells can be baked a day ahead (store the cooled shells in an airtight container); fill them shortly before serving. The baked shells also freeze well; thaw before filling.

# Rustic Red Raspberry Turnovers

*Yields 12 petite turnovers.*

**For the pastry:**

2 cups (9 ounces) bleached all-purpose flour

14 tablespoons (1¾ sticks) chilled unsalted butter, cut into 1-inch pieces

1 large egg, lightly beaten

2 tablespoons granulated sugar

1 tablespoon chilled heavy cream

2 teaspoons fresh lemon juice

1 teaspoon table salt

**For the berry filling:**

4 teaspoons granulated sugar; more as needed

1 tablespoon all-purpose flour

½ teaspoon ground cinnamon

¼ teaspoon ground nutmeg

2 cups (8 to 10 ounces) fresh red raspberries, rinsed and air-dried or patted dry with paper towels

1 to 2 tablespoons milk

**It's best not to rinse the berries until just before using. Toss with the sugar and spices after you've rolled and cut the dough.**

**Make the pastry:** In a food processor, combine the flour, butter, egg, sugar, cream, lemon juice, and salt and pulse until the dough starts gathering together in big clumps. Turn the dough out onto a work surface and gather it together. Divide the pastry in half. Pat each half into roughly a square shape about 1 inch thick, wrap each in plastic, and chill for 20 minutes.

Line a rimmed baking sheet with parchment. Lightly flour your surface and, using a floured rolling pin, roll out one square of the pastry into a 9x14-inch rectangle. If the dough is too sticky, dust it too with a little flour. Cut the dough into six rounds, each about 4 inches in diameter. Remove the excess dough from around the rounds and discard or save for another use. Run a metal spatula under each round to separate it from the counter.

**Make the filling:** In a large bowl, stir the sugar, flour, cinnamon, and nutmeg. Add the raspberries and gently toss to coat. Taste and add more sugar if the fruit seems tart.

**Assemble the turnovers:** Put a heaping tablespoon of raspberries (three to six berries, depending on size) in a single layer on one half of each dough round. Press gently to flatten the berries a bit. Dampen the pastry edges with a little water and carefully fold the other side of the dough over the berries to make a half moon. Press the edges of the dough together with your fingers or the tines of a fork. If any small cracks formed in the dough, pinch them together as best you can with damp fingers. Use a spatula to transfer the turnovers to the baking sheet. Repeat this process with the remaining half of the pastry dough and the rest of the berries.

When all the turnovers are assembled, refrigerate for at least 15 minutes and up to 4 hours. Meanwhile, position a rack in the middle of the oven and heat the oven to 400°F.

When ready to bake, brush the tops of the turnovers (but not the edges or they will get too brown) with the milk and sprinkle with sugar. Bake until golden brown, 20 to 25 minutes. Transfer to a wire rack to cool. Serve warm or at room temperature. —*Janie Hibler*

## Making buttery, tender shortbread pastry dough

This versatile dough can be used for everything from tarts to turnovers. The dough is quite soft, but all the butter in the recipe makes it forgiving and easy to work with. When baked, the crust is very tender—like a shortbread cookie.

Pulse all the ingredients until damp clumps start to form.

Finish the dough by hand so you don't overwork it; turn it onto a counter and gently press together.

# Bumbleberry Pie

*Yields one 9-inch pie;*
*serves six.*

## For the shortbread pastry:

2 cups (9 ounces) bleached all-purpose flour

14 tablespoons (1¾ sticks) chilled unsalted butter, cut into 1-inch pieces

1 large egg, lightly beaten

2 tablespoons granulated sugar

1 tablespoon chilled heavy cream

2 teaspoons fresh lemon juice

1 teaspoon table salt

Non-stick cooking spray

## For the filling and topping:

1 cup fresh blueberries; plus a small handful for garnish, picked over for stems

1 cup fresh strawberries; plus a small handful for garnish

1 cup fresh red raspberries; plus a small handful for garnish

¾ cup granulated sugar

3 tablespoons cornstarch

Kosher salt

⅔ cup water

2 tablespoons unsalted butter

1½ tablespoons fresh lemon juice

1 cup heavy cream

2 tablespoons confectioners' sugar

½ teaspoon pure vanilla extract

**There's no such thing as a bumbleberry—it's a name pioneer cooks gave to dishes made with a combination of berries. The crust for this pie is very tender—almost like a shortbread cookie—but sturdy enough to stand up to berry juices.**

**Make the pastry:** In a food processor, combine the flour, butter, egg, granulated sugar, cream, lemon juice, and salt and pulse until the dough starts gathering together in big clumps. Turn the dough out onto a work surface and gather it together. Shape the dough into a 1-inch-thick disk, wrap in plastic, and refrigerate to firm a bit, 20 to 30 minutes. You want the dough to remain pliable enough to roll, but not so soft that it's sticky and difficult to move once it's rolled out.

Lightly flour your surface and rolling pin. Roll out the dough into a ⅛-inch-thick round. (Run a dough scraper under the dough after every few passes of the rolling pin to prevent sticking and reflour the surface as necessary.) Lay the rolling pin in the center of the crust, fold the pastry over it, and transfer it to a 9-inch pie pan. Gently press the dough into the pan. Trim the overhang to about ½ inch. Fold the overhang under to build up the edge of the pastry; crimp to flute the edges. Prick the entire surface, including the sides, with a fork. Cover loosely and refrigerate for half an hour. Meanwhile, heat the oven to 400°F.

Apply a light coating of nonstick cooking spray to one side of a piece of foil that's slightly larger than the diameter of the pie pan. Line the pan with the foil, oiled side down, going up and over the edges, and fill with pie weights, raw rice, or dried beans. Set the pan on a baking sheet and bake for 20 minutes, then carefully remove the foil and pie weights and bake until the crust is golden brown, about another 15 minutes. Transfer the pie crust to a wire rack and let cool while you make the filling.

**Make the filling:** Gently rinse the berries and spread them on a paper towel-lined baking sheet to dry (keep the berries separate). Hull the strawberries and slice them ¼ inch thick. Combine the 1 cup blueberries, the granulated sugar, cornstarch, ¼ teaspoon kosher salt, and the water in a medium saucepan. Set the pan over medium heat and bring to a boil, stirring frequently. Cook, stirring constantly, until the mixture turns deep purple, thickens, and becomes translucent instead of cloudy looking, 1 to 2 minutes once the mixture begins bubbling. Remove from the heat and stir in the 1 cup strawberries, the butter, and lemon juice.

Sprinkle the 1 cup raspberries over the bottom of the pie crust, then pour the filling over the top. Refrigerate until firm, about 4 hours. The pie can be made to this stage up to 12 hours in advance.

Just before serving, in a medium bowl using an electric mixer, whip the cream, confectioners' sugar, and the vanilla to medium-firm peaks and mound on top of the filling. Scatter the remaining berries over the whipped cream for garnish. Serve immediately. —*Janie Hibler*

# Contributors

_Fine Cooking_ would like to thank all the talented and generous contributors who have shared their recipes with our readers.

**Bruce Aidells** is the founder of the Aidells Sausage Company and one of the country's foremost authorities on meat; his most recent book is _Bruce Aidells's Complete Book of Pork_, written with Lisa Weiss. He lives in Berkeley, California.

**Pam Anderson**, a contributing editor for _Fine Cooking_, is the author of many cookbooks, including _The Perfect Recipe_. She is also the food columnist for _USA Weekend_ magazine.

**Jennifer Armentrout**, a graduate of the Culinary Institute of America, is the test kitchen manager and senior food editor for _Fine Cooking_ magazine.

**John Ash** teaches wine training and cooking classes around the world. He's also an award-winning cookbook author, whose latest book is _Cooking One on One: Private Lessons from a Master Teacher_.

**Karen & Ben Barker** are the chef-owners of Magnolia Grill in Durham, North Carolina. Karen and Ben have each won numerous citations, including the coveted James Beard award. The couple has written a cookbook called _Not Afraid of Flavor_, and Karen's book on American desserts, _Sweet Stuff_, was released by the University of North Carolina Press.

**Jessica Bard**, formerly a _Fine Cooking_ staffer, is a cooking instructor and a freelance food writer and stylist.

**Paul Bertolli** is the former chef of both Chez Panisse and Oliveto restaurants. He's the author of the award-winning cookbook _Cooking by Hand_ and is now the founder of Fra' Mani Salumi.

**David Bonom** is a New Jersey-based food writer and recipe developer.

**Julianna Grimes Bottcher** is a freelance food writer and recipe developer and the owner of a food consulting business, Flavor Matters, Inc.

**Joanne Chang** headed the pastry kitchens at several highly regarded Boston restaurants before going to New York City to study under François Payard at his patisserie. Joanne is now the chef-owner of Flour Bakery + Café in Boston.

**Robert Danhi** is a chef, culinary instructor, and food service consultant based in California. He is a former instructor The Culinary Institute of America in Hyde Park, New York, and he continues to consult for them as well as for the American Culinary Federation.

**Tasha DeSerio** was a cook at Chez Panisse Restaurant & Café for five years. She currently teaches and writes about cooking and is the proprietor of Olive Green Catering in Berkeley, California.

**Abigail Johnson Dodge** is a contributing editor to _Fine Cooking_ and a cookbook author; her book _The Weekend Baker_ was nominated for a 2005 IACP award. Abby was the founding director of _Fine Cooking's_ test kitchen.

**Tom Douglas** is a leading chef in the Pacific Northwest, as well as a cookbook author. He owns Dahlia Lounge, Lola, Etta's, Palace Kitchen, and Dahlia Bakery in Seattle, Washington.

**Allison Ehri** is _Fine Cooking's_ test kitchen associate and food stylist.

**Janet Fletcher** is a cookbook author and an award-winning staff food writer for the _San Francisco Chronicle_. She writes frequently on food and wine for national magazines.

**Laura Giannatempo**, an associate editor for _Fine Cooking_, is a graduate of the Culinary Arts Program at New York's Institute of Culinary Education (ICE). She honed her culinary skills as a catering cook for The Cleaver Co. and as a line cook at The Green Table Café in New York. She was also an assistant editor at _The Magazine of La Cucina Italiana_. She is the author of _A Ligurian Kitchen: Recipes and Tales from the Italian Riviera_.

**Suzanne Goin** is the chef and co-owner of Lucques and AOC wine bar in Los Angeles. Her book, Sunday Suppers at Lucques, won a James Beard award.

**Joyce Goldstein**, the former chef-owner of Square One in San Francisco, is a prolific cookbook author who teaches and writes about cooking. Her latest book is _Antipasti_.

**Lauren Groveman** is a private cooking teacher, as well as the author of _Lauren Groveman's Kitchen: Nurturing Food for Family & Friends_. She has hosted television shows and a weekly radio show for which she won a 2001 James Beard Foundation Award.

**Gordon Hamersley** is the chef-owner of Hamersley's Bistro in Boston. Gordon is the recipient of many culinary awards and the author of the award-winning cookbook _Bistro Cooking at Home_.

**Lisa Hanauer** is a former chef-restaurateur who now writes about food and teaches preschool. She lives in Oakland, California.

**Kate Hays** is the chef-owner of Dish catering, based in Shelburne, Vermont, where she also does recipe testing, development, and food styling.

**Janie Hibler**, an expert on foods of the Pacific Northwest and the winner of a James Beard award, has written five cookbooks including, most recently, _The Berry Bible_.

**Heather Ho** was a graduate of Boston University and the Culinary Institute of America. She was the pastry chef at Windows on the World in New York City in 2001.

**Martha Holmberg** is the food editor of _The Oregonian_ newspaper in Portland, Oregon. She is the former editor and publisher of _Fine Cooking_ magazine.

**Arlene Jacobs** is a chef and cooking teacher in New York City; for many years, she worked with acclaimed chef Jean-Georges Vongerichten.

**Sarah Jay** is a former daily newspaper reporter. She was the managing editor of *Fine Cooking* for many years and is now a freelance food editor and writer.

**Elizabeth Karmel** is widely known as one of America's top grilling experts. Her most recent cookbook is *Taming the Flame: Secrets to Hot* and *Quick Grilling and Low-and-Slow BBQ*.

**Eva Katz** is a frequent contributor to *Fine Cooking*. She has worked as a chef, caterer, teacher, recipe developer and tester, food stylist, and food writer. Eva is on the advisory board of the Cambridge School of Culinary Arts.

**Joanne Killeen & George Germon** are the chef-owners of the famed Al Forno in Providence, Rhode Island. Joanne and George are co-authors of the book *Cucina Simpatica*.

**Ris Lacoste** is the award-winning executive chef of 1789 Restaurant in Washington, DC. A member of the National Board of Directors for the American Institute of Wine and Food, Ris also serves on the board of the Marriott Hospitality Public Charter High School.

**Ruth Lively** writes the In Season column for *Fine Cooking* magazine. She is the former editor of *Fine Gardening* magazine.

**Lori Longbotham** is a food writer and the author of several cookbooks, including *Luscious Lemon Desserts* and *The Scoop: How to Change Store-Bought Ice Cream into Fabulous Desserts*. In her 25 years in the food business, she has worked as a chef, caterer, recipe tester and developer, and food editor.

**Tony Mantuano** is the chef-partner of the acclaimed Spiaggia restaurant in Chicago and the author of *The Spiaggia Cookbook*.

**Jennifer McLagan** is a Toronto-based food writer and stylist and the author of the IACP award-winning cookbook *Bones*. She has worked as a chef in her native Australia as well as in London and Paris.

**Alice Medrich** is a leading chocolate expert and baker. She is the only person to be a three-time Cookbook of the Year winner. Her latest book, *Chocolate Holidays*, is a revised edition of one of her earlier books, *A Year in Chocolate*.

**Perla Meyers** is a cooking teacher and author of eight cookbooks. Born in Austria, raised in Spain, she now lives in New York. Her most recent book is *How to Peel a Peach and 1001 Other Things Every Good Cook Needs to Know*.

**Susie Middleton** is *Fine Cooking's* editor and a blue-ribbon graduate of the Institute of Culinary Education.

**Thai Moreland** was born and raised in Vietnam. She now lives in New York City.

**Leslie Glover Pendleton** is a recipe developer, cooking teacher, food stylist, and the author of *Simply Shrimp, Salmon and (Fish) Steaks*.

**Nicole Rees** co-wrote the revised edition of *Understanding Baking*, a book on the science and technique of baking, as well as its companion recipe book, *The Baker's Manual*. She works as a baker, food writer, and food technologist in Portland, Oregon.

**Rick Rodgers** is a dynamic cooking instructor who teaches classes all over the country and has written more than twenty cookbooks, including *The Carefree Cook* and *Carefree Celebrations*.

**Tony Rosenfeld**, a contributing editor to *Fine Cooking*, lives in Boston, where he also works as a food writer and restaurant consultant. His first cookbook is *150 Things to Make with Roast Chicken and 50 Ways to Roast It*.

**Lynne Sampson** is a former chef at The Herbfarm restaurant near Seattle and is now a food writer, editor, and recipe tester. She teaches cooking classes from her home in eastern Oregon's Wallowa Mountains.

**Katherine Eastman Seeley** is a food writer and pastry chef who honed her baking skills at the French Culinary Institute and in top New York kitchens, including Bouley Bakery.

**Joanne McAllister Smart** is *Fine Cooking's* special issues editor. She's also the co-author of Scott Conant's *New Italian Cooking* and Gordon Hamersley's *Bistro Cooking at Home* and the editor of *Fine Cooking's Cooking New American*.

**Molly Stevens**, a cooking teacher, cookbook author, and contributing editor to *Fine Cooking*, is the author of Williams-Sonoma's *New England*, and co-wrote *One Potato, Two Potato*. For her latest book, *All About Braising: The Art of Uncomplicated Cooking*, Molly nabbed both a James Beard and an IACP cookbook award.

**Suneeta Vaswani**, the author of *Easy Indian Cooking*, has been teaching Indian cooking for close to 30 years. Suneeta was born in Bombay, India, and now lives in Houston.

**Joanne Weir** has written seven cookbooks, including the recently re-released *From Tapas to Meze* and *Weir Cooking in the City*, which is a companion to her PBS television series of the same name. Joanne cooked for five years at Chez Panisse and spent a year studying with master cooking instructor Madeleine Kamman.

**Laura Werlin** is a leading expert on American cheeses. She's the author of several cookbooks, including the award-winning *The New American Cheese*. Laura is on the board of the American Cheese Society.

# Index